THE RESOLUTION 2.0
"SANKALPA"
ONE RESOLUTION CAN CHANGE YOUR LIFE

VISHAL MADHAV SHEVLE

BLUEROSE PUBLISHERS
India | U.K.

Copyright © Vishal Madhav Shevle 2024

All rights reserved by author. No part of this publication may be reproduced, stored in a retrieval system, or transmitted in any form or by any means, electronic, mechanical, photocopying, recording or otherwise, without the prior permission of the author. Although every precaution has been taken to verify the accuracy of the information contained herein, the publisher assumes no responsibility for any errors or omissions. No liability is assumed for damages that may result from the use of information contained within.

BlueRose Publishers takes no responsibility for any damages, losses, or liabilities that may arise from the use or misuse of the information, products, or services provided in this publication.

For permissions requests or inquiries regarding this publication, please contact:

BLUEROSE PUBLISHERS
www.BlueRoseONE.com
info@bluerosepublishers.com
+91 8882 898 898
+4407342408967

Paperback ISBN: 978-93-6261-761-3

Cover design: Rishav Rai
Typesetting: Rohit

First Edition: May 2024

About the Author

Vishal Shevle is the Founder of 'CVtoSuccess,' a Training platform company in NLP Training and grooming for professionals.

Vishal is an inspired professional driven by a vision to make a difference by motivating and inspiring professionals, corporate workers, and entrepreneurs to achieve their maximum potential.

He has worked with MNCs for over 20 years in various cross-functional roles.

Qualifications

Senior Management Program @IIMA – Indian Institute of Management, Ahmedabad

EMBA – Business Management & Operations – GNIMS Mumbai – G.N. Khalsa College

B. Com, M. Com

LL. B (Law Graduate)

Certified **Master Black Belt Six Sigma** Professional

APICS Certified Supply Chain Professional (CSCP)

Certified Trainer (MEPSC & NSDC – *Govt of India Initiative*)

Certified **NLP Trainer** (Neuro-Linguistic Programming)

Certified **Sports Nutritionist**

Yoga Certified Trainer & Practitioner

Acknowledgments

I am immensely thankful to the almighty & my grandparents Lt. Shri Pandurang Vitthal Shevle and Lt. Shrimati Radha Pandurang Shevle, who have been the core source of blessing to inspire this book, The Resolution 2.0 "Sankalpa."

My father Madhav and mother Meera for their blessing from the heavenly abode.

Let me take a step further and offer Gratitude to all associated with making this book a reality.

To one and all- my daughter "Aaradhya" for being the source to help me see the divine in a child and inspiring me to believe "I can do it". Another source is my wife Aarti for being there throughout the journey and my immediate family for their valuable feedback.

A kind word of appreciation towards the team of editors, who helped me in all causes.

Lastly the publisher- Blue Rose Publishing for accepting to publish this book.

Thank you, with all Gratitude and Faith, Let the light guide us all.

Why This Book

One fine day I decided not to take up any resolutions that do not materialise or get weakened while moving ahead. And this made me feel, that rather than taking resolutions and failing them, let's not take them.

As it's said, by Bruce Lee, *"I do not fear the man who knows 10,000 moves, but a man who has practiced one move 10,000 times,"* he means the things that we do time and again will be our weapons to success.

I have learned meditation, and practiced yoga for years helping me dive deep into the philosophy of life and leading me to a word called *"Sankalp."* I learned the way to take Sankalp by way of Yogic methods; and to my surprise, the resolutions taken came true holistically. Practicing this over the years, I have come to believe that these practices can help everyone. With this intention, I share here my stories, wisdom, and methods used, in the form of this book Resolution 2.0 *"Sankalpa."*

Preface

Resolution - The Sankalpa, is an ancient technique that, when practised correctly, accelerates holistic attainment of resolution. In this book, we explore the four fundamental facets of life - Physical, Mental, Spiritual, and Financial well-being. Each aspect contributes significantly to our life journey; however, focusing excessively on one may overshadow the others. We aim to embark on this journey, enriching it with the wisdom of Sankalpa realisation, effectively managing ourselves, and nurturing every dimension for a full expression of divine energy.

Throughout the book, we are using Resolution & Sankalpa words interchangeably.

Resolution 2.0 is new way to take up your Resolution, The Sanskrit word for it is "Sankalpa".

Introduction

The world is akin to a divine "Dream" within the mind of God, with each resolution - or Sankalpa - representing a thread in this cosmic tapestry. Time and again, we embrace these resolutions, perhaps most notably during the New Year, and yet, they often remain unfulfilled.

But what if I were to introduce a method to actualize these Sankalpas, addressing the complexities of life?

Consider the prospect of harnessing your energy with purpose towards achieving your aspirations.

Imagine utilising your senses - sight, sound, touch, smell, and taste - to fully immerse yourself in the world and enhance your experiences.

Contemplate the notion of using your mind to embed your resolutions seamlessly into your daily routine, making them a natural part of your being.

And what if I suggest that by manifesting a Sankalpa-Resolution at the speed of light, you could unlock the immense potential of your subconscious mind.

Furthermore, by honing your life skills and embracing personal development, you can align the various aspects of your life to support the realisation of your Sankalpas.

Indeed, a Sankalpa possesses the transformative power to guide your inner voice and shape your reality. Within the yogic tradition lies a method for taking Sankalpas that facilitates their holistic manifestation.

Contents

PART I
RECTANGLE OF LIFE

1. Energy, Spirituality & Self 4
2. Body, Mind & Wealth 22

PART II
POWER OF MIND

3. Conscious, Subconscious & Unconscious Mind 61
4. Mind & You 80
5. Desire & Will 97
6. Sankalpa The Resolution Realisation 105
7. Emotions 119

PART III
LIFE & YOU

8. Attitude 140
9. Life Essential Skills 152
10. Relationships 161
11. Values 174
12. Happiness 182

13. Pack A Punch For Life...... 189
14. Dare To Think...... 195
15. Love "Let It Dissolve" 201
16. Climax - The Art To Channelise The Life Force...... 209
17. Be An Athlete...... 215
18. Discipline...... 224
19. Success...... 237
20. Win "You Will Win" 245
21. Adopting A Modern Yogic Life...... 251

PART IV
SOUL

22. Law of Universe...... 258
23. World Within You...... 276
24. Inner Voice...... 291

PART V

25. Holistic Way To Realise Your Resolutions...... 300

PART I
RECTANGLE OF LIFE

The Four Quadrants of Life

We will see that the integration of the four life dimensions fuelled by the life force can create a remarkable impact. Through prioritising Physical well-being, cultivating Mental awareness alongside essential life skills, and harnessing the power of Light Speed through Sankalpa, we can undoubtedly foster a transformative, and a holistic life experience.

1. Physical Health: Self-awareness begins with understanding your physical body. This involves recognizing your body's needs, such as proper nutrition, exercise, and rest. By listening to your body's cues, you can make informed decisions about diet, exercise routines, and sleep patterns, leading to improved physical health.

2. Mind- Emotional & Mental Well-being: Self-awareness extends to your emotional state. It involves acknowledging your emotions, understanding their triggers, and learning how to manage them effectively. Self-awareness also encompasses your mental well-being. It involves recognizing thought patterns, beliefs, and cognitive processes that influence your behaviour and decision-making. With this awareness, you can identify and address negative thought patterns, promoting better mental health and cognitive functioning.

3. Spiritual Well-being: Understanding your spiritual self involves exploring your values, beliefs, and sense of purpose. It's about connecting with your inner self, seeking meaning, and aligning your actions with your core values. This introspective journey can lead to a more profound sense of fulfilment and spiritual well-being.

4. Financial Well-being - Here's how I perceive it: Until one achieves financial stability, there comes a time when everything seems to be at a standstill. Financial independence paves the way for a better quality of life – encompassing essentials like clothing, shelter, and

food, which require monetary resources. However, subscribing to the belief that money holds no significance would be deceiving oneself. While it's true that wealth isn't the sole defining aspect of life, dismissing its importance would be misguided. True wealth lies within the mind, and in the upcoming sections, we'll delve deeper into exploring this quadrant.

Chapter One

Energy, Spirituality & Self

SPIRITUAL WELL BEING - Energy

What is Energy?

Energy is the purest form of God's love that spreads across the universe to bind every element together. When you open the curtain of your room in the morning and the sunlight comes in, the light and the warmth you see, and feel is the most vibrant form of energy. Energy is not just that, but everything.

The ancient Sanskrit expression "Aham Bramhmasmi," which translates to 'I am Brahman' or 'I am the ultimate energy,' signifies the idea that I am intricately connected to the universe, and everything exists within me. He who dwells in me. I am him and within him.

The universe resonates with energy on various levels, and individuals can align with the universal flow. This concept echoes the profound words from the Puranas (Hindu Scriptures written during the 3rd Century), "Je Pindit Te Brahmandi," conveying the notion that the entirety of the cosmos resides within each individual.

Five Elements

The universe, including the human body, is composed of five fundamental elements known as "Panchamahabhutas": earth (prithvi), water (jala), fire (tejas), wind (vayu), and space (akasa). Each element represents a distinct state of matter, with earth symbolising solidity, water representing liquids, air encompassing gases, fire symbolising transformation, and space serving as the foundation for spiritual experiences. Understanding these elements is crucial for grasping the natural laws governing our world. The human body contains these elements in varying proportions, with water being the most abundant at approximately 72%, followed by earth, air, fire, and space. This recognition highlights our profound connection to the natural world and emphasises how these elements influence both our physical and spiritual experiences, showcasing the interconnectedness between humans and the universe.

There are three forms of energy

- Physical – Doing physical activities, picking up stuff, or moving around
- Spiritual – Core energy that is omnipresent
- Mental – Emotions, feelings, & logical thinking

Napoleon Hill in his book, 'Think & Grow Rich' says, you cannot see electricity, but you know how to use it. You need not know what it is made of. You don't need to see energy, It is already showered, and you have to use it to its fullest potential. You are the storehouse of energy.

Experience Energy

If you want to experience energy in its purest form, try rubbing your palms for 10 seconds hold them close without touching each other and feel the energy that transcends between your palms. Some might experience the heat and the warmth; some might feel a tugging the palms closer. This is the energy within us. If you do not feel anything from this exercise, then try stopping your breath for a couple of seconds. You will feel that there is something within you that is asking you to release your breath, to breathe easily, and to live. Energy is an inherent part of us and is primarily within us. We need the willingness to access this path. Energy is universal wi-fi and free flowing within us and around us.

Energy can also be experienced by consciously practising-

- Prayers
- Blessings
- Deeper understanding
- Gaining universal wisdom
- Attaining a higher connection with the cosmic world

Spiritual Energy

Spiritual energy is omnipresent, and we can experience it by practising spirituality.

Spirituality is a way of understanding ourselves and the world around us that goes beyond the physical and material. It is a search for meaning and purpose and a connection to something larger than us. Spirituality can help us to live more fulfilling and harmonious lives.

In other words, spirituality is not just about what we can see and touch. It is also about our inner world, our values, and our beliefs. It is about finding our place in the universe and connecting with something greater than ourselves.

Spirituality can be expressed in different ways, including religion, meditation, yoga, prayer, and spending time in nature. It is a personal journey, and there is no one right way to be spiritual.

Quantum Physics and Spirituality

Spirituality is the search for meaning and purpose in life and a connection to something larger than oneself. Many people believe that spirituality and quantum physics are interconnected. Quantum Physics describes the behaviour of Matter and Energy at its most fundamental level, including atoms, electrons and photons, their behaviour which seems odd to work in real world. Just like an experiment of Yogi to turn 'dirty water' into 'rose water' or some miracles where the Yogi appears to be seen at two places at the same time.

From a spiritual perspective, our vibrational frequency is a measure of our spiritual awareness. When we have a high vibrational frequency, we are more connected to our true selves and the divine. Here is how you can consciously create high vibrational frequency -

Your Thoughts

Every thought you have sends out a vibration into the universe. This vibration eventually comes back to you. So, if you have negative thoughts and feelings, those energies will eventually come back to affect you. This is why it is so important to be mindful of the quality of your thoughts and to try to cultivate more positive ones.

The Company You Keep

The people you spend time with have a big impact on your vibrational frequency. When you are around happy people, you start to feel happy too. But if you are around people who are always complaining and negative, it can bring you down and make you feel negative too.

The Songs You Listen

Music has a powerful influence on our emotions and our vibrational frequency. The lyrics of the songs we listen to can have a big impact on our thoughts and feelings. If we listen to songs with positive lyrics, it can help us to raise our vibrational frequency and attract positive things into our lives.

A word devoid of meaning is merely a sound, much like devotional songs lacking an impact on the mind, seem to be mere noise. However, there may be a benefit in their energetic resonance, influenced by environmental factors. Typically, songs accompanied by visuals can leave a lasting impression on the mind. Choose music that elevates you energetically, lifting your spirits to greater heights.

The Things You Watch

Watching movies, TV shows, or other content that depicts violence, tragedy, or other negative events can hurt your vibrational frequency. When your brain sees this type of content, it interprets it as real, and triggers a release of stress hormones, such as cortisol and adrenaline. This can make you feel anxious, stressed, or even depressed. On the other hand, watching content that is positive and uplifting can have a positive impact on your vibrational frequency.

Your Environment

Your surroundings, both at home and at work, can have a big impact on your vibrational frequency. If your surroundings are cluttered or disorganised, it can lower your vibration. But if your surroundings are clean and tidy, it can raise your vibration.

When you take care of your environment, you are saying to the universe that you are ready to receive more good things. It is important to appreciate and care for what you already have.

Your Speech

Complaining and speaking negatively about situations and people hurts your well-being. It is important to break the habit of criticising and speaking negatively about others. Instead, take responsibility for your own choices in life. When you complain, you are focusing on the negative aspects of your situation. This can cause anger, resentment, and frustration. It can also lower your vibrational frequency and attract more negative experiences into your life.

Practice Gratitude

Expressing gratitude is a great way to raise your vibrational frequency. When you are grateful, you are focusing on the positive aspects of your life. This can help you to feel happier and more optimistic. It can also attract more good things into your life.

Saints and yogic practices across India have been holding the flag of spiritual energy for all of us to be able to access ourselves in the highest form. They have helped people to know their self. There are many stories of these saints which are beyond our comprehension. They have placed themselves at such a high level that sometimes it is even out of human understanding that such things are possible.

My Spiritual Experiences-

My Grandfather who lived until the age of 97 years, lived a life on three pillars - faith, discipline, and service.

Faith :- The moment I hear about my grandfather, the quote of his rings a bell in my ear that says –

"Ram naam laduu

Gopal naam ghee

tu ghol ghol pee tu ghol ghol pee."

This means the name of God is like sweets, you remember to grace his divinity by gulping the sweetness of his name and keep chanting the name of the lord.

He had immense faith in God that was seen through his word and action, never being disappointed being a kind gentleman walking around with wisdom and the name of lord on his lips.

Discipline :- He followed, his morning ritual keenly over each day getting up as early as 5 am and doing his yoga practices with chanting and prayers, afterward taking a long walk ensuring each day to pray to the Sun God during the sunrise, throughout the day meal times were marked and even the night bedtime.

Service :- Above all his practices, he ensured to help people around with his wisdom, spiritual insight, and kindness.

I remember whenever I used to come home after long playing hours my feet used to pain, he would rub my feet with both his hands chanting the name of the lord, I could feel the warmth of his palms then and now too, it was something magical.

He widely spoke about the sound of life within, you need to have keen sight to hear the beauty of life in small things.

Neem Karoli Baba

Neem Karoli Baba was a Hindu saint and a strong devotee of Lord Hanuman. He practised bhakti yoga and kept chanting the name of Lord Ram. He never gave any chanting or prayers to his followers

Energy, Spirituality & Self

but asked them to chant 'Ram Ram.' His simple message was, 'Love Everyone and Serve Everyone.'

Surprisingly, some stories make us feel how evolved a person can be through his/her spiritual practices. Once a disciple approached Baba. The disciple was stashed with a good quantity of potent drug tablets. These were very strong and even one tablet could knock a person down. The disciple told this to Babaji and Babaji asked him to show him the stuff. The disciple was apprehensive as the drug was very strong. The disciple gave one tablet to Babaji, and Babaji asked what would happen with just one, and he extended his hand to ask for more. The disciple was scared that more drugs would do harm to Babaji or knock him off. But Babaji came forward and took all the stuff from the disciple and consumed it all at once. The shocked disciple kept looking for some severe outcome, as bad as loss of life, but Babaji continued to be in his senses, without a trace of any hangover or effect. He was happy and blissful. He said people who connect with higher forms of themselves, overcoming their karma remain unaffected by all these things. Things are beyond good and bad for them. However, the beings who do not practise spirituality or interconnectedness remain affected.

I have rich experiences from the spiritual wisdom of India. I have been practising meditation for over a decade now. After reading about all his miracles I wanted to see what a bhakti yogi can do, and I was on my quest. I was a non-believer of Bhakti Yoga and seeking my answers. I went to visit Neem Karoli Baba's ashram at Kainchi Dham, Uttarakhand in 2021.

Once in his ashram, I bowed down to the idol of Neem Karoli Baba. I sat and prayed that I wanted to feel your energy. I want my dreams to come true. But I couldn't see any sign of this happening. Dejected, I was walking back to return. While nearing the gate, I heard a sound from a gentleman from the administrative office, who was a staff there. He asked me about my experience so far, and if I have had my prasad. From our conversation, he kind of judged my unsaid dejection.

There was a glint in his eyes, a spark, and with a happy face, he asked me to go to a shade at the mountain cliff that was adjacent to the administrative room where Babaji meditated. The man asked me to bow down at this place. I thought I had come all this way; I might as well do what this man is telling me. I went to this shade; it was a small one built beside the mountain cliff. On the mountain cliff, Ram, Ram was written everywhere. I went and bowed down here. Just then I felt some upswing of energy, and on some instinct, I felt like sitting there and meditating. I sat there and meditated. It appeared to me that I had been in meditation here for hours, but when I opened my eyes, I saw that the actual time was not more than 20 minutes. Such was the effect of meditation that I did not feel happy, sad, excited, or anxious, but I was in the moment. One unusual thing was the name 'Ram' kept chanting in my mind all day like I had switched on some tape on auto mode.

Throughout the day, I found myself immersed in the chanting of the name "Ram." Even as I entered the car, where the driver had been chatty for the past few days, I remained absorbed in this meditative chant. There was a moment when the driver seemed poised to initiate conversation, but I just looked at him and a silent understanding passed between us, and he refrained from speaking. The uninterrupted repetition of "Ram" filled me with a profound sense of bliss, akin to quenching a deep thirst with pure water after days of longing. It was as if I was drinking from the fountain of love through the continuous recitation of "Ram, Ram, Ram."

What Is A Guru?

The word guru is split in two; 'Gu' stands for dark, and 'Ru' stands for light. Guru is the one who takes us from dark to light. It could be yourself if you are consciously aware. It could be your teacher or even nature. A guru is not a person, but an element, a tatva.

Ramana Maharishi

In 1896, Ramana Maharshi departed from his familial home and embarked on a journey to the sacred mountain of Arunachala in Tiruvannamalai. There, he entered into a state of profound meditation spontaneously. Over the subsequent years, he remained deeply absorbed in spiritual contemplation, completely detached from worldly matters. This period of intense introspection and self-examination ultimately led to his realisation of the true essence of the self.

Ramana Maharshi's teachings primarily centred around the practice of self-inquiry, known as Atma-vichara, as a pathway to understanding one's true nature. He stressed the significance of asking oneself, "Who am I?" and turning inward to uncover the core of the self beyond the confines of the ego-mind. According to his philosophy, the ultimate aim of human existence is to recognize this pure consciousness, which transcends time and remains immutable.

Renowned for his silent presence, Ramana Maharshi often imparted his teachings through silent transmission rather than a verbal discourse. His aura exuded an overwhelming sense of peace and awareness, profoundly impacting those who encountered him. Many seekers experienced spontaneous awakenings or profound insights simply by being in his vicinity and sorting out their problems.

His form of meditation is to observe, not react. Once you do this every form of action, imaginative fear, bother, and doubt vanishes. Every form of energy comes from you, and when you observe, all these challenges vanish. The energy drops down.

Any form of meditation you do, you will feel happy and blissful.

I visited his ashram at Tiruvannamalai, Tamil Nadu and stayed there for a couple of days to practise meditation. Usually, it is an effort to get to the meditative state irrespective of your practice and experience, but what I observed of this ashram is, that there is something mystical about it, and you tend to slip into your meditative state effortlessly.

The way of Ramana Maharishi is to connect with your deeper sense with profound wisdom of your own inner light.

Bhatt Kaka

I was just a young adult completing my college. I was learning my way into the world. I was active in sports and that led me to practise yoga. Growing up in India has helped me to understand yoga practices and its meaning. At such a tender age I knew it was a way to know oneself. One needs to practise meditation or a yogic practice to know oneself within.

I was so oriented in seeking myself that I tried my ways. I had read somewhere, you got to ask what you are looking for, and I asked for spiritual guidance in the form of a guru.

One fine day I was introduced by one of my friends to a person called Bhatt Kaka. Bhatt Kaka appeared like a normal man, and not a Yogi or someone who meditated or would be fit to be my guru. He was wearing jeans and a cream-coloured kurta. The one remarkable thing I observed about him was, his eyes glittered like diamonds. He had a glow on his face. He stood apart from all of us.

My friend Swapnil introduced me to Bhatt Kaka stating I want to learn meditation. He just looked at me and said, "Okay come back after one month, and try to practise celibacy for those 30 days." Well, I was just a young adult then. Yet I showed up on the 31st day as he asked me to. He initiated me in Sri Vidya Sadhana, giving me a mantra to be said in a specific way. He told me to have faith in the path I had chosen for myself.

I started my journey in meditation with his blessings and guidance. There were also other disciples around to help and motivate me to practise meditation. I felt it's all about the people around you that make you who you are.

Bhatt Kaka used to tell the disciples to practise what is told. To have patience and believe in the path. He was a 70-year-old man, when I met him first, but was youthful in his appearance. He gave all the credit to the path he followed and inspired me to walk on the same.

Bhatt Kaka meditated for all his life. He was a married man. His way of yogic practice - Grihasthashram, a married family man who follows certain disciplines and is a patient disciple of YOG. I know it's difficult to understand having a family and being a Yogi, however, this man taught and preached the art of walking the path of Yogi while being around our people.

He meditated daily for hours. In particular, he never slept at night. Whenever we would go to sleep, he would sit in his chair which would be somewhere from around 10:00 pm until morning 6:00 am to 7:00 am. He would be meditating the whole night. His schedule was simple- during the daytime, he would do all the activities to help people and support his family, while at night he would do his meditation. At the age of 75, his eyes glittered like diamonds and his face radiated content and blissfulness. Regardless of anything happening in his life, he would be able to connect with everyone with kindness, love, and gratitude. His words sometimes were mystic and at times very simple and practical.

He rode a 350 CC bullet at the age of 75. Once he picked up his bullet and I looked at him in amazement, he smiled and told me, "You should be able to do this when you are my age." He credited this youthfulness to his yogic practices.

Seeing all the disciples progressing on the path of meditation, I felt they were bestowed with a new form of meditation or mantra. One day, I asked Bhatt Kaka, "Is there a new form of mantra meditation that others know, and I don't?" He smiled and replied, "Do what is given to you. You have been taught all that you want to know."

I was the youngest in the group. I was naive and anxious to learn more. I used to be very keen to talk with my guru and have a good discussion about some of my problems like he used to discuss with others. But every time I went to him with my problem, he smiled, and magically the problem disappeared. At least from my mind.

One fine day I was in a hurry to have a solution for my biggest problem then and wanted to talk to him. He looked at me and didn't say anything. I was unable to utter a word, but he kept talking about his experiences. He asked me for a high five which was his habit and asked other people too. I went with my stubborn ego and wanted him to talk about my problem. But he joked and laughed. I was dejected and angry and decided to go back. While I was going back and was about to open the door, he didn't utter a word, but I could hear, "Stop for a while." I didn't know who it was, but I could hear the words. I *stopped, I never saw him get up from his seat while I walked to the door, but at the very next moment, he was beside me and stood there for nearly five minutes. With him around I was feeling the force of his energy coming into my body like a gust of air- light and warm. Something in me was shifting. I didn't know what was happening, just that I could feel his grace. Now I could breathe more clearly. I was in that moment; when the big problem was not valid anymore, and it just vanished.*

It took me years to understand the above experience. Now when I introspect the way he showered the energy with grace, it does help me enlighten, and understand the very nature of self. I believe that if you help a man with food, you help him for a moment or day, if you help a man with money, you help him for a day or time being, But if you educate a man, you help him for life. All the more influential is that if you help a person with spiritual grace, you will help him eternally.

Transformation by Breath

On the journey of spirituality, I have learned to keep myself open for the experiences, some logically fitting into the scheme of things, and some with no logical explanations. I met another person who made a sea change in the very tiny dot of my life. He transformed me by letting me follow the method of 'stay aware' by following 'Shwasa' (Breath).

The flow of breath is intriguing. If you learn to observe and sometimes immerse yourself, it can make you dissolve as if the world is one.

I saw a procession of Paramhansa Satchidananda while I was coming from work, the procession was followed by his disciples and some of his followers. I thought, who is he to have such a procession. The thought left me pondering and I walked away. Few days later, I accidentally bumped into temple and an ashram that was built and run by Paramhansa Satchidananda Trust. I got a chance to meet this Yogi (Swami) there.

He enquired with his deep voice, full of love, "How are you?" His deep voice penetrated my soul, I don't remember the answer that I spoke out, but I remember I was full of joy and peace.

Swamiji, use to stay away from city and his town was in the interiors of Madhya Pradesh. In his Ashram I met with a soul; a sanyasi called Jagdish Baba who managed the ashram. His appearance was that of a yogi, with a full-grown white beard, long hair tied into a pony at the back, and his eyes with the shining glory like that of a child. His words were full of wisdom, love, and spoken with lot of care.

This man transformed me, not by mere advise or words. He showed me the way by helping me find respect with the tasks I did. His way of Sankalpa was to stay aware and follow one's breath. He was a man of discipline, wisdom and more importantly kind, and patient. Merely being with him one would feel immense love and respect. He was a very kind Sanyasi I ever meet. I feel for a person to transform you, as a guru or master, he needs to be besides you to help you find your way.

Jagdish Baba told stories of Mahabharata, Ramayana, and some of his experiences that helped me find answers to my questions. Sometimes when I went to meet Jagdish Baba, he merely answered my questions without me even asking him.

Every time, I had a query he helped me to find it in my own way by putting a query and asking me to observe my breath. And then, my mind would uncover and solve the question. Even the craziest of the problem that I thought were, he installed faith in me to believe they will soon be solved and taken care of.

One thing that I learned from him is to breathe in a different way, thinking every moment is a new breath, and we should embrace it one at a time.

Energy & Self

Energy is the purest form of God's Love. It extends across the universe to every element to get every element together. It is present in everyone and the moment you realise this, you shall connect with the supreme. Energy is in the rain that you see, it's in the winds, the sun that scorches or gives the tender heat on a cold day. Energy is all around us in various forms and to experience it we primarily have to breathe. Pure unadulterated air is the richest source of life and an ultimate form of energy. This is the basic phenomenon of light and energy.

Can you differentiate yourselves from your breath?

If I ask you to hold your breath for 10 seconds, just 10 seconds and see now how you feel. Breath is the universal way to connect to the global wi-fi of God. In the absence of it, you look at your connection with the world, the divine and yourself. Thus, it is of utmost importance that you work on your breath and the way you work to maintain your hair, your face, your physique, or other body parts. Although breath seems intangible, it is the core of life. Let its precious presence be nurtured towards a satisfying life.

Thoughts come to us from a desire or a will. All thoughts will revolve around a desire.

Heart Chakra

The heart chakra, often referred to as the fourth chakra in the traditional system of seven main chakras, serves as the epicentre of unconditional love and emotional balance within the human energy system. When this chakra is in a state of equilibrium, it facilitates the harmonious flow of love, compassion, and empathy, not only towards others, but also towards oneself. This balance creates a profound sense of inner peace and connection with the world around us.

Conversely, when the heart chakra is out of balance or blocked, it can manifest as a range of negative emotions such as fear, anxiety, hurt, and even hatred. These emotions can create a sense of constriction or tightness in the chest, often described as feeling emotionally closed off or distant. The saying that "the opposite of love is fear" underscores how fear and negativity can disrupt the natural flow of love and compassion from the heart chakra.

Healing and balancing the heart chakra is an ongoing process that involves various practices aimed at restoring its energy equilibrium. Meditation, yoga, deep self-reflection, and acts of kindness towards oneself and others are among the methods used to promote healing and balance in this vital energy centre. Through these practices, individuals can gradually release emotional blockages, let go of fear and negativity, and open themselves up to experiencing and sharing unconditional love.

Living a life centred around the principles of the heart chakra is a rewarding journey filled with growth and transformation. Embracing love, compassion, and emotional harmony leads to greater resilience, improved relationships, and a profound sense of interconnectedness with all beings. While the process of activating and balancing the heart chakra may require time, effort, and dedication, the positive impact on one's well-being and ability to experience and share unconditional love makes it undeniably worthwhile.

1. Balancing your Heart Chakra: A powerful tool for opening and balancing the heart chakra is meditation. During meditation, you can focus your attention on the heart centre, imagining a warm, green,

or pink light expanding from this area. As you meditate, release any negative emotions, and cultivate feelings of love, forgiveness, and compassion. Regular meditation helps create a strong connection to your heart chakra and promotes emotional well-being.

2. Heart Chakra Activation: Self-love and self-compassion are fundamental for heart chakra activation. Treat yourself with kindness and understanding. Practise positive self-talk, acknowledge your worth, and forgive yourself for past mistakes. By nurturing self-love, you create a strong foundation for opening your heart to others.

3. Heart Chakra Alignment: Nourishing your body with good food and maintaining a healthy lifestyle can positively impact the heart chakra. Consume foods that are not only physically nutritious but also energetically nourishing. Fresh, whole foods with vibrant colours can help align your energy centres, including the heart chakra. Staying physically healthy can support emotional well-being.

4. Deepen Heart Chakra Connection: Prayer, or any form of spiritual practice that resonates with you, can be a powerful way to activate the heart chakra. It allows you to connect with a higher power. Prayer can instil feelings of love and compassion, both towards yourself and others, deepening your heart's chakra activation.

Remember that the process of activating and balancing the heart chakra is a personal journey, and it may take time and patience. Making these practices a part of your daily life can help you cultivate a deeper sense of love, compassion, and emotional well-being. Ultimately, openly expressing your emotions from the heart and upholding a clear conscience can attract the essential energy to your heart chakra and initiate its activation.

Chapter Two

Body, Mind & Wealth

Health is a holistic term. But if we go to understand it, it is a total of different aspects that classify you as a healthy person. Health can primarily be classified as – Strength, non-pathology, cardiovascular and agility. They are all interconnected and relatively affect each other.

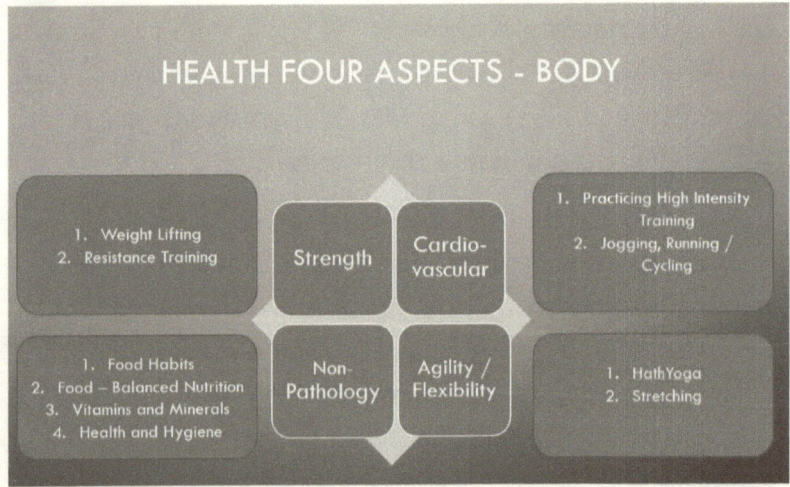

There are common misconceptions surrounding weight loss and health. Some believe that simply shedding pounds equates to improved health. However, being on a diet doesn't necessarily equate to good health. For instance, fasting for a couple of days might result in a quick 2kg weight loss, primarily from water content. However, once you cease this fasting or dieting regimen, you're likely to rebound to your initial weight, which can be demoralising.

The paramount objective should not solely revolve around dieting but rather prioritise overall health and well-being.

In today's world, food has transcended its basic role as a necessity; it has evolved into a symbol of style, a trend, a craving, and even a lifestyle. People no longer view food solely as a means to acquire essential nutrition and sustain themselves. Instead, we've become discerning about our food choices, meticulously timing our meals. Religious dietary practices are often disregarded, and a substantial portion of the food we consume is laden with chemicals to prolong shelf life, but unfortunately, it lacks the minerals, vitamins, and nutrients our bodies require daily.

In the face of these nutritional deficiencies, our overall health suffers, resulting in weakened immunity and a heightened susceptibility to diseases. Regrettably, our departure from healthy eating habits and nutritious meals has given rise to lifestyle disorders such as diabetes and hypertension, among others. These trends underscore the significance of making informed and wholesome dietary choices.

Just like the quality of your food, the consistency of your dietary habits is crucial, and so is your hygiene. Prioritising oral hygiene is essential, and brushing your teeth twice daily should not be seen as optional but as an ingrained habit. Being mindful of your breath and how you present yourself to others after meals is equally vital. Much like body odour, bad breath should be kept in check. It can be repulsive not only in professional settings but also during personal interactions and intimate moments.

Strength

Strength pertains to the characteristic or condition of having physical power. Muscles play a crucial role in enabling us to perform activities such as walking, running, lifting objects, and numerous other functions.

The development of strength can be achieved through activities like resistance training and weightlifting.

Weightlifting

Weightlifting, across its diverse variations, holds a pivotal position in upholding a well-rounded and healthy lifestyle.

Weightlifting has the potential to elevate your confidence levels. Each instance you manage to lift weights evokes a profound sense of accomplishment. Additionally, there are noticeable transformations in your physique. Even if your objective isn't to bulk up significantly, you're likely to observe some degree of muscle definition. Moreover, strength training is an effective means of calorie expenditure, contributing to improved physical fitness.

Weightlifting goes beyond building muscle and can positively impact your physical and mental well-being. It can boost your confidence, transform your physique, aid in weight management, and contribute to long-term health. Whether your goal is to become a competitive bodybuilder or simply to lead a healthier lifestyle, incorporating weightlifting into your fitness routine can be highly beneficial.

Enhanced posture is a physical benefit of weightlifting that can have a positive impact on your self-confidence. When you have good posture, you stand up straighter and taller, which can make you look and feel more confident. Good posture can also help to improve your breathing and reduce back pain.

Muscle-building exercises often lead to improved sleep patterns. This is because exercise helps to tire your body and mind, which can make it easier to fall asleep. Exercise also releases endorphins, which have mood-boosting effects that can help to improve sleep quality.

Exercise is effective in reducing anxiety and depression. This is because exercise helps to increase the production of endorphins, which have mood-boosting effects. Exercise can also help to reduce stress levels and improve sleep quality, both of which can contribute to improved mental health.

Weightlifting specifically can improve your mental alertness, cognitive abilities, and memory. This is because weightlifting helps to increase blood flow to the brain, which can improve brain function. Weightlifting can also help to build new brain cells and connections, which can improve cognitive function.

Physical weightlifting offers a range of health advantages, which encompass:

- Enhanced cardiovascular health, resulting in a stronger and healthier heart.

- Elevated metabolic rate, contributing to better calorie burning and weight management.

- Controlling blood sugar levels and reducing the risk of diabetes.

- Enhanced bone density, fortifying the skeletal structure.

- Potential reversal of the effects of Osteoporosis in advanced age.

I know of a middle-aged relative who led an extremely sedentary lifestyle. He avoided exercise, stretching, and weightlifting altogether, essentially allowing his body to become inactive and stiff. He even hesitated to lift weights at home, resulting in a frozen and unconditioned body.

One day, out of no choice he had to lift a heavy gas cylinder and place it in its designated spot. In the process, he ended up injuring his tailbone. The pain he experienced was excruciating, and it persisted for years.

This incident prompts us of how important it is for both men and women to maintain physical strength and flexibility. As parents, we may need to lift our children, and individuals of any age may find themselves wanting to lift loved ones, or as housewives, perform everyday tasks like carrying groceries and vegetables. Strength is an inherent quality in every human being, and it's crucial to nurture and develop it healthily and functionally.

Resistance training, which is also known as weightlifting and strength training, involves engaging in exercises where you exert force to overcome a form of resistance. Resistance, in this context, refers to any force that makes a physical movement more challenging.

The simplest way of resistance training involves utilising your body weight to perform a variety of exercises. Activities like push-ups, pull-ups, and planks leverage gravity as the natural resistance. Alternatively, you can introduce resistance by incorporating dumbbells into your workout routine, which enables exercises like deadlifts, bicep curls, and bench presses. Starting with a minimum of 10 repetitions of push-ups per day and gradually increasing to 100 can be an effective approach. Additionally, resistance bands offer another excellent way to engage in resistance-based exercises.

Cardiovascular

Cardiovascular exercise is characterised as any form of physical activity that elevates and sustains your heart rate over an extended duration. This heightened activity prompts your respiratory system to operate at a faster and deeper pace. Your blood vessels dilate to transport increased oxygen to your muscles, and your body releases natural pain-relieving substances known as endorphins.

Cardiovascular exercises encompass a wide range of activities, including skipping, walking, brisk walking, swimming, boxing, cycling, hiking, using stairs, and even dancing. If you're not inclined towards gym workouts, there's no need to confine yourself indoors; you can engage in these diverse cardio exercises to enhance your heart rate and overall fitness.

Typically, a regular human being maintains a heart rate falling within the range of 60 to 100 beats per minute. While this range can vary among individuals, it serves as a general guideline. Some individuals have achieved the remarkable feat of maintaining a lower heart rate and consequently living longer lives. We are familiar with many sages who, through disciplined practices and controlled breathing techniques, have accomplished this and extended their lifespans well beyond the average human age.

Even athletes and sports professionals have honed the ability to regulate their heart rate. Take, for instance, a runner who exerts maximum stamina and energy during a race, causing a significant increase in heart rate. Yet, through dedicated practice and discipline, they can swiftly regulate and return their heart rate to a normal range once the race concludes.

Cardiovascular health is intricately linked to both your physical and mental well-being.

Agility

Agility is the ability of the body to quickly change direction or position.

The capacity to swiftly alter your body's position or change its direction is referred to as agility. It is a fundamental element of physical fitness crucial for achieving success in numerous sports, including team sports like football and hockey, as well as individual sports such as tennis and squash. However, agility isn't solely for sports; it is beneficial for everyday activities as well. Maintaining agility can help you retain a youthful feeling, particularly in your lower back. Achieving and preserving this agility can be accomplished through various means, such as practising Hatt Yoga, a highly structured and disciplined form of yoga.

Engaging in routines like Surya Namaskar, also known as Sun Salutations, is highly recommended. Starting with at least six rounds of Surya Namaskar, divided into three sets of two rounds each, is a good beginning. It's essential to maintain a 10-15-second interval between each set. Throughout these activities, controlled breathing assumes a critical role, connecting your energy and mental well-being while promoting nervous system healing and enhancing the flow of energy.

Here are some yoga poses that you can practise every day to enhance your agility.

1. Sitting and Forward Bending:

Sit with your legs extended in front of you. Inhale deeply, and as you exhale, slowly bend forward from your hips, reaching toward your toes. Keep your back straight and try to touch your toes and reach as far as you comfortably can.

You can also do this stretch while you are sitting on chair.

Benefits: This exercise stretches your hamstrings, and lower back, and improves flexibility in your spine.

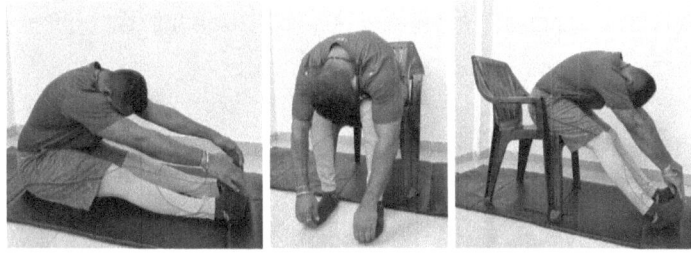

2. Bhujangasana (Cobra Pose):

Description: Lie on your stomach with your palms placed beneath your shoulder. Inhale and lift your upper body, arching your back, while keeping your lower body grounded. Look upward.

You can also practice this asana while sitting on chair to give a quick relaxation.

Benefits: Bhujangasana strengthens the spine, opens the chest, and helps improve posture.

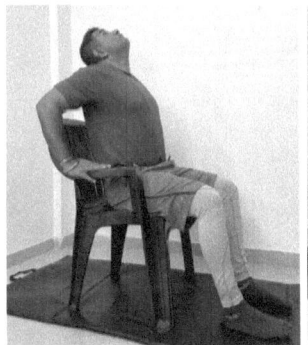
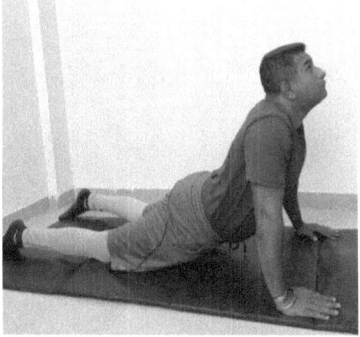

3. Tadasana (Tree Pose):

Stand tall with your feet a width apart. Inhale as you raise your arms over your head, palms facing each other. Stretch your whole body upward, stretching the spine.

Another way to practice while sitting and standing is Tadasana.

Benefits: Tadasana enhances posture, stretches the spine, and promotes a sense of balance and alignment.

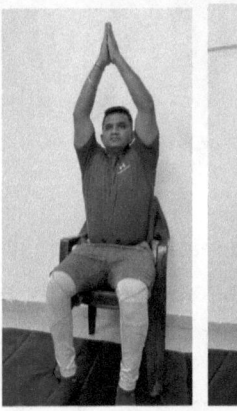

4. Vajrasana (Thunderbolt Pose) and Vajratadasana:

Vajrasana involves kneeling on the floor, sitting back on your heels, and keeping your spine straight.

Vajratadasana is an advanced variation where you interlock your fingers behind your back, straighten your arms, and lift your chest.

Benefits: Vajrasana helps improve digestion, posture, and flexibility. Vajratadasana further enhances chest opening and flexibility in the upper body.

These simple exercises can be incorporated into your daily routine to enhance agility, flexibility, and overall physical well-being. Remember to perform them with proper form and gradually increase the duration or intensity as your body becomes more comfortable with these movements. Always listen to your body and consult with a yoga instructor or healthcare professional if you have any concerns or medical conditions.

As the renowned saying goes, "Your body is a sanctuary". While you visit a temple to devoutly pray, it's equally vital to tend to your body through various methods, such as engaging in physical exercises and sports activities. However, it's crucial to adhere to a structured routine that includes warming up, performing exercises, and concluding with a proper cooldown.

Food

If we look throughout the world, there are different concepts about food set by region, religion, beliefs, values, and culture. These patterns are based on several factors of work, culture, climate, endemic stuff, and beliefs. And these beliefs have been passed on through generations.

With every generation the patterns change, the work habits change, the lifestyle changes, but our food patterns have remained the same. It is important that we know the gap. Today we stay in a world of Aladdin's Magic Lamp, where the genie gets us our food right on our tables in the form of food delivery apps.

It is easy to live such a lifestyle. Enjoying things is becoming a priority. What makes it challenging is the ease of things. But remember, food should make you feel energetic and blissful, and not lethargic.

I was overweight. When you get overweight you face different life challenges. Every day is a difficult journey and then of course my friends around asked, "How do you feel about yourself?" Leave aside the physical appearance, but being overweight comes with illness. And most of the time, you do not accept yourself to be overweight or fat.

Ironically, I was a sportsman from my teens till my early 20s and extremely fit. After graduating and starting a job, I continued working for corporations for 20 long years. During this span, I did not realise when I shifted from being a fit sportsman to an overweight employee. I worked hard and challenged myself to lose weight four times. And then, once I was fit, I slipped on the routine and discipline, and I gained weight again.

Each time losing weight did work. The very first time I left all the junk foods and had a lot less food that helped me to reduce. But with this, I experienced low energy and fatigue. After controlling for a few months one fine day, I lost control and went back to my normal diet. Things got worse. I started putting on again.

Then I started running. This time I had a little better diet in terms of quantity as compared to my first time. I continued this for a few months and went around the marathon running for a good 25 - 30 minutes daily six days a week. I again lost weight. But because of the running activity, it took a strain on my body, and I lost control again and gained weight again.

However, over the different attempts and self-experience, I have realised that to be in good shape one has to have balanced nutrition.

What I have learnt over the last six years of having balanced nutrition is very important to have an understanding of the right food and food habits. Last six years I have diligently been working on my exercise regime, and yoga, and have maintained my fitness level, keeping my weight well under control.

Under the concept of Balanced Nutrition, it becomes very important to understand that the concept of diet as having less food is a farce.

Dieting would deplete certain vitamins, and minerals which can cause mood swings and can cause you even to stress. All these might make you lose control one day. You must understand the foods – carbohydrates, fats, proteins, minerals, and vitamins and how eating them in the right proportions can solve many of your worries, and this systematic eating diligently is balanced nutrition.

So, the term is "Balanced Nutrition" and not Dieting.

I asked a lot of people about what the size of your stomach is. Surprisingly, not many knew about it. The stomach is the size of your two fists joined together. We consider the entire abdomen as our stomach and gobble food. Yoga says that you need to have food just 25% of your stomach and the rest 25% water. 50% of the space you need to digest food. Understanding the stomach is very important for your benefit. Everybody is unique, there is no peculiar balanced nutrition diet that would be good for a person.

Let's take the example of milk. Milk is said to be very healthy and of course, it does have certain benefits. But taking milk at the wrong time can worsen things. Like milk taken in the morning with rotis or bread would give you a hard time to digest. Milk in itself is a complete meal and it needs to be taken on an empty stomach. After taking milk you should not eat anything for the next 45 minutes to digest it. If you understand the mechanism of your stomach, half of your eating and digesting challenges are solved.

Certain foods are healthy for you, at certain periods. But consuming them at the wrong time will not be healthy. This is how it is. The basic rule of food is you should be sensitive towards your stomach. Digestion takes a minimum of 2 to 3 hours, and this gives you lethargy and heaviness.

Luke Coutinho, an established Nutritionist says, *our bodies possess innate intelligence and mechanisms that guide us on when to eat, how much to consume, and when to stop. Hunger and thirst are natural signals ingrained within us, constantly communicating when to nourish ourselves and when to hydrate. Pain serves as another message from the body, indicating its needs. It's important to recognize the distinction between physical hunger and emotional hunger, which may stem from various emotions such as sadness, anger, or happiness. Emotional eating may lead to overeating or undereating, and at the same time, true physical hunger is felt in the stomach. Waiting for about 10 minutes can help discern whether it's genuine hunger or an emotional urge. If hunger persists, it's time for a nutritious meal. This interplay between feasting and fasting aligns with the natural functioning of the human body.*

Let's discuss the timing of meals and the amount of water we should drink. Our bodies possess innate intelligence and mechanisms that guide us on when to eat, how much to consume, and when to stop. Hunger and thirst are natural signals ingrained within us, constantly communicating when to nourish ourselves and when to hydrate. Pain serves as another message from the body, indicating its needs. It's important to recognize the distinction between physical hunger and emotional hunger, which may stem from various emotions such as sadness, anger, or happiness.

Today we are so accustomed to age-old food habits that we don't want to explore what is needed. It's important to unlearn them and understand our gut. If you stay aware of yourself, about your stomach, I'm sure you will understand which foods are good, what are the good timings, and what are the good food habits.

I will share with you the generic rules of food habits and food. I understand with your current food habits, and your sensitivity towards your stomach it's going to be difficult to trust the aspect of balanced nutrition.

To understand your requirement of energy and to fulfil that energy what nutritional needs to be taken care of? One thing is sure, you have to be self-aware, self-afraid of your stomach and the food that you consume. The food that we have is for nutrition, it needs to be absorbed well. A good healthy relationship depends on the space a stomach gives to digest its food. Life is not merely about longevity, it's more about how fit you live. It's not how many days, how many years, how many decades you have lived, but you can live. Are you living a healthy life? Are you living a life to breathe? Are you living a full life? That's what I call living healthy.

A fit body would have a better expression of life and, a higher expression of self. The human body depends upon food as its fuel. This fuel helps build strength, gives specific nutrients, keeps away pathological issues, improves mental and physical health as well as enhances longevity if taken in an orderly form.

A body that is well supplemented on different foods, at periodic intervals can keep you energised and active. However, some foods might make you feel lethargic and need to be avoided. Sometimes, we cannot refuse the urge to have a dessert on an already heavy stomach, and then we are ourselves calling for lethargy.

In some cases, or most, the digestive system also plays a major role in processing the food. What you eat and how you eat will decide your trajectory through the digestive system. Meat and other non-veg foods take the most time to digest whereas fruits can be easily digested. Our digestive system is a magical machine that works on our brain signals, and each one of us should know how it works.

Digestive System

What is the function of the digestive system?

The purpose of your digestive system is to efficiently transform the food you consume into the essential nutrients and energy required for your sustenance. Additionally, once it has completed this process, it effectively segregates your solid waste, known as stool, and prepares it for elimination during a bowel movement.

Why is digestion important?

Digestion is essential because it extracts vital nutrients (carbohydrates, proteins, fats, vitamins, minerals, and water) from the food and drinks you consume. These nutrients are crucial for energy, growth, and cell repair, ensuring your body functions properly and stays healthy.

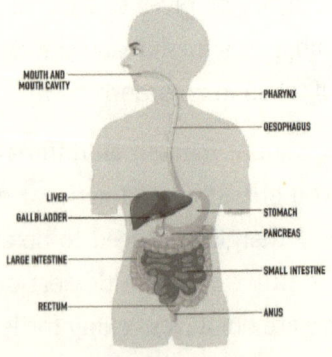

DIGESTION PROCESS

What organs make up the digestive system?

Your digestive system consists of the gastrointestinal tract, featuring the mouth, oesophagus, stomach, small intestine, large intestine, and anus, complemented by supporting organs such as the pancreas, gallbladder, and liver. Together, they function harmoniously to process food and nutrients.

Mouth

Digestion begins in the mouth, even before eating. Saliva is triggered by the sight and smell of food. Chewing and saliva further break down food for absorption. Swallowing moves it into the throat and oesophagus.

Oesophagus

The oesophagus, near the windpipe, receives food during swallowing. The epiglottis prevents choking. Muscular contractions move food to the stomach. Before that, the lower oesophageal sphincter relaxes to allow food in and then contracts to prevent acid reflux or heartburn.

Stomach

The stomach is a container for food, where it mixes with enzymes that break it down. Stomach cells secrete acids and enzymes to aid in this process, and once the food is sufficiently processed, it moves to the small intestine.

Small Intestine

The small intestine is divided into duodenum, jejunum, and ileum. It's a 22-foot muscular tube that breaks down food using pancreas enzymes and liver bile, aided by peristalsis. The duodenum focuses on breaking down food, while the jejunum and ileum absorb nutrients into the bloodstream.

Initially, semi-solid, small intestine contents turn liquid due to water, bile, enzymes, and mucus. After nutrient absorption, the liquid residue moves to the large intestine (colon).

Pancreas

The pancreas releases digestive enzymes into the duodenum to break down proteins, fats, and carbohydrates. Additionally, it produces insulin, which enters the bloodstream and serves as the primary hormone for sugar metabolism in the body.

Liver

The liver's primary role in digestion is processing nutrients from the small intestine. It also produces bile for fat and vitamin digestion. Beyond that, it functions as the body's chemical factory, generating essential chemicals, while also detoxifying harmful substances, including drugs.

Gallbladder

The gallbladder stores and concentrates bile produced by the liver. It subsequently releases this bile into the duodenum of the small intestine, facilitating the absorption and digestion of fats.

Colon

The colon, a 6-foot-long muscular tube, processes waste, turning liquid remnants into solid stools by removing water. Stool, mostly food debris and beneficial bacteria, is stored in the sigmoid colon until elimination, which takes about 36 hours. When the descending colon is full, it empties into the rectum to start bowel movements.

Rectum

The rectum is an 8-inch passage connecting the colon to the anus. It receives stool, temporarily stores stool, and signals the need for evacuation. Sensors in the rectum notify the brain, which decides whether to release the contents. If allowed, the sphincters relax, and the rectum contracts to eliminate the stool; otherwise, the sensation temporarily subsides.

Anus

The anus, the end of the digestive tract, is a 2-inch canal with muscles and sphincters. Its upper lining detects and signals the nature of rectal contents, whether liquid, gas, or solid.

What Body Type Are You?

What is your Body Mass Index required to maintain a healthy body? Strictly, it's going to be how and what type of genetics you have. So, it's never going to be size. It's always going to be a matter of breath. How is the life force within you? Is it towards the full form of expression and this expression would be better by way of balanced nutrition?

Balanced nutrition would have aspects of carbohydrates, fats, and proteins, also with requirements of certain vitamins & minerals. The body if you see is an amalgamation of chemical reactions. If these reactions happen to their fullest, you will be healthy. For which you need good levels of juices flowing through your body. It should be taken care of by the food that you eat, being absorbed well by the body.

A self-aware person will usually have a very fit life regardless of his appearance. Appearance is just one of the facets that you can see. More than happiness, it's the flow of energy that keeps you going, and this flow will be uninterrupted.

Calories Count Chart

Nutrient	Energy Produced	Broken down into	Function
Carbohydrates	1 g = 4 Kcal	Glucose	Energy
Proteins	1 g = 4 Kcal	Amino acids	• Muscle Protein synthesis
Fats	1 g = 9 Kcal	Fatty acids	• To make essential fat (like cell membrane), sex hormones & many other functions.

Macro-Nutrients Source Chart

Food Group	Food Sources	Macronutrient
1. Cereals/ Grains/ Millets	Rice, Wheat, Jowar, Bajra, Corn, Ragi, Chapatti, Bread, Idli, Poha, Upma, Dosa, Kurmura, Popcorn, Cornflakes, Wheat flakes, Oats, Muesli	Mainly Carbohydrate
2. Vegetables	Palak, Methi, Lettuce, Beans, Bhindi, Cabbage, Cauliflower	Carbohydrate
3. Fruits	Banana, Mango, Apple, Pear, Orange, Guava, Sweet Lime etc.	Carbohydrate
4. Pulses/ Legumes/ Dals	Soyabean, Chana, Rajma, Chole, Moong, Masoor, Matki and their dals	Carbohydrates + Protein
5. Animal Food	Egg, Chicken, Fish, Mutton	Protein + Fat
Food Group	Food Sources	Macronutrient
6. Milk And Milk Products	Curd, Milk, Paneer, Cheese	Carbohydrate + Protein + Fat
7. Fats/Oils	Cooking Oil, Ghee, Butter	Fat
8. Sugars	Jaggery, Sugar, Honey	Carbohydrate
9. Nuts & Oilseeds	Almond, Walnut, Pista, Peanut	Fat + Protein + Carb
10. Roots & Tubers	Potato, Sweet Potato, Raddish, Beetroot	Carbohydrate

Macro-Nutrients

For your understanding, it's better to know what happens when food is consumed, what happens when we eat carbohydrates, proteins, and fats, and how they help is important. In a broader and general sense understanding carbohydrates, proteins, and fats would give you an understanding of what you need to consume.

Carbohydrates are an energy fuel, and it gives you energy to work.

Proteins give you muscle power and strength.

Fats can be good and bad fats. Fats give you vital nutrients.

Understanding food and food habits is going to be your biggest piece of work. To apply these towards ensuring balanced nutrition the general rule of the food habit is, to use time. What time of the day are you having your meals? Some people would be high on fire element, That person would need his first meal early in the morning. Some people like me who are high in the element of water, can take the first meal a little later. I take my first meal close to noon during lunchtime. My morning time is mostly used to let the creative energy flow and to do workouts. If I work out, I eat the first meal after my workout around 9- 10 am.

Food Habits

Whatever you eat, it has to come in a disciplined manner if you think about healthy longevity for your body. Often eating the right things in the wrong way can have a toll, or eating the right things at the wrong time can be harmful too. It's important to understand when your body needs food. You should observe your episodic hunger pangs, and the food craving cycle and thus feed your body in that discipline and time. Remember, everybody is different, so one diet food chart or table of standard information might not fit your body and lifestyle. Be aware, be informed and make your food habits accordingly. Habit, because anything that is done in a regular and disciplined manner would give assured results.

To maintain a healthy and balanced eating routine, it's essential to adhere to several key practices. Firstly, ensure you never skip meals, as this can disrupt your metabolism and lead to overeating later in the day. Instead, plan your meals and snacks ahead of time to make nutritious choices readily available.

Keeping a food diary can be an effective tool for monitoring your eating habits, helping you identify patterns and areas for improvement. Moreover, limit nighttime eating to prevent excessive calorie intake before bedtime.

Hydration is crucial, so make it a habit to drink plenty of water throughout the day. When cravings hit, try delaying or distracting yourself to steer clear of heavy eating. If boredom sets in, choose physical activity as a helpful substitute.

Pay close attention to your meals by avoiding distractions like TV, work, driving, or standing while eating. Consume your meals in a designated setting, preferably at the kitchen table, for undistracted eating habits.

Monitoring portion sizes is vital for controlling calorie intake but remember to allow yourself a variety of foods without rigidly forbidding any particular item. Be your cheerleader by offering self-encouragement and seek support from a trusted person who can help keep you motivated and accountable on your journey.

Remember, it's important to be kind to yourself. Don't dwell on lapses; instead, view them as opportunities for growth. Approach healthy eating as a long-term lifestyle change rather than a short-term fix. Finally, if you choose to use a scale to track your progress, do so mindfully and limit weigh-ins to no more than once a week, as weight fluctuations are normal. Ultimately, prioritise making consistently healthy food choices to support your overall well-being.

Quantity of Food

In this part of the world- India, we have around four meals. The major three are – breakfast, lunch, & dinner. Few people even have evening snacks. The size and portions of the concept here are usually eating lot of Chapatis - the Indian bread, which may cause trouble based on your gut. Then eating rice in a large quantity gives you a lot of glucose spike. And if the energy is not consumed it turns into fat. The question is, do you need this large amount of energy? As you need energy for the working of different body functions, the question is - How much energy do you need for your work?

We are eating based on assumptions which have been going on for ages. We feed on chapati and rice more than required and then complain about all the troubles that we are having because so much energy is put together which is not consumed. It then shows through lethargy, fat deposits and indigestion. The small intestine is an engine for us to operate our body. Now, if our tank is overloaded, it's not going to be efficient. Rather we are putting more load and damaging it. So, understand the quantity to eat. Every person is unique, every person's job is unique, every person's profession is unique, and so is their need. Their mental habits are unique. The mental work also absorbs or requires energy. So, what is required specifically for you, is important to understand.

I was discussing with another friend the importance of the consumption of milk. He said, my grandmother said that milk is healthy and to have half a litre of milk every morning. He approached me seeking advice on weight loss and improving health, expressing concerns about feeling lethargic after consuming milk. Observing his situation, I couldn't help but notice the contrast between him and his grandmother. While his grandmother was actively involved in farming, he led a sedentary lifestyle at his desk job. Despite my observations, he remained steadfast in his belief that milk was still healthy. At that point, I decided to let the matter rest.

The key takeaway is that people need to be open to learning, unlearning, or even discarding certain beliefs and practices to see what works best for them.

The Aspect of Time

"Your circadian rhythm is a 24-hour internal clock that is running in the background of your brain and cycles between sleepiness and alertness at regular intervals. It's also known as your sleep-wake cycle," states the National Sleep Foundation.

Circadian rhythm, or our natural body clock, controls many biological activities in our body, including metabolism. In the morning, when the sun is up, our metabolism is high, and our bodies are more sensitive to insulin. This allows us to use the energy from food efficiently and feel alert and energized. In the evening, when the sun goes down, our metabolism slows down, and our bodies become less sensitive to insulin. This prepares our bodies for rest and cell repair.

I have known a friend who is a diabetic for many years now. He has tried numerous ways to bring his diabetes under control. Over the last couple of years, he has been living an active lifestyle. Yet, six months back he had a car accident and had a frozen shoulder. Despite active physiotherapy, his frozen shoulder pain keeps him awake at night, and he can only sleep at 4 in the morning. His health spiralled down because his circadian clock changed. His blood sugar was so high that it impacted his vision to a considerable extent. He is struggling with the consequences and needs a turnaround of his existing lifestyle.

Experts believe that aligning our mealtimes with our circadian rhythm can have many benefits, including:

- Weight loss: When we eat in sync with our circadian rhythm, we are more likely to burn calories efficiently and lose weight.

- Improved endurance: Eating at the right times can help us to improve our endurance and performance during exercise.

- Reduced risk of Type 2 diabetes: Aligning our mealtimes with our circadian rhythm can help to reduce the risk of developing Type-2 diabetes.

- Lower blood pressure: Eating at the right times can help to lower blood pressure.

When it comes to food consumption before a workout, the timing is important. If you are going to do a high-intensity workout or running, it is generally recommended to go on an empty stomach. This is because your body will burn more fat for energy when you are working out on an empty stomach. However, it is important to listen to your body and see how it reacts.

The amount of food you eat before your workout also depends on your body type. Genetically thin people may need to eat a small amount of food before their workout to avoid feeling lightheaded or nauseous. However, naturally heavier people may be able to work out on an empty stomach without any problems.

Ultimately, the best way to determine how much food to eat before your workout is to experiment and see what works best for you. Pay attention to how your body feels and listen to your intuition. The most important thing is to find a balance that allows you to work out hard and feel good without feeling sick or uncomfortable.

Chewing the food

An essential aspect of maintaining healthy eating habits involves the proper chewing of food rather than hastily swallowing it. When we chew our food thoroughly, it becomes mixed with saliva, which in turn aids in the digestion process once the food reaches the stomach. It's advisable to make a conscious effort to chew each mouthful at least around 32 times before swallowing, ensuring that the food is effectively broken down into a nearly liquefied consistency. This practice not only eases the workload on the stomach but also promotes more efficient digestion.

Furthermore, the role of water in digestion cannot be understated. Incorporating water into our eating routine can significantly enhance its benefits for the body. Drinking water slowly and steadily while in a seated position can optimise its effects on the digestive system. By being mindful of both chewing habits and water consumption, we can actively contribute to better digestion and overall well-being.

There is a medical fact behind drinking water preferably by sitting and not standing.

"Sitting while drinking water helps our kidneys filter it better. When we stand and drink water, the fluid quickly passes through our stomach without being filtered. This can cause impurities in the water to settle in our bladder and can damage our kidneys."

Time to Digest

The third thing, the big rule of balanced nutrition is the gap between sleep and your last meal is strictly to be put in a time gap of minimum two to three hours. I would say it depends on a person who can digest food in less time.

The time gap is really important. What happens is people usually have a late-night dinner and then sleep for the next hour or half. Some people say I cannot sleep if my stomach is empty. You need to understand that while you sleep, you're not letting your organs rest.

Waiting a few hours after dinner before going to bed can also help to improve sleep quality. When you eat a large meal before bed, your body has to work harder to digest the food, which can make it difficult to fall asleep. Additionally, the body temperature rises after eating, which can also make it harder to fall asleep. Waiting a few hours after dinner allows your body to digest the food and return to its normal temperature, which can help you to fall asleep more easily.

Finally, waiting a few hours after dinner before going to bed can help to prevent weight gain. When you eat a large meal before bed, your body has more calories to store as fat. Additionally, the body produces more insulin after eating, which can also promote the storage of fat. Waiting a few hours after dinner allows your body to use up some of the calories from the meal before storing any as fat.

A Clear Gut

Proper digestion plays a pivotal role in maintaining a healthy gastrointestinal system, ensuring the efficient elimination of waste from your body each morning. If you encounter difficulties in achieving regular bowel movements, it raises a red flag regarding your digestion. The benefits of optimal digestion extend beyond just physical comfort; they encompass a clear and rejuvenated gut, elevated energy levels, and stable moods. Prioritising and nurturing proper digestion can lead to a positive effect that contributes to your overall well-being.

Sleep is one of the most important parts of life. We sleep for one-third of our life. The moment you practise an empty stomach sleeping for a few days, you're going to feel energetic in the morning. The first thing that is going to change is the perception of life because now you'll be full of energy and once, you're full of energy the expression of life changes. Let the flow of energy happen, let it flow like a kid, let it grow, let it grow each night. Ensure you take care of your sleep on a good mattress, in a good clean room. Sleep well aware of yourself and with all the love you need, to experience the fullest.

To Clean the Gut

You might be familiar with various liquids recommended for bowel cleansing, each with its benefits. However, if you're unable to follow those methods, here's a simple alternative: drink at least 1-2 glasses of water or gulp down enough to stimulate bowel movement. Hot water is beneficial, and lukewarm water is optimal, but if heating water isn't feasible, room-temperature water will suffice.

Culture of Party

The next big thing in food habits is the perception of partying. The perception of enjoyment of your taste buds. To adjust to society and status, people have accepted a set level of living. Eating and drinking out at untimely hours. Eating unhealthily, usually fried foods.

We live in an age where some things are important, friends, a bottle of wine, business meetings over drinks. Such social and professional obligations are necessary, but it is important to know your health. It is better if you understand the foods which are good and bad. Again, with good foods, the quantity matters and so it is with bad foods.

So, if you want to party, go, and educate yourself with certain foods that are okay to have once in a while. Be strict in your discipline. Life is more of food habits, and you need to be open-minded to understand what works best for you.

Work-Stress Relationship

Stress eating presents a significant challenge for many, driven by various factors like daily pressures, screen time, and emotional turmoil. Awareness of triggers and cultivating healthy coping mechanisms are key to combating this habit.

In a 2014 survey by the American Psychological Association, 33% of Americans admitted to overeating or consuming unhealthy foods due to stress. Nutrition plays a crucial role in stress management; however, stress often leads to cravings for sugary, fatty, and salty foods, aggravating the situation.

Opting for high-fibre, protein-rich foods, while avoiding processed items and sugary drinks, can help mitigate stress-related eating patterns. Adequate sleep, confiding in a trusted individual, regular exercise, and relaxation techniques such as yoga or meditation are also beneficial.

Personal experimentation and perseverance are vital in discovering what dietary and lifestyle strategies work best. Despite setbacks and weight fluctuations, maintaining a disciplined routine has enabled long-term weight management, health, and overall well-being.

Self-Management

Everything starts with the self. Handling and balancing the different aspects of you like health, emotion, spiritual well-being, and more. Self-understanding is what needs to be practised toward self-management. Self-awareness and self-understanding serve as the foundational pillars for a fulfilling and balanced life. Here's an elaboration on how focusing on oneself can lead to better management of various life aspects:

Interpersonal Relationships: Self-awareness enhances your ability to relate to others. By understanding your own emotions and reactions, you can better empathise with others and navigate conflicts more effectively. It also enables you to set healthy boundaries and maintain healthier relationships.

Personal Growth: Self-awareness is a vital driver of personal growth. When you understand your strengths, weaknesses, and areas for improvement, you can set meaningful goals and work toward self-improvement. Continuous self-reflection and learning become catalysts for personal development.

Life Balance: Self-awareness aids in achieving balance in life. By assessing your priorities, values, and energy levels, you can make conscious decisions about how to allocate your time and resources. This balance leads to a more harmonious and fulfilling lifestyle.

Decision-Making: Self-awareness plays a pivotal role in decision-making. It allows you to align choices with your values, assess potential consequences, and make informed decisions that resonate with your authentic self.

Resilience: Self-understanding fosters resilience. When you know your strengths and limitations, you can approach challenges with greater confidence and adaptability. Failures and setbacks are seen as opportunities for growth rather than insurmountable obstacles.

In essence, everything does indeed start with self-awareness and self-understanding. It's an ongoing practice that enables you to lead a more authentic, balanced, and purpose-driven life, fostering well-being across various dimensions of your existence.

Wealth

When your blood is circulating freely in your body, you are healthy. When money is circulating freely in your life, you are economically healthy.

One of the reasons the rich get richer, the poor get poorer, and the middle class struggles with debt is that the subject of money is taught at home and not in school.

-**Rich Dad Poor Dad.**

Contrary to the beliefs of our parents, and their parents and their parents, we have been under the influence of notions held by them in terms of money. Money as a valuable lesson has indeed been transcended to us at home, through whatever beliefs our parents and forefathers have held. Therefore, we all have never received standard lessons on money, as other topics are taught academically.

We all have grown up hearing some erratic beliefs about money from our parents that –

Does money grow on trees?

Money is hard to earn.

Money is evil.

We must supersede these home-taught beliefs on money and accept some proven ways which have been helping people achieve their money goals.

I have included the fourth pillar - finance in complete well-being because I feel that even after adjusting and optimising all the other aspects of your life, your money angle remains the most important. Leading a certain lifestyle needs money, having the discretion to enjoy your work under stress means the support of money, relaxing your mind when others are racing calls for money. Money is responsible for all aspects of our lives in this scenario, in this time.

This book is a game changer, highlighting and changing the way people think about money. Here's an excerpt from the book, "Rich Dad Poor Dad."

"One dad had a habit of saying I can't afford it. The other dad forbade those words to be used. Instead, he insisted I ask, "How can I afford it?" While one is a statement, the other is a question. One lets you off the hook and the other forces you to think. My soon-to-be rich dad would explain that by automatically saying the words. "I can't afford it." your brain stops working. By asking the question, "How can I afford it?", your brain is put to work. He was fanatical about exercising your mind the most."

Concept of Money – Physical and Mental Money

The concept of money extends beyond the physical, encompassing its mental dimension and how we manage it.

Money plays a paramount role, in influencing various facets of our existence, including our physical well-being, mental state, and overall health. When one's financial situation is stable, it can have a positive impact on maintaining balance in these other crucial domains of life: the body, mind, and health.

Aspect	Physical Wellbeing	Mental Wellbeing
Financial Stability	Stability in finances contributes to affording nutritious food, healthcare, and physical activities, leading to better physical health.	Reduced financial stress enhances mental clarity, reduces anxiety, and promotes emotional well-being.
Managing Money	Requires discipline in budgeting, saving, and spending, which can translate into healthier lifestyle choices, such as	Discipline in financial management fosters cognitive focus and decision-making skills, enhancing mental

	prioritising essential needs over impulse purchases.	acuity and reducing distractions.
Impact on Life Balance	Financial stability enables individuals to allocate time and resources to maintain a balanced lifestyle, including regular exercise, adequate sleep, and leisure activities.	Reduced financial worries allow for better concentration, productivity, and engagement in activities that promote mental well-being, such as hobbies and social interactions.

To attract money, you should focus on wealth. It is impossible to bring more money into your life when you are noticing you do not have enough, because that means you are thinking thoughts that you do not have enough. Focus on not having enough money, and you will create untold more circumstances of not having more money. You must focus on the abundance of money to bring that to you.

-The Secret

Discipline of Credit Card

I've observed individuals earning, for instance, around 30,000 to 40,000 per month, yet holding a credit card with a limit of 3 lakhs, which is 10 times their monthly income. This decision is often considered unwise.

A prudent approach to managing a credit card is to maintain a credit limit that is in the range of 20% to 30% of your monthly salary. For instance, if your monthly income is 1 lakh/month, it would be advisable to have a credit card with a limit of Rs. 20,000 to 30,000.

It's crucial to avoid falling into the high-interest rate trap, particularly with personal loans. Home loans can be restricted to one with average interest rates.

Mental Money

Mental money is basically how you look at money. What are your values and beliefs about money?

"Mental money" refers to the psychological and emotional relationship an individual has with money. It encompasses their attitudes, values, beliefs, and behaviours concerning financial matters. Here's an elaboration on the concept of mental money:

1. How you think about Money:

A person's money mindset is the foundation of their mental money. It's the set of beliefs and attitudes they hold about money. For example, some individuals may have a scarce mindset, believing that there is never enough money, leading to a fear of financial insecurity. Others may have an abundance mindset, believing that opportunities for wealth are plentiful and attainable through effort and smart choices.

2. Values and Beliefs:

A person's values and beliefs about money are deeply rooted in their upbringing, culture, and personal experiences. These can include beliefs about the importance of saving, investing, or spending money on experiences rather than possessions. Some may value financial security above all else, while others prioritise enjoying life in the present.

3. Financial Aspirations:

Mental money influences the financial goals one sets. A person with a strong belief in saving may prioritise long-term financial security, while someone who values experiences might set goals related to travel or personal development. These goals reflect an individual's values and beliefs about what money can achieve.

4. Financial Discipline:

Mental money significantly impacts spending and saving habits. For instance, someone with a belief in frugality and minimalism may practise budgeting and prioritise saving. Conversely, individuals with a belief in indulgence and immediate gratification may accumulate debt through excessive spending.

5. Mental Relation:

Money can evoke strong emotions, and a person's mental money can influence their emotional response to financial situations. For example, someone with a fear of financial instability may experience anxiety or stress when faced with unexpected expenses, while another person may approach such situations with confidence and problem-solving skills.

6. Decision-Making:

Mental money plays a pivotal role in financial decision-making. It affects choices related to investing, spending, budgeting, and debt management. People with a growth-oriented money mindset may be more inclined to seek financial education and make informed decisions.

7. How it affects the well-being:

Mental money can significantly impact an individual's overall well-being. A healthy money mindset can contribute to reduced stress, improved relationships (especially regarding joint finances in partnerships), and a sense of control over one's financial life. Conversely, negative, or unhealthy mental money can lead to financial stress, conflict, and emotional turmoil.

Understanding and assessing one's mental money is crucial for achieving financial goals and maintaining a healthy relationship with money. It enables individuals to identify, and challenge limiting beliefs, cultivate a positive money mindset, and make more informed financial decisions aligned with their values and goals.

Break Your Existing Patterns

"Brain can create reality" when you carry the perceived reality in mind. We have seen astounding examples of the law of attraction and the power of manifestation.

Are you contemplating ways to enhance your financial situation? Do you aspire to increase your income beyond your current earnings? The good news is that you can draw wealth into your life. "You can attract money".

However, it's important to clarify that attracting money doesn't entail quitting your job or simply waiting for money to magically materialise. Instead, it involves adopting a disciplined approach to managing your finances and being mindful of your spending habits. This process also requires introspection, including an examination of your values and beliefs about money.

Furthermore, setting clear financial goals is a pivotal step. The more precise and detailed your goals are, the more likely you are to manifest them. In the realm of businesses, growth may occur in substantial leaps, while for salaried individuals, it might be more gradual but definite.

Consider this analogy: Imagine the Universe intends to offer you a 50% increase in income, but you're only requesting a 15% raise. In this scenario, you may unintentionally limit your potential for financial growth. Who is at a loss then?

I recall a conversation with a friend who owns a recruitment consultancy business. We were casually discussing the concept of business growth and attracting wealth when he shared an intriguing anecdote about one of his candidates.

This particular candidate possessed a rare IT skill at a beginner level and was currently earning a salary of 3.5 lakhs per annum. Surprisingly, he received a job offer from my friend's client with a whopping 100% hike, taking his potential new salary to 7 lakhs per annum. However, as the joining date approached, the candidate became unresponsive, leaving everyone puzzled. My friend and his team embarked on a quest to track him down, scouring various social media platforms and communication means. Despite their efforts, the candidate remained elusive, and the joining date passed without a word.

Finally, the candidate resurfaced and explained. Astonishingly, he had received an even more lucrative offer of 35 lakhs per annum, an opportunity he simply couldn't resist. You might wonder if this sounds too good to be true, but it wasn't. Based on the initial offer of 7 lakhs, he secured a second offer of 21 lakhs from another company. However, it was the third company that extended the jaw-dropping 35-lakh offer, citing a high-priority project requiring his rare skill set.

This story serves as a reminder that, even as a salaried individual, setting your intentions on attracting opportunities can lead to remarkable outcomes. After all, visionaries like Jeff Bezos and Steve Jobs never initially envisioned running multi-million-dollar empires.

An individual's beliefs and values hold significant sway over their path in life. It's crucial to recognize that the size of a business is not what matters most; it's the idea and the potential behind it. Every business starts as a concept on paper, and both entrepreneurs and salaried individuals have the capacity for growth and success.

Market dynamics and news about impending recessions, job losses, pay reductions, limited job opportunities, and shifting landscapes can sometimes be demoralising. However, it's essential to remember that change is an inherent and inevitable part of life. Rather than letting these challenges deter you, consider adopting a discerning approach. Focus on absorbing only the information that is pertinent and beneficial to your personal and professional growth.

Consciously embracing the idea of wealth can, indeed, attract prosperity into your life. It can start with a simple affirmation: "I am prosperous. I am wealthy." This positive mindset shift can set the stage for a more abundant and fulfilling journey.

The clear steps to being wealthy –

1. What you aspire to do with the wealth?
2. What change will you bring once you are wealthy?
3. How much of wealth do you need now? Define it clearly 'in terms of an exact amount.'

Once you have clear definition, please ensure to believe that you deserve and have faith to be wealthy.

4. Action to be taken – Visualise your wealthy life, How will it be when you will be wealthy?
5. Now live it mentally.
6. Let all your logical thoughts relax.
7. Mark the time and date to earn the desired wealth.

Above all, you need faith to embrace being mentally wealthy.

PART II
POWER OF MIND

The mind is by far the most complicated and least understood aspect of a human. But what is the mind?

I had this encounter with a Buddhist Monk while visiting a monastery and asked him, "What is mind?" He asked me to follow him as he performed an activity with me to explain the mind. He asked me to sit in a comfortable position and close my eyes. Then he instructed me to breathe in about 3 times and relax. He then said,

"While sitting in this relaxed position, see yourself reaching your home."

Suddenly, I did not find myself in that room anymore; but I was at my door. He instructed, now can you see your mother opening the door asking you to freshen up and while you are freshening up, you can now smell your favourite dish. You go to the kitchen to see your mother cooking your favourite dish.

You are happy, ecstatic, and at that moment you hug your mother, and she serves you your favourite food. You have it, and in a blink, you are now back in the monastery. "Breathe back 3 times, you have come back to where you are" . I hear.

The monk asked me to open my eyes and asked, "Did you experience the mind?" And indeed, you did. You journeyed to places, felt emotions, and saw scenes unfolding—all within the scope of your mind. The monk continued, "Now, are you aware of the power of your mind?" I nodded, realising the immense potential lying within. But then, the monk posed a challenge: Can you harness this power even in times of trouble?"

Initially sceptical, I wondered how happiness could coexist with problems. Yet, the monk assured me that it's possible – in a powerful way- By Harnessing the Power of the Mind.

Chapter Three

Conscious, Subconscious & Unconscious Mind

Sigmund Freud, a notable figure in the world of psychology, emerged as a prominent researcher in the field of the mind. Hailing from Austria, he contributed a plethora of theories, including his conceptualization of the levels of the mind. These divisions are recognized by Freud as the three tiers of awareness: the conscious, the subconscious mind, and the unconscious.

According to his framework, our mental processes unfold within the dynamics of these distinct levels.

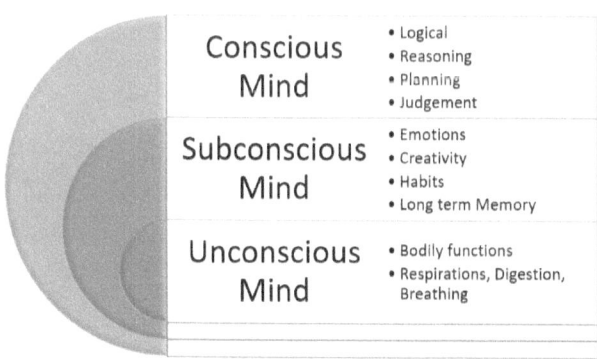

Conscious Mind

The conscious mind encompasses various cognitive functions essential for daily functioning. It involves rationalisation, enabling individuals to analyse situations logically and make reasoned decisions. Willpower originates from the conscious mind, driving goal-directed behaviour and the ability to resist impulses. Short-term memory allows for the temporary storage of information, facilitating immediate tasks and problem-solving. Additionally, planning, critical thinking, and judgement are fundamental aspects of the conscious mind, enabling individuals to strategize, evaluate options, and make informed choices for both short-term and long-term outcomes.

Subconscious Mind

The subconscious mind operates beneath the surface of conscious awareness, influencing behaviour and thought patterns. Long-term memory storage occurs here, retaining vast amounts of information accumulated over time. Emotions, deeply rooted in the subconscious, shape perceptions and reactions to stimuli, often guiding decision-making processes. Creativity flourishes in the subconscious realm, where innovative ideas and solutions can emerge freely without the constraints of conscious limitations. Moreover, habits form and reside within the subconscious, driving automatic responses and routines that streamline daily life.

Unconscious Mind

The unconscious mind oversees vital bodily functions autonomously, regulating the pulse rate, respiration, and immune system without conscious effort or awareness. It operates seamlessly in the background, ensuring these physiological processes continue smoothly and efficiently. This running of the brain functions instinctively, without requiring deliberate thought or conscious intervention from the individual.

Western Vs Indian Thought Process

The Western way of living is defined by planning, affirmations and execution taking a strategic approach involving both the conscious and subconscious mind. Their methodology is driven from the conscious to the subconscious which involves reprogramming a set of values, ideologies, and practices to make a new start or progress.

The Indian way of living is driven by energy. We act from the subconscious making our conscious alert. We have been doing this through ages in the form of dhyana, yoga, and meditation. We believe in awakening and transfer of energies over positive affirmations and planning.

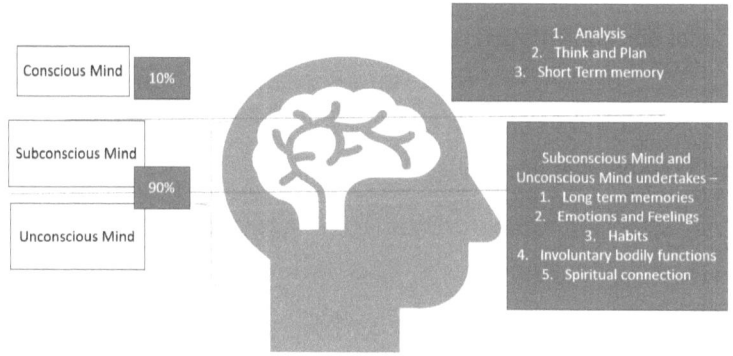

Conscious Mind, Subconscious and Unconscious Mind

Conscious Mind

The conscious mind acts as the centre of our consciousness, actively managing thoughts, perceptions, and choices in the present moment. It operates like the captain of a ship, steering our actions according to our comprehension of our surroundings. Through nurturing mindfulness and self-awareness, we unlock the potential of our conscious mind to mould our thoughts, behaviours, and ultimately, our destinies.

Your conscious mind is your rational or analytical mind. It lacks memory and can only focus on one thought at any given moment.

The conscious mind encompasses all that currently resides within our awareness. It encompasses thoughts and emotions that arise from engaging with information or conversing with others. These mental activities can manifest prominently or subtly within our mind's scope. A defining trait of the conscious mind is the unwavering awareness we possess, regardless of the specific location where thoughts and emotions emerge.

Scientists believe that your conscious mind makes up less than 10% of the mind's total operational power and is responsible for -

1. Collecting Information: Your conscious mind constantly receives input from your senses—what you see, hear, touch, taste, and smell. It's responsible for taking in information from the outside world and your thoughts and feelings.

2. Analysing and Processing Data: Once information is gathered, your conscious mind processes it. This involves recognizing objects, people, and situations, as well as understanding the meaning and importance of the information.

3. Finding Patterns and Connections: Your conscious mind is skilled at identifying patterns and making links between different pieces of information. This ability to compare and contrast is vital for solving problems and making decisions.

4. Decision Making and Directing Actions: A key role of the conscious mind is making decisions. It evaluates options based on processed data and recognized patterns, and then chooses a course of action. It also directs the body to carry out these decisions.

5. Mindful Responses: Your conscious mind enables you to respond thoughtfully to situations. It allows you to consider the consequences of your actions, weigh various options, and select the most suitable response.

6. Managing Short-term Memory: It holds information in your immediate awareness, enabling you to manipulate and work with it.

7. Conscious Awareness: When something is in your conscious mind, you are aware of it. This means you have a direct and active focus on that information or thought.

It's important to note that the conscious mind has limited capacity. It can only hold a relatively small amount of information at any given moment, and it requires cognitive effort to process and maintain that information. This limitation is one reason why we often rely on the subconscious mind for routine tasks and automated behaviours, freeing up the conscious mind for more complex and critical thinking.

The conscious mind works wonders when practising manifestation through:

- Affirmations: Positive statements to reprogram the subconscious mind
- Visualisation: Mentally picturing your desired outcomes
- Daily Practice: Consistent habits to reinforce progress
- Goal Writing: Setting clear intentions and reviewing them regularly

- Journaling: Reflecting on experiences and tracking growth

- Embracing a Positive Attitude: Cultivating optimism and gratitude to attract positive outcomes

Mita is a Stage Theatre Artist, and her journey towards her dream of becoming an actor was not an easy one. She faced numerous challenges and setbacks along the way, each one threatening to derail her aspirations. Despite her burning passion for acting, she found herself constantly battling self-doubt and the paralysing fear of failure, which often left her feeling overwhelmed and defeated.

It was during one particularly low moment that Mita crossed paths with a mentor who would change the course of her life. This mentor introduced her to the profound concept of the conscious mind – the seat of awareness, capable of shaping intentions, making decisions, and executing purposeful actions. This idea intrigued Mita, sparking a newfound determination to explore the power of her own conscious mind.

With renewed vigour, Mita began her journey of self-discovery and empowerment. She started by setting clear and achievable goals for her acting career, breaking them down into manageable steps that she could pursue methodically.

Her first fight was to get up and search for an art school from where she could take an acting course.

Getting up every day and keeping herself motivated to go for the course.

Practising time and again what she has learnt.

She started keeping a journal documenting her every day.

She started observing, evaluating, and analysing her performance.

She sought feedback on her work.

She started planning and improving her strength.

She had mental clarity and kept a commitment to herself.

It was an effort as her existent life pattern did not have any such schedule and aspirations, and she was doing things out of the box. She also delved into the practice of visualisation techniques, vividly imagining herself on stage, exuding confidence, and grace in every performance. She even visualised winning awards and being recognised. This exercise not only fuelled her ambition but also helped her cultivate a deep-seated belief in her own abilities, gradually eroding the walls of self-doubt that had held her back for so long.

As Mita devoted herself wholeheartedly to her art, she began to notice subtle shifts in her thoughts and behaviours. She became more disciplined in her practice, investing countless hours honing her skills and refining her technique. Most importantly, along the way, she learned to silence the nagging voice of self-doubt, replacing it with affirmations of confidence and unwavering belief in herself.

All along, Mita had learnt a valuable lesson – that the conscious mind is a formidable tool that can be harnessed to shape our reality and manifest our deepest desires. By setting clear intentions, staying focused on her goals, and taking purposeful action, she was able to overcome her setbacks and achieve her dreams.

Subconscious Mind

The subconscious mind operates as the powerhouse fuelling our beliefs, behaviours, and feelings, operating beyond our conscious awareness. It acts as the automatic pilot guiding our thoughts and actions, shaped significantly by past experiences and conditioning.

Through comprehending and reshaping our subconscious beliefs, we can unleash our complete potential and foster beneficial transformations in our lives.

The subconscious mind influences our thoughts, feelings, and behaviour without us being consciously aware. It is like a hidden operating system that runs in the background, controlling our bodily functions, processing information, and making decisions.

The subconscious mind exerts a potent influence on our thoughts, emotions, and actions, operating beyond our conscious recognition. While the conscious mind is focused on the present moment, the subconscious mind is constantly working behind the scenes to help us navigate our lives.

The majority of our brain's activity occurs within our subconscious mind, storing thoughts, emotions, and memories from our conscious awareness.

The subconscious mind tends to draw us back towards our comfort zone, which is familiar and predictable. This is because the subconscious mind is programmed to keep us safe. It associates change with uncertainty and risk, so it tries to prevent us from doing anything that might put us in danger. The subconscious mind is like a bouncer at the door to our conscious mind. It only lets in information that it thinks is safe.

As a young man brimming with dreams and aspirations, Rajesh often found himself overwhelmed by the complexities of daily life. The pressures of adulthood seemed to weigh heavily on his shoulders, leaving him feeling scattered and unsure of how to turn his aspirations into tangible achievements.

Rajesh was short of hope. He grappled with self-doubt and uncertainty, often finding himself at the mercy of negative thought patterns that hindered his progress. He struggled to navigate his emotions, feeling overwhelmed by the constant barrage of stress and anxiety.

One day amidst all his struggles, Rajesh stumbled upon a book that would change the course of his life – the book was based on the concept of the subconscious mind. Intrigued by the idea that his thoughts and beliefs held the key to shaping his reality, Rajesh saw a ray of hope to change his existing ways of life.

- *Determined to take control of his life, Rajesh turned to mindfulness and self-awareness techniques from the book as his guiding lights.*
- *He began to cultivate a deeper understanding of his thoughts and emotions, identifying patterns and triggers that influenced his behaviour.*
- *He started meditating.*
- *Through introspection and reflection, he gained invaluable insights into the inner workings of his subconscious mind.*

It was a long journey with this newfound awareness, Rajesh learned to harness the power of positive thinking and intention setting. Instead of dwelling on past mistakes or worrying about the uncertain future, he focused his energy on the present moment, cultivating a mindset of gratitude and abundance.

Beyond all this, he understood that mere awareness wasn't enough – he needed to take deliberate actions to manifest his dreams into reality.

Not later, Rajesh began to witness tangible results in his life. He found the courage to pursue his passions, breaking free from the shackles of fear and self-doubt that had held him back for so long.

Power of Subconscious Emotions

The actress Frieda Pinto whose movie won Oscars 'The Slumdog Millionaire, "I would describe myself simply as a working actor. When it comes to preparing for roles, my approach has been somewhat unconventional. Unlike many actors who have formal training from acting schools, I've forged my path by immersing myself in the world of cinema. I've spent countless hours watching films, studying the performances of various actors, and delving into autobiographical material to understand the intricacies of human behaviour."

While her sister attributed Freida's success to her manifestation power.

She says, "Freida finds immense joy in a quirky habit of hers was standing before the mirror, envisioning herself receiving the prestigious awards. It's a playful routine where she poses questions to herself and responds, creating an amusing scenario. Even before her journey into receiving actual awards and delivering heartfelt thank-you speeches, Freida had been practising her acceptance speeches in front of the mirror. It is her dedication and the power of visualisation long before such success materialised."

Unconscious Mind

The unconscious mind is a repository of emotions, thoughts, desires, and memories that exist beyond the scope of conscious awareness. Within this framework, the majority of the material stored in the unconscious is often regarded as unacceptable, or distressing, encompassing sensations like pain, anxiety, or inner conflicts. According to Sigmund Freud, the unconscious exerts an ongoing influence on our behaviour, even when we remain oblivious to these underlying forces.

Our unconscious mind possesses incredible power and plays several vital roles in our daily life:

1. Essential Bodily Functions: It manages the majority of our body's essential functions, such as breathing, digestion, sleep, heart rate, and temperature regulation, all without requiring our conscious intervention. It even controls our reflexes.

2. Guarding Mechanism - Our unconscious mind serves as a guardian of the status quo. When you attempt to initiate change, it can make you feel uneasy because it instinctively seeks to maintain what is familiar and perceived as safe. This resistance to change is a protective mechanism.

3. Emotional Portal: The seat of our emotions resides in our unconscious mind. It is responsible for generating and processing a wide range of emotions, influencing how you feel in response to various situations and stimuli.

4. Innovation and Inspiration: Our unconscious mind is the wellspring of imagination and creativity. It gives rise to innovative ideas, artistic inspiration, and novel solutions to problems. It's where our creative thinking flourishes.

5. Forming Patterns: Our habits, both beneficial and detrimental, are developed and sustained within our unconscious mind. It's the domain where routines and automatic behaviours are established and perpetuated.

6. Instincts: In times of perceived danger, our subconscious mind triggers automatic responses, such as the fight-or-flight reaction. It can prompt us to run, freeze, or take immediate action to address threats, all without conscious thought.

7. Memory Databank: Our unconscious mind serves as the repository for long-term memories. It stores past experiences and information, which it can retrieve when needed, influencing our decisions and behaviours based on past learning.

Our unconscious mind is a powerhouse that operates in the background, shaping our thoughts, emotions, and actions, often without our explicit awareness. Understanding and harnessing its capabilities can be a powerful tool for personal growth and self-improvement.

The unconscious mind can lead to certain challenges like:

1. Anger: Unconscious feelings of anger can surface unexpectedly in situations where they may not seem warranted. These repressed or hidden emotions can result in sudden outbursts or passive-aggressive behaviour, often leaving both the individual experiencing them and those around them puzzled by the intensity of the reaction.

2. Bias: Unconscious biases are attitudes or prejudices that individuals may hold without being consciously aware of them. These biases can affect decisions, judgments, and behaviours in ways that may be discriminatory or unfair. Becoming aware of these biases is crucial for combating discrimination and promoting equity.

3. Compulsive Behaviours: Unconscious thoughts and desires can drive compulsive behaviours. These behaviours can be distressing and interfere with daily life.

4. Difficult Social Interactions: Unresolved conflicts or hidden emotions can make social interactions challenging.

5. Distress: Unconscious distressing memories or emotions that are repressed can continue to generate psychological discomfort. This

distress may manifest as anxiety, depression, or other emotional difficulties, even if the person is not consciously aware of the source.

6. Relationship Problems: Unconscious feelings and desires can play a significant role in relationship dynamics. For instance, unresolved childhood issues or hidden insecurities may affect how individuals interact with their partners, leading to communication breakdowns or patterns of behaviour that cause strife in the relationship.

Freud's perspective on the unconscious posits that many of these issues arise because the mind seeks to protect itself from thoughts and emotions that are too emotionally charged or threatening to be consciously acknowledged.

The deepest layer of our mind, known as the unconscious, holds vast potential for personal growth. However, exploring this world is a complex practice, as it requires delving into deeply buried information.

Despite its elusive nature, the unconscious mind exerts a substantial influence on our behaviours. It quietly moulds our actions, frequently escaping our conscious awareness.

In the Indian Yogic system, it is believed that certain aspects of our experiences transcend our comprehension and originate from past lives. Energies, carrying "Samskara" from previous lives, influence our current existence. To navigate these energies, understanding the unconscious mind is essential. Yogis who perform miraculous feats or healing often operate within this energetic domain, offering a broader perspective on life and existence beyond the ordinary.

Ajita, initially seen as rational and composed, carried unresolved emotions, and buried memories shaping her behaviour. Through vivid dreams, she confronted past traumas, stirring deep emotions she couldn't grasp. Determined to understand, she tried taking a journey of self-discovery, exploring her unconscious mind's depths. Therapy and introspection revealed insights into her fears and desires. Unravelling her past, Ajita pieced together her identity and embraced her vulnerabilities. Listening to her unconscious whispers, she found guidance towards self-awareness and growth. Each revelation liberated her from past shackles, paving the way for a purposeful future. Ajita learned that by delving into her unconscious, she could unlock profound transformation and inner peace, realising the vast wisdom beneath conscious awareness.

How Your Subconscious Mind & Unconscious Mind Operates

The human brain constantly receives sensory input from our five senses, which are then stored as memories. However, only a small fraction of these memories is actively recalled, with estimates suggesting that between 95% and 99% are forgotten.

Nevertheless, these memories remain stored within our brains and can be accessed through techniques such as hypnosis. Psychological research indicates that our experiences, particularly those from early life, profoundly shape our thoughts and behaviours. Despite most of these memories not being consciously accessible, they exert a significant influence, accounting for an estimated 90% to 95% of our behaviour.

Comparable to the autopilot system of an aeroplane, the subconscious mind operates behind the scenes, regulating bodily functions and numerous daily activities without conscious awareness.

For example, we don't have to think about how to breathe or walk. Our Unconscious mind does it for us automatically. The Unconscious mind also helps to regulate our body temperature, heart rate, and other vital functions.

Our Subconscious mind holds our memories, beliefs, and feelings. It also helps with our emotions, creativity, and gut instincts. It's really strong and can help us do better in life. For example, it can help us build good habits, do well in tasks, and face tough situations.

Here's an excerpt from the book- 'The Power of Subconscious Mind.'

Watch your thoughts! All frustration is due to unfulfilled desires. If you dwell on obstacles, delays, and difficulties, your subconscious mind responds accordingly, and you are blocking your own good.

All your experiences and everything that enters into your life depend upon the nature of the mental building blocks which you use in the construction of your mental home.

The ideas which you harbour, the beliefs that you accept, and the scenes that you rehearse in the hidden studio of your mind.

Busy your mind with the concepts of harmony, health, peace, and goodwill, and wonders will happen in your life.

Brain & Mind Correlation -

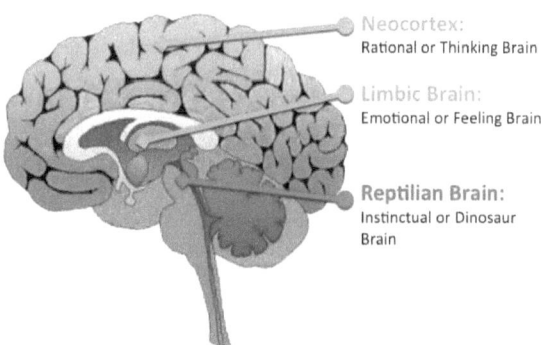

The correlation between the brain and the mind is a fundamental topic in neuroscience, psychology, and philosophy. Here's a brief overview:

Overall, while the exact nature of the correlation between the brain and the mind remains a subject of ongoing research and philosophical debate, it is widely accepted that there is a profound and intricate relationship between these two aspects of human experience.

Reptilian Brain

The reptilian brain, the oldest segment of the human brain, governs fundamental bodily processes including hormonal regulation, body temperature maintenance, blood pressure control, and hunger management. It also influences our emotional responses and can be impacted by our recollections. For instance, recalling a joyful memory triggers hormone release by the reptilian brain, inducing feelings of happiness, while concurrently reducing blood pressure and heart rate, fostering relaxation and increased joyfulness. Given its primal nature, the reptilian brain drives our most basic instincts related to survival and reproduction, as well as overseeing vital bodily functions such as heart rate, respiration, and thermoregulation. Additionally, it oversees essential needs like hunger and thirst, propelling us to consume food and fluids as necessary and ensuring adequate sleep patterns.

Our ancestors lived in a dangerous world, and they had to be constantly on the lookout for danger. If they saw a mammoth, they didn't have time to think about what to do. They had to react immediately. The reptilian brain is very good at keeping us alive. It is always on the lookout for danger, and it is quick to react when it senses a threat. For example, if you see a snake, your reptilian brain will automatically trigger the fight-or-flight response. When we are in danger, the reptilian brain takes over. It sends signals to our bodies that prepare us to fight or flee. Our heart rate increases, our breathing becomes shallower, and our muscles tense up. This allows us to react quickly to danger without having to think about it.

Despite the modern world being comparatively safer, our brains retain an inherent predisposition to remain vigilant for potential threats, potentially resulting in anxiety and hindering experimentation with novel experiences.

In the case of children raised in neglectful or abusive surroundings, the reptilian brain may operate in hyperactive mode, perpetually poised for danger. Consequently, this heightened state of alertness can impede their ability to absorb new knowledge and develop.

Hunger, sexual arousal, addiction, stress, social status, and safety are certain things that activate the Reptilian brain. Understanding the mechanisms of the reptilian brain enables us to harness control over it and exercise greater mindfulness in decision-making.

NEO-CORTEX - NEW BRAIN (UPPER PART OF BRAIN)

The term "neo-cortex" refers to the outer layer of the brain, specifically in mammals, which is responsible for higher-order brain functions such as conscious thought, spatial reasoning, sensory perception, and language. It is the most developed part of the brain in humans and plays a significant role in cognitive processes.

The mind, on the other hand, is a more abstract concept often used to describe the collective aspects of consciousness, thought, perception, emotion, and imagination. It encompasses both conscious and unconscious processes, including those that occur within the neo-cortex and other parts of the brain.

The relationship between the neo-cortex and the mind is complex and not fully understood. While the neo-cortex is crucial for many higher cognitive functions associated with the mind, it is just one component of the broader neural networks and structures that contribute to mental processes. Additionally, factors such as emotions, memories, and subconscious processes also play essential roles in shaping the mind.

Understanding the relationship between the neo-cortex, brain, and mind is a central focus of neuroscience and psychology research, aiming to unravel the mysteries of human cognition and consciousness.

SUBCONSCIOUS MIND (MID-BRAIN)

The limbic brain, also known as the old cortex, is an evolutionary older part of the brain compared to the neocortex. It includes structures such as the hippocampus and the olfactory cortex. While the neocortex is associated with higher cognitive functions, the limbic brain is involved in more primitive functions such as emotion, memory, and instinctual behaviour.

The subconscious mind refers to the aspects of mental processing that occur below the level of conscious awareness. It encompasses a wide range of automatic processes, including emotions, habits, intuition, and bodily functions. Many subconscious processes are mediated by structures within the limbic brain and other brain regions associated with emotion and memory.

The limbic brain plays a crucial role in shaping subconscious processes, particularly those related to emotional responses and the consolidation of memories. For example, the hippocampus, a part of the limbic brain, is involved in the formation and retrieval of memories, both conscious and subconscious.

Understanding the interplay between the limbic brain and the subconscious mind is essential for comprehending various aspects of human behaviour, including emotional reactions, learned behaviours, and the processing of sensory information. Research in neuroscience and psychology continues to explore the complex relationship between brain structures and subconscious mental processes.

Conscious & Subconscious Mind Understanding

When we first learn to drive, every action requires conscious effort and attention. We carefully follow instructions on how to operate the vehicle, constantly reminding ourselves to check the mirrors, shift gears, use the brakes, and steer. It feels like a deliberate process, where we are fully engaged in every aspect of driving.

However, with time and practice, driving becomes second nature. The actions that once required conscious thought now seem to happen effortlessly. We can hold conversations, listen to music, or even make phone calls while driving, all while still safely navigating the road. It's as if our subconscious mind has taken over the task of driving, allowing us to perform complex actions without needing to consciously think about each step.

This transition from conscious to subconscious driving highlights the difference between the two states of mind. When we drive consciously, we are actively aware of our actions and decisions, requiring effort and attention to perform tasks. In contrast, driving with the subconscious mind involves automatic responses and ingrained habits, where actions occur without conscious thought.

While we can't drive with an unconscious mind, as that would pose significant safety risks, we can certainly perform basic bodily functions like breathing while unconscious. However, the ability to drive safely relies on the engagement of our conscious and subconscious minds working together harmoniously, allowing us to navigate the complexities of the road with ease and efficiency.

Chapter Four

Mind & You

I know that you know what's mind by now, have you ever tried to experience the Power of your Mind? For sure you must have seen or felt an amazing power like you were long desiring a material thing or a specific dish and suddenly you are bestowed with that by your mother. You are taken aback by this surprise. WOW! How amazing it is. Now if I say that the application of some practices can help you manifest your goals, desires much faster, just like a miracle. Would you be interested in exploring it?

Law of Attraction

During my car buying experience, I kept seeing the same brand and colour of car while travelling which I wanted to buy. It seemed peculiar, but I realised it was likely because my mind was tuned into those specific details, making me more aware of them. This phenomenon occurs because our thoughts and focus often attract corresponding experiences or observations.

During my college days, when I was actively involved in playing cricket at the university level, I had a close friend who served as both a confidant and an intelligent advisor. He was a year or two older than me and pursued his studies diligently at one of Mumbai's premier institutes - IIT. Despite his studious nature, I sensed a positive envy from him towards my lifestyle, as he immersed himself in academics while I dedicated my time to sports.

During one intense discussion we had, an acquaintance interrupted us. He did this a couple of times before too. He spoke foul and used cuss words. When he interrupted us this time with some local slang and cuss words to get our attention, I was frustrated and asked my friend, "Why does this person speak such indecent language?" In response, my insightful friend remarked, "His mind is full of shit, so he talks shit." In that candid conversation, my friend highlighted that our words often reflect the contents of our thoughts and emotions.

The following is an experiment that involves a 24-hour task:

During the first day (24 hours), set a conscious intention to focus on observing a particular thing, like yellow butterflies or purple feathers. No special actions are needed—just set the intention and stay attentive. Notice whether your awareness affects the frequency of those specific items you're looking for.

Or you carry this experiment on to the second day too, you will find the same result.

I did this experiment for a day and had planted a thought of seeing a parrot. Seeing a parrot in my area was rare. In fact, I had not seen a parrot for years in the place I used to stay. That evening, I could see 4-5 parrots in my nearby vicinity. How is that? I was just amazed.

I have realised that with your deep love or crush, you kind of wish that you can see that person repeatedly, and you are blessed with her or him. I know for sure someday you might have experienced this.

The purpose of this experiment is to demonstrate three fundamental concepts:

1. Your perception of reality aligns with your focus and intentions. In simpler terms, you tend to notice what you anticipate or purposefully seek.

2. The possibility exists to discover anything you actively search for or have in mind.

3. The most transformative notion is that altering your search criteria leads to a corresponding change in the occurrences within your surroundings.

Ultimately, the significant realisation is that adjusting your search parameters directly influences the composition of your experiences.

Practices

What you practise dwells in you and makes you what you are. However, in the infinite scope of things, it is important we are able to realise the blessings we have in our life. We need to create a habit of living some mental practices

Certainly, let's elaborate on these mental practices:

1. Gratitude: Practising gratitude involves acknowledging and appreciating the positive aspects of your life, both big and small. It's about focusing on what you inherently have over what you want. By regularly taking time to reflect on the things you're grateful for, you cultivate a positive mindset and shift your attention away from negativity. Gratitude has been shown to improve overall well-being, reduce stress, and enhance relationships.

2. Feeling Happy: Engaging in activities that make you feel good is essential for your mental and emotional health. These activities can vary from person to person and might include hobbies, spending time with loved ones, pursuing creative endeavours, or simply enjoying nature. When you prioritise activities that bring you joy and

satisfaction, you create moments of happiness that contribute to a balanced and fulfilling life.

3. Blessings: Blessing others and around with wholeheartedness, counting your blessings involves recognizing the positive aspects of your life and acknowledging the good things that come your way. It's a way to shift your focus from challenges to the fortunate circumstances you experience. By regularly acknowledging your blessings, you reinforce a positive perspective and cultivate a sense of contentment and abundance.

4. Generous: Being generous involves giving back or responding in kind to the positive actions or gestures of others, I strongly emphasise donating and doing charity in whatever action or kind you can. When you engage in giving, you create a cycle of goodwill and kindness. This can strengthen relationships, foster a sense of community, and contribute to a positive social environment. Reciprocation is not only about material things but also about emotional support, understanding, and empathy.

5. Prayers: Prayer with faith can work wonders, regardless of which faith you follow, it will make life fulfilling and content.

These mental practices are interconnected and contribute to your overall mental and emotional well-being. They help shape your mindset, influence your interactions with others, and contribute to your sense of fulfilment and happiness. By incorporating these practices into your daily life, you can cultivate a more positive and resilient outlook, which can have far-reaching effects on your overall quality of life.

Affirmations

Affirmations consist of positive declarations that you repeatedly tell yourself, aiming to foster a positive mindset and impact your thoughts, emotions, and behaviours. Affirmations can address various aspects of your life, such as self-esteem, health, relationships, and success. By consistently affirming positive beliefs, you reshape your thought patterns and enhance your overall well-being.

However, here are a few things that should be avoided in your affirmations.

- Negative Talk

Avoiding negative self-talk is crucial. Negative statements, whether about yourself or your abilities, can undermine your confidence and limit your potential. The absence of negativity creates space for positive thoughts and affirmations to thrive.

- I Won't and I Don't

Using "I won't" and "I don't" in the context of avoiding unhealthy habits or behaviours empowers you to make conscious choices aligned with your goals. This phrasing reinforces your commitment to positive actions and steers you away from actions that don't serve your well-being.

- Maybe

"Maybe" opens the door to possibilities. It's an acknowledgment that outcomes aren't set in stone and that uncertainties exist. Embracing "maybe" invites a flexible and adaptable mindset that's open to various outcomes.

- I Will Try

"I will try" signifies your willingness to act and make an effort. Even if success isn't guaranteed, the act of trying is valuable in itself. This approach encourages a growth-oriented perspective, where learning from attempts is just as important as achieving the desired outcome.

Incorporating positive affirmations into your daily routine can lead to a transformation in your thought patterns and overall outlook on life. Remember that the key is consistency—regularly engaging with affirmations strengthens their impact on your mindset and well-being.

How to Structure Affirmations?

The art of writing affirmations is to write in such a way that they are already coming true. And, when you write them or say them repeatedly and believe in them, they often come true.

But there is a way in which affirmations are written. Affirmations need to be positive. They need to be visualised in the mind already before putting them down on paper.

They can be written in the following manner-

- Identify the area where you want to see a change. Identify the specific task and create an affirmation for it as you have already achieved it.

I want to pursue a degree.

I want to hike Kilimanjaro.

I want to get the 'Best Student Award' for this academic year.

- Write affirmations in present tense as if you are living it now.

I am Happy.

- You need to feel it and visualise it as if it is already happening.

I am Rich / Wealthy.

- Remove any negative tags, words and doubting phrases.

I don't want to get sick!!

Now here the intention is not to get sick which is correct, but you see the sick word with don't is not recognised by mind, and the command can be taken to get sick.

Rather, the best way of affirmation will be -

I am Healthy, Strong, and living a Healthy Life.

I am fit, energetic with 70 kgs of weight (here you can put your desired weight).

Faith and beliefs work wonders. Affirmations with feeling, energy, belief, and faith are sure to make an impact. Affirmations are great to guide the conscious mind and eventually they will drop to the subconscious level by way of practising with energy, patience, and faith. However, you need to be sure to use words and phrases.

The Power of Positive Affirmations:

1. 360% Mindset Shift: Positive affirmations redirect your thoughts away from self-doubt and negativity. They reinforce constructive beliefs about yourself and your capabilities, fostering a growth mindset.

2. Confidence Booster: Regularly repeating positive affirmations can boost your self-esteem and confidence.

3. Stress Reduction: Positive affirmations have been shown to reduce stress and anxiety.

4. Goal Achievement: Affirmations align your thoughts with your goals. They create a mental framework that supports your efforts toward achieving your aspirations.

5. Resilience: Affirmations contribute to emotional resilience. They provide a positive anchor during challenging times, helping you maintain a balanced perspective.

Self-Image

Self-image refers to the mental perception one holds of oneself, influenced often by upbringing and conditioning. It serves as a reflection of our thoughts and attitudes, shaping our actions and eventual outcomes.

Philosopher Cooley once remarked, *"I am not what I think I am, and I am not what you think I am. I am what I think, you think, I am,"* illustrating the subjective nature of self-perception.

Physical appearance need not conform to societal standards of beauty, such as fairness, a beautiful face, or a good build, but rather should reflect qualities like grooming, dressing well, strength, health, and hygiene. In some cultures, the concept of beauty may differ, emphasising individual uniqueness.

Mental self-image involves maintaining resilience against external influences, staying grounded in personal values and beliefs amidst diverse thoughts and expressions.

Emotional self-image entails prioritising self-care and emotional balance, avoiding overinvestment in emotional responses to external stimuli.

In essence, nurturing a positive self-image involves holistic self-care across physical, mental, and emotional dimensions, embracing individuality and inner strength.

Self-image encapsulates a person's self-perception, encompassing their internal assessment of who they are, how they believe others perceive them, and the aspirational version of themselves—their ideal self. These notions encompass various aspects, including how one sees their physical appearance, personality traits, competencies, values, and ethical beliefs. Furthermore, they encompass how an individual perceives their alignment with societal norms associated with masculinity and femininity.

Do a small activity- Stand in front of a mirror for just two minutes and see how your mind sparks a bunch of thoughts. We first think of the physical attributes, perhaps our skin, our blemishes, our hair texture, our build, our physique, our dressing sense and then eventually our thoughts drift to our inner self, are we happy? Are we sad? Are we missing something? Are we expecting? Are we waiting?

This short mirror moment can make you think about how you are doing and what you want to improve. It's like a reminder to keep growing and becoming better. But remember, while it's good to work on yourselves, you should also accept and be kind to who you are right now.

If what you see is not enough, change. As simple as it may seem, if you are not satisfied with what you see, you have the power to make changes in your appearance or your life.

Self-image should be more seriously considered over the opinions of others. It's you who know yourself more than anyone else.

Meditation

Meditation is a state, it's an expression of true self, where you need to connect with your inner self.

I learnt the various forms of meditation from my master (Guru). One of the prominent forms that I practised is known to be Srividya, it's a practice that combines Mantra, Tantra, Energy practices, Raj yoga, and Bhakti Yoga. Mantra is a sacred word, or combinations of words given to you by your master to practise and repeat. Tantra is the way of doing things. Energy practise is believing in a higher form of energy and having love & faith in the path you are bestowed with. This path does require a certain number of rituals to be followed, ensuring you daily practice meditation. It is also important that you restrict your active sexual life. By that – I do not mean celibacy, but sexual discipline. As you practise daily, you are for sure bestowed with the divine experience, and of course meditation makes you calmer, and stay connected. Eventually, you derive -Siddhi - a certain level of proficiency based on your karma.

My Guru used to meditate from 10 pm to 6 am. In fact, he never slept. He would claim in meditation you are more relaxed, and you can achieve much more than sleep. Every morning and throughout the day, his eyes shone like diamonds. Seeing his grace, I did try and meditate for hours together, initially starting from 45 mins to 1 hour, and then extending even to 2 to 3 hours. I remember one fine day I was sitting for about 5 to 6 hours or more. In my college days, I could put more effort into my Meditation practice, but a few years down the line, while working in the corporate world, I was still connected to Meditation and did practices. Though the number of hours dropped, my practice was intact. One thing which I have understood is, you need to initially put in hours to practise, and then it becomes a habit. The moment it becomes a habit you do not need to put in those additional efforts to hit that meditative state.

My Guru told me, "Meditation can be done anywhere, and anytime. It just means you are in a meditative state if you are at work. Doing what you are doing is a form of meditation, be it any work, it can be sweeping the floor of your house or store. You can also meditate at a club where you can hear loud noises, if you can hear your own voice and feel your inner connection, and the energy rising within you, you can be in a meditative state. Once you are in a meditative state, mere noise won't bother you. You will automatically stay away from the energy that pulls you down as you would understand the real nature of your own self."

Vishal M Shevle

MEDITATION is being in a "MEDITATIVE STATE"

Meditation is not about the hours you sit in a position still doing your practice going into ZERO thought. I have never understood the concept of ZERO thought. How do you recognise your zero thought in meditation? If you recognise your zero thought in Meditation, zero thought is also a thought, You need to understand thoughts are going to be coming and going. One- you need to understand the source of it, why are thoughts coming the way they are? Believe me for sure, there is a reason. Second - you can stay a mere observer, the more you get involved the thoughts might drag you in. That's why you need a way to meditate, by chanting a Mantra which can dilute the thoughts or raise your awareness.

Also, what matters is a day consisting of 24 hours, and not the only hours that you meditate. If you need to attain peace and calm, you need to practise being meditative for 24 hours. Don't look at this as an act of work, it's the innate nature of human to be blissful, if you stay meditative while you are not mediating I am sure your hours of Meditation will be lot fruitful, you will be able to connect better and get your practices going in a better way.

Also, it is important to understand why you want to do meditation. The foremost thing that comes to mind is Concentration, to Focus and Prioritise. Concentration is not removing thoughts or controlling them. To concentrate we use certain methods to make our mind empty, meaning no thoughts or less thoughts.

Meditation encompasses an array of techniques deliberately designed to foster an elevated state of awareness and concentrated focus. This practice is not only transformative for consciousness but also boasts a range of psychological benefits.

Extensive research attests to the multi-faceted impact of meditation, spanning both physiological and psychological specialisations. Physiologically, meditation yields several favourable outcomes, including a reduction in physical arousal, a decrease in respiration rate, a lowering of heart rate, alterations in brain wave patterns, and a notable decrease in stress levels.

Importantly, meditation has seamlessly integrated into various therapeutic approaches, with mindfulness-based stress reduction being a prominent outcome. This therapeutic method incorporates mindfulness and meditation together to aid individuals grappling with stress, depression, anxiety, and other mental health challenges. By cultivating mindfulness and introspection, meditation offers a comprehensive avenue for enhancing psychological well-being.

Once, a sage was journeying through a kingdom and found refuge under a tree. While he rested, a passing warrior approached him and remarked, "Esteemed sage, as you traverse our lands, it is fitting to pay a visit to our king."

Perplexed, the sage inquired, "For what reason should I do so?"

The warrior responded, "The king's benevolence is renowned. You could be a recipient of his generosity, gaining wealth and riches."

Curious, the sage questioned, "As a wanderer, what purpose would wealth and riches serve me?"

The warrior answered, "They could bring you contentment."

Calmly, the sage countered, "Contentment is what I currently embrace."

This tale encapsulates the intricate cycle of existence – what one seeks might not align with another's desires, and while contentment suffices for some, it may not be the same for others.

The Most Prominent Meditation Types:

Omkar (OM) Meditation: -

We know this form of meditation by chanting OM. The effective way to chant OMKAR - OM is by starting with AAAUUUUUUMMMMMMMMM (the NADA or the flow of the sound) helps to raise the energy level of the vibration of OM. If done in a certain way it elevates the spiritual vibration of the body.

AAA UUUUUU MMMMMMMMM

The AAA comes from the core, UUUUUU you can extend and MMMMMMMMM try to extend further. With this you will feel the vibration level in the body rising. Try doing this early in the morning or evening preferably on an empty stomach. As you extend the MMM to the last part, you will see the vibrations moving upward toward your forehead and circulating over the crown chakra.

Not only the spiritual benefit of doing OM, but you can also see your voice also improving. You would be clearer and more confident; the mind would be able to focus better, and you can easily achieve the experience of spiritual elevation.

Doing it daily, repeating Omkar for about 11 times and then extending the practice counts as your appetite helps in the long run.

- **Chakra Meditation**

Chakras, a fundamental concept in Hinduism, constitute integral components of an interconnected energy network within the body. The word "chakra," derived from Sanskrit, translates to "wheel," signifying one of the seven pivotal junctures within this energetic system.

Each of these energy centres functions like a spinning wheel, emanating vibrations of energy. The equilibrium of your chakras is influenced by the frequency at which they vibrate – a higher frequency corresponds to a greater state of balance.

Chakra Meditation is practices that have prevailed from ancient times, Good to be done under a good guide, Guru, or Master.

- **Visualisation Meditation**

Visualisation meditation is a method that centres on promoting sensations of relaxation, serenity, and tranquillity through the mental creation of positive scenarios, images, or entities.

This technique entails immersing yourself in a vivid mental depiction of a particular scene, utilising all five senses to infuse it with intricate details. Additionally, it encompasses the practice of summoning the presence of a cherished or revered individual, aiming to internalise and embody their virtues and attributes.

- **Mantra Meditation**

Mantra meditation holds a significant place in various teachings, notably within Hindu and Buddhist traditions. This form of meditation employs a repetitive sound to achieve mental clarity. The chosen sound can take the form of a word, a phrase, or a specific sound, with "om" being a widely recognized example.

The mantra can be vocalised audibly or silently. Upon continuous chanting of the chosen mantra, a heightened state of alertness emerges, enhancing your connection to the surroundings. This heightened awareness facilitates the exploration of profound levels of consciousness.

- **Movement Meditation**

While yoga is often the first association with movement meditation, this approach encompasses a broader spectrum of activities, such as:

- Walking
- Engaging in gardening
- Practising qi gong
- Participating in tai chi
- Exploring various gentle forms of movement

Movement meditation constitutes an active practice, utilising bodily motion to facilitate a heightened bond with your physical self and the immediate present.

- **Focused Meditation**

Focused meditation centres on directing concentration through any of the five senses. As the name implies, this method is particularly suitable for individuals aiming to enhance their focus and attentiveness.

Examples of practices within focused meditation include:

- Utilising mala beads for counting
- Engaging in attentive listening to a gong
- Gazing intently at a candle flame
- Counting breaths to maintain focus
- Contemplating the moon's appearance

- **Mindfulness (Vipassana) Meditation**

Mindfulness meditation involves attentively observing the thoughts that flow through your mind without attaching judgments or engagement to them. Your role is simply to witness and acknowledge any recurring patterns.

This technique harmonises focused concentration with heightened awareness. While concentrating on an object or your breath, you simultaneously observe bodily sensations, thoughts, and emotions, without becoming entangled in them.

Meditation Process

Prepare your mind for meditation.

1. Find a comfortable position, whether seated cross-legged, on a chair, or lying down on a yoga mat, mattress, or bed.

2. Begin the process by closing your eyes, gently shift your focus to your breath, pay attention to the sound of your breath, the sensation of air entering and leaving your body, and its temperature. Observe the thoughts and emotions that pass through your mind.

3. Use your breath as an anchor to stay present in the moment. Let it be your point of focus.

Being Mindful

As a teenager I was very fascinated with meditation and was just learning it. I had heard and read a lot about meditation and was aware that different people experience it in different ways. While some see a white light meaning enlightenment, others are able to see colours.

It was in 2005 when Mumbai was under floods. I used to stay in Badlapur, on the outskirts of Mumbai, and the situation was the worst in our vicinity. The dams had let out water, and the water levels were alarmingly high as water had engulfed the ground floor of our building where I resided. Thus, we had to stay with our neighbours on the 1st floor. It was nighttime and I was unable to sleep. I thought of meditating. I sat in my meditation stance and started meditating. After a while I could see some yellow orange light illuminated in front of me. I was excited and surprised momentarily as I assumed I was seeing the divine light and excited that I had attained enlightenment. I could see this for a while, but then recollected the controversy I read about coloured light associated with enlightenment, and on an impulse, I opened my eyes. I was in front of a shocking scenario. The neighbours TV was in front of me, and it was burning, and the flames were the orange yellow light I saw.

I immediately woke up everyone and the fire was doused. I was able to avert a major disaster that day with my consciousness and awareness. However, I was still naïve at meditation and looking for my enlightening moment.

It is good to be aware and educated about things. If I kept my eyes closed thinking it was indeed the light of the divine, an accident would have hurt most of us there, but that mindfulness helped me and my neighbours that day.

Meditation, Guru, & Leader, or Master to follow

The nature of every soul is to be blissful. Meditation occurs to be a natural way in which we learn to understand our soul – spirit / energy. To understand you need to practise a certain path to help you open the energy channel that flows throughout the body.

While you learn a certain form of meditation or follow a leader or a master, you need to understand that we are in our journey of life, and are a traveller, and the meeting of your guru is for a certain reason. As your guru too is a traveller too and at some point, in life you two will part ways. In this scenario, we need to practise an awareness not to completely submit and epitomise this guru as a God. While people treat their gurus as Gods, it should be rather living the learnings of the guru and implementing them, over idolising a human as God. Emotionally linking with a guru might possibly derail you from your purpose, and after all both you and the guru are on individual transient journeys.

As emphasised earlier guru is a mere element, in each one of us and prevailing across the Universe.

Chapter Five

Desire & Will

Desires are like seeds that are planted in our minds.

Why do we desire the things that we do desire?

Desire is the rising emotion that leads you to want something, and the certain pleasure associated with it.

When we see something that we desire, it registers in our brain and can start to grow. Even if we don't consciously think about it, the desire can still be there, influencing our thoughts and actions.

It's like you are walking on the road, and you see someone sitting in an open restaurant having wholesome breakfast. It might be your favourite food or even might not be, but it will give a slight energy to your brain at that moment and register it. And when you are having your breakfast, you might remember that food item. That's a very subtle way a desire is planted in our mind.

Imagine you are treated to a buffet spread. You take a cursory glance at everything, initially indecisive, but after seeing the entire spread, you feel like eating one or two items, and you eat only those. It is due to a desire registered in your mind before trying those food items. Perhaps, you like only those food items. A desire might arise out of a will, curiosity, need, and sometimes even the absence of something.

Desires can arise from many different sources, both internal and external.

Internally what can trigger a desire is –

- Will: We may desire something because we want to achieve a particular goal or experience something new. For example, we may desire to learn a new language, start a business, or travel the world
- Curiosity: We may desire to learn more about something or experience something new. For example, we may desire to meet new people, try new foods, or visit new places.
- Need: We may desire something because we need it to survive or thrive. For example, we may desire food, shelter, water, and love.
- Absence: We may desire something because we are missing it or don't have it. For example, we may desire a loving relationship, a sense of purpose, or financial security.

The external source that can trigger our desires are -

Seeing something in the past: We may desire something because we saw it and liked it. For example, we may see someone wearing a beautiful dress and then desire to buy one for ourselves.

Hearing of it: We may desire something because we heard about it, and it sounded interesting or appealing. For example, we may hear about a new salon that has opened and then desire to try it out.

Experiencing it: We may desire something because we had a positive experience with it in the past. For example, we may have experienced a certain coffee brand and want to keep ordering it.

Feeling it: We may desire something because we feel a strong need for it. For example, we may feel hungry and then desire to eat something.

Coming from deep within, spiritual: We may desire something because it is connected to our core values or beliefs. For example, we may desire to live a life of service to others or to make a difference in the world.

Imagine if you are the only man/woman on this earth, will you be doing the thing you are doing right now? Perhaps No!! You would be fighting for survival.

Imagine, if you were the only person left on Earth, you would need to find food, water, shelter, and clothing. You would also need to protect yourself from wild animals and other dangers. This would be a daunting task, and it would require all of your attention and energy. You would not have time to do things like watch TV, read books, or go for walks in the park. You would be too busy trying to stay alive.

Of course, some people might find ways to make their survival more enjoyable. For example, they might build a beautiful home or create a garden. But even these activities would be focused on survival, not on leisure.

The point is that if you were the only person left on Earth, your life would be very different from what it is now. You might miss communicating with people, fight with loneliness, and most of all struggles to find food.

It would be a challenging life, but it would also be a meaningful one. You would be fighting for your own survival, and you would be the only person responsible for your own well-being. This would give you a sense of purpose and accomplishment.

When we are exposed to the values of society, we are often drawn to wealth, luxury, and status. These desires can motivate us to achieve our goals, but they can also conflict with our other desires, such as the desire to be happy and fulfilled.

For example, imagine you are stressed out preparing for an exam. You see a trailer for a movie that you really want to watch, but you know that you should be studying. This is a conflict of desires. To resolve this conflict, you need to decide what is most important to you. Watching the movie will give you momentary happiness, but studying will help you achieve your long-term goal of clearing the exam and being successful, then you need to choose the latter.

However, it is also okay to indulge in short-term desires from time to time. If you have a long-term goal, but you are still feeling drawn to watching the movie, then it is okay to give in to that desire, as long as you are mindful of your priorities and don't let it derail your long-term goals. The important thing is to be aware of your desires and to choose the ones that will lead you to a happy and fulfilled life.

Your desires shape your entire being, from your thoughts to your actions to your will. As a result, you are constantly tempted by short-term desires, even though you know that your long-term goals are more important. This is the crux of the matter.

When we say I want to achieve a certain thing having seen it, and you might not get successful at times, because it has not dropped into the subconscious mind as a desire. Anything that has dropped into your subconscious mind, the core, it would never fail. Because the moment it goes to the subconscious, you will do things that are in tandem with that outcome. And it will come very naturally.

So, if you feel a certain thing or want a certain thing, think about what you really desire. Our conscious mind is constantly bombarded with information, but only a fraction of it reaches our subconscious mind. This is why we may say we want to achieve something, but we don't always succeed. Our subconscious mind is where our true desires reside. Once a desire is planted in our subconscious mind, it becomes our driving force. We will naturally take actions that are aligned with our goal, and we will succeed.

Therefore, if you want to achieve something, focus on what you truly desire. Think about it deeply and let it sink into your subconscious mind. The more you focus on your desire, the stronger it will become. Eventually, your subconscious mind will take over and drive you towards your goal effortlessly.

Many businesses fail because the calling has not really set in the core of their subconscious mind as a desire. They must have seen something, and it must have appealed to them, and they felt the need to do it. Because any path you take, there are going to be challenges, or even stringent problems. And if you can overcome a challenge or problem around your core desire, it is your calling, and you will sustain it. But if you have just seen it and want to do things then there is a good chance that if there is a push coming back, the resistance might not be there, and the sustenance is taken hit, while you might just give up.

Imagine a restaurant business, there might be many who start a restaurant business, but they are hardly able to sustain it. They have only seen and known that the restaurant business is lucrative, but it's not their calling, they are not driven to it with a passion to make it work, and hence gradually this short-term desire fades away.

Like laughter, you cannot measure laughter, it's just there. You cannot even measure the love between a child and a mother. Regardless of everything, bonding is just there. In fact, a loving life is built over time, and it just does not happen overnight, and you really like it, and will never be able to measure it. Do you have that strong connection with the goal you have planted? Be it success or failure, you like doing it. You do it irrespective, and eventually the success comes due to your visualisation of that success.

When we have a strong connection to our goals, we are more likely to succeed. This is because our subconscious mind is working with us, driving us towards our desired outcome.

Imagine that you have a goal to write a book. You have a strong connection to this goal because you are passionate about writing, and you believe that your book can make a difference in the world. You spend time visualising yourself finishing your book and having it published. You also take consistent action towards your goal, writing for a few hours every day.

Your subconscious mind is working with you to achieve your goal. It is driving you to take action, even when you are tired or unmotivated. It also helps you to overcome obstacles and challenges.

As a result of your strong connection to your goal and your consistent effort, you are able to achieve your goal and write your book.

Some people express their deep love, but in a subtle way. Others express their love more outwardly, with flowers, gifts, and public displays of affection. Similarly, some people achieve success in a low-key way, while others are more flamboyant. Although it is possible to achieve success without being flashy or glamorous.

Here the importance of will matters. Will is the driving force behind our actions. It is what allows us to overcome obstacles and achieve our goals. We can grow our will by visualising our success. When we visualise, ourselves achieving our goals, we are sending a message to our subconscious mind that we are serious about achieving them. This helps us to stay motivated and focused.

Imagine that you have a goal to start your own business. You visualise yourself sitting in your own office, running your own company. You see yourself meeting with clients, making deals, and growing your business. You also visualise yourself achieving your financial goals. You see yourself paying off your debts, buying a new house, and taking your family on vacation.

By visualising your success, you are sending a message to your subconscious mind that you are serious about achieving your goal of starting your own business. This helps you to stay motivated and focused, even when things get tough.

When you have a clear vision of what you want to achieve, you are well on your way to success. However, it is important to be patient and let your desires develop fully before you start to doubt yourself or give up. You can also choose from many different paths to success. However, many people start to doubt themselves and their abilities when they try to achieve their own success. They may worry about how they will achieve their goals, or whether they are on the right path. They may also be influenced by the judgments of others.

The real problem is that people are confronting their desires before they have even had a chance to fully develop. Your desires should be strong and unwavering, like a mountain. No matter what obstacles you face, your desire should stay intact.

If you can develop a strong desire for success and let it develop fully, you will be well on your way to achieving your goals.

And this will happen only if it's at your core. If you have not walked the path before, do not judge, and leave it there. Take steps, don't doubt where they are leading you, these doubts will kill your desire, disturbing your faith and your will.

It is important to be aware of how our desires are influenced by external sources so that we can make conscious choices about how we respond to them. We don't have to be slaves to our desires. We can choose to focus on our inner values and goals, and to let go of desires that are not aligned with our true selves.

Chapter Six

Sankalpa The Resolution Realisation

Life is a Sankalpa in the Dreams of God, Life was first made in the thought by a Resolution or Sankalpa in the mind of God "Brahma," as the saying goes, "We are part of the Brahma - Aham Brahmasmi." If a life has come into existence by a Sankalpa / Resolution it becomes necessary to know the art of Sankalpa or ways to make it more effective.

The process of making resolutions, often done on New Year's Eve, is a familiar practice. These resolutions typically arise from a need or a lingering task that we feel compelled to address. For instance, a common resolution is to get fit and achieve six-pack abs. We may take action by purchasing a gym membership and initially commit to the routine. However, over time, old patterns may resurface, leading to feelings of guilt or self-doubt, and we may give up, attributing it to laziness. This cycle repeats, with promises to start anew on the next Monday or month, but often these intentions falter quickly. What if there were a specific method to approach resolutions that would lead to a more holistic achievement, considering various aspects of life?

The First Flight

In the 18th century, the idea of human flight was considered impossible. However, the Wright brothers believed that it was possible. They dedicated their lives to developing a flying machine, and in 1903, they made history with the first successful airplane flight.

Of course, the Wright brothers could not have achieved their goal without the support of others. They had the help of engineers, mechanics, and financial backers. They also had the support of the public, who were fascinated by the idea of human flight.

The Wright brothers' invention was a major breakthrough, but it was only the beginning. In the years since their first flight, many other people have contributed to the development of aviation. Today, we have airplanes that can fly faster than sound and travel all over the world.

This example shows that it takes a combination of individual creativity and collective support to make great ideas a reality. One person may have the vision, but it takes others to help make that vision a reality. Here one Sankalpa to build a way to travel faster made the difference to ensure all things fall in place over a period of time.

A goal is a Sankalpa conditioned to achieve and give.

To grasp the essence of Sankalpa, one must first understand its various levels. Sankalpas manifest throughout our day, ranging from surface-level intentions to those rooted deep within our subconscious and unconscious mind. For instance, a surface-level Sankalpa might arise when we see a car we admire, leading us to express a desire to own it someday. On an emotional level, during moments of anger or conflict, we may make resolutions to confront or prove ourselves to others in the future. These resolutions are driven by our emotions and subconscious reactions.

At an unconscious level, our minds absorb and emulate traits or behaviours from our surroundings, shaping our personalities without conscious awareness. For instance, admiring and idealising our boss may lead us to unconsciously adopt similar traits or behaviours over time. Understanding these levels of Sankalpa provides insight into how our thoughts and intentions influence our actions and perceptions.

Sankalpas carries significant power, as experienced by moments when our thoughts seemingly manifest into reality. Whether it's recalling someone and encountering them shortly after or craving a specific treat only to find it presented before us, these occurrences are often attributed to the strength of our Sankalpas. When our desires, emotions, or visualisations are deeply rooted and intense, they possess the potential to materialise. This phenomenon aligns with the concept that 'What exists within us is reflected throughout the universe.' Thus, we are interconnected with and influenced by universal energy. Each day, we are showered with this 'Divine Energy,' and it's up to us to harness it effectively. By remaining conscious and aware, we can channel this energy to fulfil our intentions and resolutions. Failure to do so may result in the energy dissipating, akin to the rule of gravity. Therefore, by understanding and utilising this energy wisely, we can empower our Sankalpas to manifest and shape our reality.

A resolution done with intensity has a lot of potential to change the destiny too, it helps to connect with the divine energy and drive the path ahead to manifest Sankalpa or Resolution. A resolution is not just a predetermined path; it is fuelled by desire - the "Sankalpa" or resolution is propelled by willpower, harnessing your core energy to pave its way. With time, you'll notice your ability to manifest your resolutions increasing, as you communicate your true desires to the universe and align your will with them safely and holistically.

Repeating your Sankalpa aids in sharpening focus and prioritisation. It's beneficial to continue your resolution practice for at least a month, as this sustains momentum and provides the necessary determination and enthusiasm to realise your resolutions in all aspects of life.

The yogic approach to desire manifestation is more rigorous than the Western approach, which focuses on visualisation. In addition to visualisation, yogic practice involves using faith to connect with the energy of the universe. Yogis often claim to perform miracles or feats that appear magical to others. However, the reality behind these occurrences lies in the power of Sankalpa or resolution. In Yogic philosophy, there are two main energy channels known as Nadi: Ida (associated with the left nostril) and Pingala (associated with the right nostril), along with a third central channel called Sushumna Nadi. The awakening of Kundalini energy, or Shakti, occurs when it passes through both Ida and Pingala, thereby activating the Sushumna Nadi. This activation of Sushumna Nadi facilitates the realisation of Sankalpas. Any Sankalpa made during this period is believed to have a higher likelihood of manifestation.

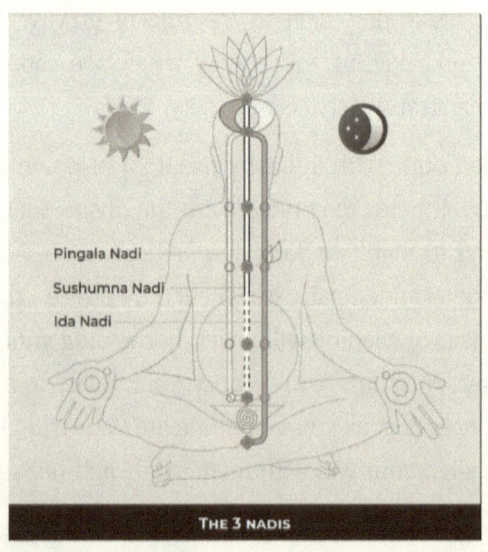

THE 3 NADIS

Let me share my personal journey. In my late twenties, after years of working in a corporate environment, I found myself gaining weight and feeling lethargic. Determined to reclaim my health, I set a goal to shed 12 kilograms, bringing my weight down from 82 to 70 kilograms. Through dedicated efforts and the repetition of mantras as part of my Sankalpa practice, I successfully achieved my weight loss goal and regained my fitness. However, a few months later, I noticed the weight creeping back up, reaching 80 kilograms again. This unexpected setback prompted me to re-evaluate my approach. While my initial focus had been solely on physical weight loss, I realised that true health and wellness encompassed more than just numbers on a scale. I embarked on a journey to understand holistic fitness and healthy living, seeking guidance from trainers and coaches. To my surprise, this journey not only transformed my physical health but also had a profound impact on every aspect of my life. I experienced positive changes in my job, family life, mental and emotional well-being. One powerful Sankalpa had changed my destiny, demonstrating the incredible potential for transformation when aligned with the right intentions.

A Holistic Sankalpa

Crafting a Sankalpa aimed at living life holistically involves addressing all aspects of one's existence. For instance, if the goal is to attain wealth, it's essential to consider the broader picture. While acquiring wealth may happen sooner or later in life, it's crucial to ensure there's a supportive family to share it with. Instead of solely focusing on personal riches, the Sankalpa should aim to enrich the well-being of the entire family under the guidance of the divine will. This comprehensive Sankalpa not only encompasses financial prosperity but also fosters family harmony and ensures good health for all involved.

A comprehensive Sankalpa seeks holistic well-being, addressing every facet of life. It prioritises vitality and health, fostering energetic living. Within the family, it promotes harmony and support, nurturing relationships and creating a loving environment. Professionally, it strives for fulfilment and growth, aligning career paths with passions and values. Socially, it emphasises meaningful connections and community contribution, enriching lives through empathy and service. At its core, this Sankalpa magnetises positivity, attracting joy and abundance into every aspect of life, serving as a guiding light towards holistic fulfilment and balance.

Aspects of Life -

Life comprises various aspects that contribute to our overall well-being:

1. Body - Health: This aspect focuses on physical well-being, encompassing factors such as fitness, nutrition, and overall health.

2. Mind - Mental Health: Mental health is crucial for emotional stability and psychological well-being. It involves managing stress, maintaining a positive mindset, and seeking support when needed.

3. Energy - Spiritual: Spiritual well-being involves connecting with one's inner self, finding meaning and purpose in life, and nurturing a sense of spirituality or higher consciousness.

4. Financial - Rich & Wealthy: Financial well-being is essential for stability and security. It involves managing finances wisely, building wealth, and achieving financial goals for a comfortable and prosperous life.

Balancing these aspects of life contributes to overall happiness, fulfilment, and a sense of harmony in one's life journey.

Sankalpa of Service

A Sankalpa of service is a powerful intention that reflects a commitment to helping others and making a positive impact in the world. It involves offering assistance, support, and kindness to others without expecting anything in return. By prioritising the needs of others above our own, we cultivate a spirit of generosity and altruism. Whether through volunteering, acts of kindness, or advocacy, we demonstrate our commitment to making a positive difference in the lives of others. Embracing a Sankalpa of service brings profound inner peace and fulfilment. By aligning our actions with values of kindness, compassion, and service, we experience a deep sense of purpose and meaning in our lives. The impact of a Sankalpa of service extends far beyond the immediate act of giving. It creates a ripple effect of goodness, inspiring others to join in acts of kindness and compassion. By embracing a Sankalpa of service, we tap into the transformative power of selfless giving, leading us on a path of inner peace, fulfilment, and collective well-being.

Making a Sankalpa for someone else, particularly an immediate family member, can lead to a quicker realisation of their desires. Not only will the individual attain their desired outcomes, but you will also experience a sense of peace, contentment, and bliss. Most importantly, it results in a boost of divine energy.

Focus & Priority

Life revolves around focus and priorities. When we claim to lack time for something, it's often a matter of priorities rather than actual time constraints. Whatever we prioritise receives our focus and attention. Sometimes, deadlines are necessary to redirect our attention. For instance, we tend to intensify our focus on studying as exams draw nearer, while we may relax when the exam is far in the future. Ultimately, it's our mindset that determines our level of preparation and engagement.

When it comes to making resolutions, such as New Year's resolutions, we often set goals or desires to achieve over time. However, maintaining the resolve to follow through can be challenging, leading to waning motivation and decreased power over time. Yet, a comprehensive approach can offer a solution. For instance, in yoga, practices like breathing exercises, Jal Neti, and Sutra Neti focus on cleansing the physical nadis, or channels, particularly in the nostrils. By incorporating such holistic practices into our resolution-making process, we can cultivate habits and behaviours that become second nature, ensuring that our goals are not only easily accomplished but also deeply integrated into our lives.

Ideal Sankalpa - One Sankalpa

An ideal Sankalpa, or resolution, is a focused intention that aligns with your deepest desires and aspirations. While you set your intention with clarity and conviction, it's essential to release attachment to specific outcomes and trust in the wisdom of the universe. Surrendering to the flow of life allows for greater flexibility and openness to unexpected opportunities and blessings.

Take a Sankalpa that encompasses all aspects of life, such as prioritising health and fitness to enhance overall enjoyment. By maintaining good health and vitality, one can experience increased energy levels, leading to improvements in family life, professional endeavours, and social interactions. This comprehensive approach acts as a magnet, attracting positivity and success across various facets of life, aligning all factors to work in harmony for personal betterment.

To achieve your resolution using the yogic approach, follow these steps:

- Identify your core desire, the thing that you truly want to achieve.
- Visualise yourself achieving your desire as if it has already happened. Feel the emotions of joy, satisfaction, and accomplishment.
- Take 3-5 deep breaths to calm your mind and body.
- Repeat or visualise yourself achieving your desire until you feel a deep sense of peace and calm.
- Whichever God you pray to chant its name repeatedly, do it 21 times every day. But if your prayer is long, say the prayer once and repeat your desire.
- Do it at least three times for the whole cycle.
- Do it at least for 40 days continuously.
- Do not judge or doubt or find deviation. Just do it!!

If you need a certain amount of money in life, don't worry about whether you are capable of achieving it or whether the environment is working in your favour. Simply start taking action towards your goal, and the environment will become conducive to your wish on its own.

- Identify your core desire. What is the specific amount of money that you need? Why do you need it? Once you have a clear understanding of your core desire, you can start to take action towards achieving it.
- Visualise yourself achieving your goal. See yourself with the money that you need. Feel the emotions of joy, satisfaction, and accomplishment. The more vivid your visualisation, the stronger your desire will become.

- Take inspired action. Start taking steps towards your goal, even if you don't know exactly how you will achieve it. The universe will provide you with the resources and opportunities that you need along the way.
- Don't be afraid to fail. Failure is a natural part of the learning process. Don't let it discourage you from continuing to take action towards your goal.

As you take action towards your goal, the environment will start to change in your favour. Opportunities will come your way, and people will be more likely to help you. This is because the universe is conspiring to help you achieve your desires.

Imagine that you need Rs. 10,00,000 to start your own business. You can start by visualising yourself with the Rs.10,00,000 in your bank account. Feel the emotions of excitement and anticipation. Then, start taking inspired action towards your goal. This could involve talking to people who are successful entrepreneurs, networking with other people in your field, and developing your business plan.

As you take action, the universe will start to provide you with the resources and opportunities that you need. You might meet someone who is willing to invest in your business, or you might find a government grant that can help you get started. The more you take action, the more the universe will conspire to help you achieve your goal.

It is important to remember that manifestation is not a magic trick. It takes time, effort, and patience. But if you are willing to put in the work, you can achieve anything that you desire.

Technique to take a "Sankalpa Or Resolution"

There are a number of ways. You need to find your most favourable technique as it will for sure impact the intensity of resolution hence driving the realisation of the Sankalpa.

1. By way of Prana

1. Start by cleansing your nostrils and freeing them up.

2. Practise KapalBhati / Pranayama for three rounds, exhaling forcefully and pushing from the lower abdomen.

3. Follow with Anulom-Vilom, alternating inhalation and exhalation between nostrils for three rounds.

4. Focus on your breath, taking deep inhales for six counts and exhales for six counts.

5. Repeat your resolution or Sankalpa 21 times during this breathwork, for three rounds.

6. Allow your Sankalpa to settle and unfold naturally.

2. By Way of Universal Energy

Connect with the Universal Energy by standing with your arms wide open, eyes closed, and faith in the divine energy. Take a moment to breathe deeply. Then, raise your arms and gently rub your palms together. Starting from your face, glide your hands over your body. Now, seek divine assistance, feeling a shift in energy. It's time to make your Sankalpa or resolution. Repeat this process three times for maximum effect.

3. By Way of Beliefs, Faith, and Mantra

This is an incredibly potent method for manifesting your Sankalpas. I've personally experienced it several times, and I encourage you to try it yourself. Here's how it works:

1. Repeat your Sankalpa silently in your mind

2. Invoke the deity or person you have faith in and chant their mantra or name 21 times

3. Repeat your Sankalpa and the entire process seven times for maximum effectiveness

4. By way of discipline, karma

Karma is the path of action. A Karma Yogi follows this path, believing in the power of action and leaving the results to divine fruition. They do not concern themselves with the outcome, although they are certainly aware of it.

5. By Way of Love

Love resides within the Heart Chakra, making it a powerful force for manifesting your Sankalpa. To realise your desires, it's essential to cultivate love for your desired outcome.

Self-doubt or questioning will only hinder your progress. The ultimate truth is that belief in your goal will bring it to fruition. By falling in love with your vision, you'll elevate your emotions and gain the knowledge needed to reach your destination.

6. Through exploration and prayerful inquiry, ignite your curiosity to seek and discover what is right for you. Before sleeping and upon waking, ask for guidance through prayer. Continuously question yourself until you uncover the answers you seek.

Sankalpa Mudra – You can take a Sankalpa mudra before taking a Sankalpa. Illustration 1 – Palms joint and fingers interlocking & illustration 2 – One Palm over another and interlocking with thumb.

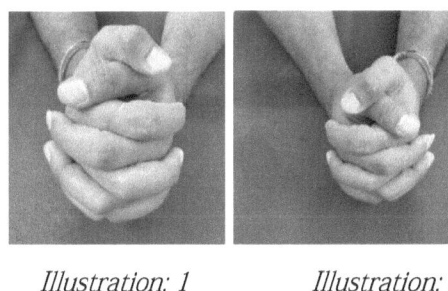

Illustration: 1 *Illustration: 2*

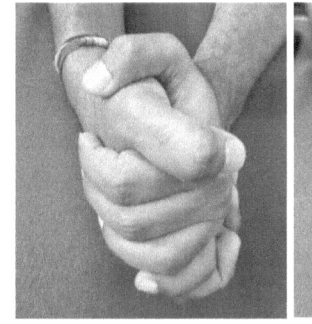 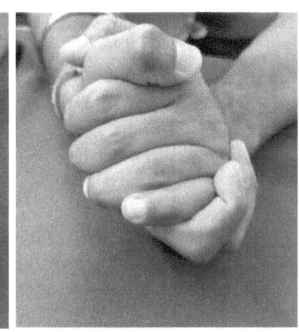

Illustration: 3 *Illustration: 4*

Moksha

When we say Moksha, it has a very deeper meaning. My Guru said, "No one can give you Moksha, but Gati." Gati is basically speed like going from Point A to Point B, metaphorically transferring from one life to another. This is dependent on factors like- how clear you are with your goals, desires and will. The stronger you are, the more inclined you are towards your goal. Some people are emotional, and if they take a hit in their emotional lives, they might stop on the way. Some want to study but might have to take a break. In all this, you sometimes have to control some desires as your pace slows down because your mind becomes inactive with these supplementary desires.

In Yog it is said that every moment has a life in itself. In that sense it means every moment has a gati, every moment has a Moksha, and that means any emotion that is held out, with prayers it gets the gati to realise or travel.

Things come to realisation when it is thought from within, it takes a form. It gets the gati to get across. When people perform pooja, it is like getting your subconscious thoughts to release. It gets that momentum, the gati, to move forward.

In mental science, there are two forms- a physical form and mental form. Like when a person is dead, the physical form passes away. But the mental form- the mind, the energy is there. That needs support to move. Usually when people see them, they mix two things. They just see the physical form, saying a person is not getting Moksha, so it is not the physical form, but the energy form that needs a release.

There are various means to do it. There are poojas, prayers, and channelizing that part of the force which is stuck within. If something is said to be done in a particular way, it takes form, it manifests, because the mind is like God's visualisation. It's the resolution you make that takes the shape.

Chapter Seven

Emotions

Human beings are emotional creatures, they experience varied emotions throughout their life. These emotions build a lot of life, and at the end of the we always judge – The emotions build our understanding of life, and based on this we judge or are judged as a personality.

How do I feel?

How did I feel?

How am I feeling?

As humans, we often gauge our emotional state based on how we feel. When someone treats us well, we experience positive emotions, but if they mistreat us, we may feel down. These fluctuations in our emotional state play a significant role in determining our overall emotional well-being. However, it's important to recognize that life isn't always smooth sailing. Despite moments of strength and happiness, challenges can arise, akin to the force of gravity pulling us back to earth. Yet, as humans, we possess the unique ability to defy this gravitational pull and elevate our emotional well-being. It's within our power to cultivate resilience and maintain higher energy levels. Learning to embrace challenges and let go of negative emotions is crucial. By nurturing ourselves and focusing on increasing our energy levels, we can overcome adversity and bounce back stronger.

Learn the art of embracing to maintain "Higher Energy levels," Believe me it's a matter of time, any emotion that leads you to pull out your core energy is not so good. Negative emotions are also a part of life, just that we fall for it or hold on too long. We need to learn "The Art of Letting go." By cultivating life's nurturing aspects to elevate your energy levels will prevent you from succumbing to negative emotions for extended periods; and you will undoubtedly bounce back.

Avoiding personal grudges and maintaining a clear conscience is essential for inner peace, which ultimately leads to bliss. However, in a competitive world, it's easy to become attached to goals and tasks, which can lead to unnecessary emotional entanglements. Dwelling on these emotions can hinder progress towards our goals. To navigate such challenges wisely, it's crucial to cultivate higher energy levels and maintain a clear conscience. Energies wield a significant influence, often observed in the charisma of celebrities whose aura resonates with positivity. Holding onto negative emotions can drain our energy and hinder our path to success.

We are our "State of Mind,"

If we get angry about one thing, it carries on,

If we are sad, it carries on,

We need to let the emotions flow.

The energy of children is remarkable in its purity and fluidity. They effortlessly release negative emotions and bounce back with enthusiasm, regardless of scolding or setbacks. Observing a child reveals a vibrant energy radiating from them, captivating anyone nearby with their sparkling eyes and infectious energy. Their unconditional love and lack of emotional attachment serve as a refreshing reminder of innocence. Children's perception of good and bad is not yet fully formed, allowing them to approach life without judgement or preconceived notions.

As individuals become educated and mature, they begin to develop self-awareness and judgement, which can dilute the pure energy reminiscent of childhood. To reconnect with this childlike energy, one can learn valuable lessons from observing children. The fundamental values, beliefs, attitudes, and perceptions we hold are integral to shaping our subconscious and influencing our perspectives and interactions with the world. Emotions are pivotal in moulding our identity and navigating life's experiences.

In an interview, Anupam Kher recounted a challenging moment in his career when he was replaced by another actor after receiving an assignment from Mahesh Bhattt. Feeling disheartened, he contemplated returning to his village. However, on his way to the station, he decided to confront Mahesh Bhattt and express his frustration. In a burst of anger and emotion, Kher confronted Bhattt, who recognized his potential and cast him in a significant role as an elderly character in an upcoming film- Saransh that ultimately turned out to be a much-acclaimed movie for Anupam Kher's iconic acting.

This instance illustrates how anger, when channelled effectively, can lead to positive outcomes. While uncontrolled anger can be destructive, controlled anger, when used purposefully and with intent, can drive individuals to assert themselves and seize opportunities.

In the case of an athlete, controlled anger can be harnessed as a source of motivation and focus, enhancing performance in competitive settings such as the ring or on the field.

However, it's essential to recognize that emotions, including anger, play distinct roles and can have varying impacts depending on the context. While "controlled anger may fuel determination and drive in certain situations, it's crucial to exercise judgement and higher intent to ensure that emotions are utilised constructively rather than succumbing to unnecessary negativity. Ultimately, it's the individual's ability to navigate and harness emotions effectively that determines their impact on outcomes.

Love possesses the remarkable ability to dissolve all negative emotions, serving as a potent force for healing and connection. Humans inherently hold immense power within them, capable of manifesting their desires and maintaining profound connections with others through the appropriate use of emotions.

Despite the fleeting nature of words, the impact of how someone made us feel resonates deeply within us. Emotions serve as the foundation of our existence, influencing our thoughts, actions, and relationships. Through our emotions we define who we are and how we interact with the world around us.

Higher the Energy - Better the Emotional Levels

Negative emotions often exert a strong grip on the mind, while positive emotions act as light feathers, granting wings to our thoughts. It's unrealistic to expect only positive experiences with emotions, as life inevitably presents us with negative ones as well—they are an integral part of the human experience. However, by learning to harness high levels of energy, we can effectively diminish the impact of negative emotions. It's not solely about experiencing negative emotions, but rather about how long we allow them to linger, as prolonged exposure can drain our core energy and leave us vulnerable. Instead of allowing negative emotions to consume us, it's essential to dissolve them within our core energy, refraining from excessive attachment to the ego, which can lead to self-harm.

If you feel a certain negative emotion and want to turn that emotion into a positive one, you can practise below steps: -

- Avoid excessive judgement; instead, acknowledge the negative feeling and consider your next steps.

- Acknowledge the presence of a negative emotion; accept it without resistance.

- Release attachment to the negative emotion and maintain awareness of your thoughts and feelings.

- Practice HVEFC (High Vibration Energy Frequency Connect) to dissolve negative emotions and cultivate high-energy vibrations conducive to positivity. Understand that accessing high energy frequencies connects you to your core divine essence, preventing you from being engulfed by downward gravitational pulls and promoting mental elevation.

How do we Practise HVEFC –

Step 1. Breathe, Put your awareness on breath

Step 2. Now, move your body – Dance or do exercise (jump, move around), Make sure to shake your body

Step 3. Next, breathe, Put your awareness back on breath

You will feel the shift in Energy level, practise & see how it feels!!!

High Energy can make a difference in life, it has the power to change your state of mind.

Positive Emotions	Negative Emotions
Calm	Irritating
Joyful	Sad
Happy	Angry
Energetic	Dramatic
Inspiring	Hateful
Courageous	Fearful
Secure	Doubtful
Content	Dissatisfied
Helpful	Selfish
Thankful, Gratitude	Arrogance

Our experiences often revolve around emotions, categorising them as either positive or negative. However, it's important to recognize that fear isn't inherently negative; it serves as a mechanism to heighten awareness and alertness. The key is to manage fear effectively, as allowing it to overwhelm us can deplete our core energy and hinder our actions. Similarly, any negative emotion, when channelled properly, can lead to improved outcomes. Take nervousness, for example; it's a common feeling before stepping on stage. Typically labelled as negative, nervousness can become debilitating if we allow it to control us, believing we can't succeed because of it. Instead, what if we reframed nervousness as something positive? By acknowledging it as a sensation of excitement and butterflies, we can embrace its beauty and allow it to settle within us, empowering rather than hindering us.

The Connection Between Emotions and Physical Sensations

Emotions are complex experiences that not only influence our thoughts and behaviours but also have a profound impact on our physical sensations. Recent studies have delved into the fascinating relationship between emotions and bodily experiences, shedding light on how different feelings manifest in various parts of the body.

While we would not take them to face value, expressing or subduing emotions can have a greater, unseen impact on your body.

- Anger, Frustration & Envy

Concentrates in the eyes, liver & gallbladder causing related physical issues like increased cholesterol, improper digestion due to an imbalance in bile creation, and the liver's reduced capacity to detoxify.

- Worry, Anxiety Or Mistrust

Sits in the spleen, stomach and pancreas creating difficulty in digestion.

- Hate, Cruelty & Impatience

Dwell in heart & small intestine causing heart palpitation, high blood pressure and chest pain.

- Fear

Makes home in the kidney, ears and bladder leading to loss of sexual energy, life force, nervous system disorder and acidity.

- Grief & Depression

Lungs, skin, and large intestines cause breathing problems, constipation, and decreased oxygen levels.

Researchers at Finland's Aalto University have produced a set of images showing where in their bodies people experience different emotions. Emotions such as anger, disgust, sadness, anxiety, shame, and happiness are often associated with specific bodily sensations. Fundamental emotions elicit heightened sensory reactions primarily in the upper chest area, correlating with changes in breathing and heart rate. Stimuli associated with the approach, such as anger and happiness, led to sensations primarily in the upper limbs. Conversely, sadness was observed to decrease activity in the limbs and evoke a reluctance to move. Sensations in the digestive system and throat region were provoked by stimuli associated with disgust. Alterations in the head region, including increased or decreased activity, were noted in response to all stimuli. Additionally, happiness was found to consistently amplify sensations across all bodily components.

The body map below shows warm colours when the feeling of emotion increases and cool colours when the feeling of emotion decreases.

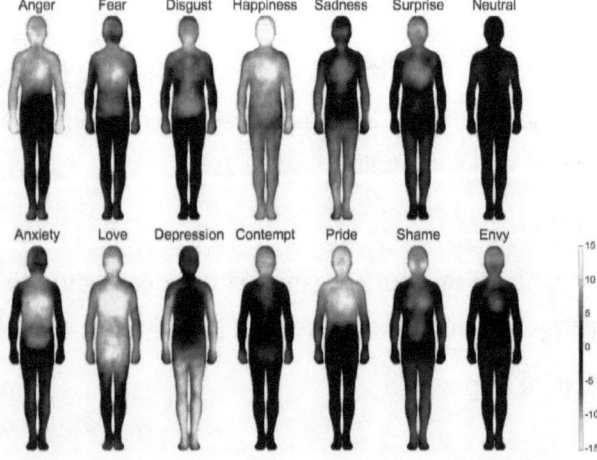

The image above, Bodily topography of basic (Upper) and non-basic (Lower) emotions associated with words.

Moreover, difficult emotions can give rise to physical symptoms such as muscle tension, tightness, feelings of heaviness or tiredness, throat constriction, aches or pains, and gastrointestinal discomfort like nausea or stomach knots. These sensations may be indicative of the body's response to emotional distress, highlighting the intricate connection between mind and body.

Furthermore, chronic emotional states have been linked to certain medical conditions such as bruxism (teeth grinding), irritable bowel syndrome, and fibromyalgia. While medical research has not conclusively proven a direct causative relationship, there is growing evidence to suggest that prolonged emotional distress can exacerbate these conditions or contribute to their onset.

One intriguing phenomenon related to the interaction between emotions and physical symptoms is somatization, where emotional distress "converts" into physical manifestations. In somatization, individuals experience real physical symptoms that have a psychological origin. These symptoms are not imagined; rather, they are the body's way of expressing underlying emotional turmoil.

Although the exact mechanisms underlying the relationship between emotions and physical sensations are still being explored, body-based therapies have emerged as promising approaches to address both emotional and physical well-being. Practices such as mindfulness, yoga, and body-centred psychotherapy aim to integrate the mind-body connection, offering avenues for individuals to explore and understand their emotional experiences while promoting overall health and resilience.

Emotions hold immense power on a mental level. Take, for instance, warriors who exhibit a profound love for their homeland, compelling them to make the ultimate sacrifice of their life or even take the lives of others. While sacrificing one's own life may seem easier, the act of taking another's life is undeniably challenging.

Your emotions can be harnessed to propel you towards success. By observing your celebrity idols and modelling your thoughts and actions after theirs, you can cultivate a deep motivation to emulate their achievements. Drawing inspiration from the lives of these stars, you'll find yourself naturally inclined to pursue similar paths of excellence, driving you to accomplish feats close to those of your favourite icons.

We have seen people impersonate Bollywood stars, their dressing style, their haircuts. There is a minor population in India who aspire to be like Sachin Tendulkar, and MS Dhoni and have caused their life to achieve where Sachin Tendulkar and MS Dhoni are today. In this endeavour, they have at least been able to make a minor change and bring a certain discipline in their life.

When individuals experience fear or nervousness, they often perceive these emotions as negative and harmful, leading to self-doubt and feelings of inadequacy. However, it's essential to recognize that fear and nervousness can serve as valuable signals, alerting us to potential risks and motivating us to take action. Rather than succumbing to these emotions, we can leverage them as catalysts for growth and achievement.

One way to transform fear or negative emotions into positive ones is by reframing our perspective. Instead of viewing fear as a hindrance, we can see it as a natural response to challenging situations, indicating that we care deeply about the outcome. By embracing fear as a sign of our commitment and passion, we can harness its energy to propel us forward, inspiring us to push beyond our comfort zones and strive for excellence.

Moreover, fear and nervousness can heighten our awareness and sharpen our focus, enabling us to take that extra mile in pursuit of our goals.

To turn fear or negative emotions into positive ones, it's essential to cultivate self-awareness and mindfulness. By observing our thoughts and emotions without judgement, we can gain insight into the underlying causes of our fears and address any irrational beliefs or negative self-talk.

Negative emotions, such as envy, can be channelled in a way that ultimately benefits us. While envy may initially lead to harmful thoughts or actions, such as wishing ill upon others or attempting to undermine their achievements, it also has the potential to drive us towards positive outcomes.

For instance, envy can serve as a motivator to strive for our own accomplishments. Instead of resenting someone else's success, we can use their achievements as inspiration to push ourselves further and reach similar levels of success. Envy when looked positively, can prompt us to take the extra mile, investing more time, effort, and dedication into our goals in order to achieve the same level of recognition or accomplishment as others.

Our emotions, whether positive or negative, stem from the same core energy within us. When we attach labels such as "positive" or "negative" to this energy, we influence how we perceive and respond to it. Instead of allowing ourselves to be consumed by negative emotions, we have the power to choose how we channel this energy.

By infusing our thoughts and actions with love and positivity, we can transform the energy within us into a force for good. Love has the power to uplift and inspire us, enabling us to stay focused on our goals and maintain a positive outlook, even in the face of challenges.

The challenge with negative energy lies in its potential to deplete one's spirit and vitality, consuming the very essence of their being. However, combating this requires cultivating a positive attitude or mindset. By remaining mindful, individuals can sustain positivity, thereby fostering positive emotions.

Emotions are deeply intertwined with the subconscious mind, influenced by past experiences, personal preferences, beliefs, and values. However, adopting a higher level of consciousness and intent empowers individuals to navigate towards positive emotions. This elevation in energy and awareness enables individuals to tap into positivity, fuelling their journey towards success, victory, or any other desired outcome.

It's essential to recognize the significant impact of our physical condition on our mental well-being. By maintaining good grooming habits and practising proper hygiene, we set ourselves up for a better sense of well-being. When feeling emotionally drained or low, a quick shower can work wonders, instantly revitalising both our physical and mental state.

Mind Over Body

Prioritising the body over the mind is a misconception. In reality, both physical, mental, and spiritual health are equally significant and interdependent.

Achieving optimal body health and mental well-being go hand in hand. A healthy body supports a healthy mind, and vice versa. Neglecting one aspect can lead to imbalances and hinder overall wellness.

Emotional Hygiene

Emotional hygiene refers to the practice of maintaining and nurturing one's emotional well-being, much like how we prioritise physical hygiene for our bodily health. Self-esteem, failure, rejection, loneliness, anxiety, and stress are all interconnected aspects of emotional health, and research has extensively explored their relationships:

1. Self-esteem: Self-esteem refers to a person's overall sense of self-worth and value. Individuals with higher self-esteem tend to handle failure, rejection, loneliness, anxiety, and stress more effectively. Conversely, low self-esteem can exacerbate negative emotions and lead to greater vulnerability to stressors.

2. Failure and Rejection: Experiencing failure or rejection can significantly impact self-esteem. Individuals who perceive failure or rejection as personal shortcomings may suffer from decreased self-esteem, which can further perpetuate negative emotions and impact mental well-being. Conversely, individuals with resilient self-esteem tend to view failure and rejection as opportunities for growth and learning, mitigating their adverse effects.

3. Loneliness: Loneliness, or perceived social isolation, can have detrimental effects on mental health. Research suggests that individuals who feel lonely may experience lower self-esteem, increased anxiety, and higher levels of stress. Loneliness can also exacerbate feelings of failure and rejection, further compromising emotional well-being.

4. Anxiety and Stress: Anxiety and stress are natural responses to perceived threats or challenges. However, chronic, or excessive anxiety and stress can have detrimental effects on emotional health. Persistent stressors, such as financial difficulties, work-related

pressures, or relationship problems, can contribute to feelings of failure, rejection, and loneliness, ultimately affecting self-esteem and overall well-being.

Research highlights the complex interplay between these emotional factors, emphasising the importance of emotional hygiene practices for maintaining mental health. Strategies such as cultivating self-compassion, building resilience, fostering social connections, seeking support when needed, and practising stress-management techniques can help individuals effectively navigate these challenges and promote emotional well-being.

Emotional well-being is in our own hands.

Developing mental awareness and maintaining a clear conscience are paramount for inner peace. Learning to let go and releasing personal grudges fosters emotional freedom. Respecting personal space and boundaries is essential in nurturing healthy relationships. Taking time to understand our mental state when alone is crucial for self-discovery and personal growth.

Additionally, practising kindness and compassion are integral components of fostering happiness and well-being. When individuals prioritise acts of kindness and cultivate a compassionate mindset, they not only positively impact others but also enhance their own sense of fulfilment and contentment.

Moreover, having a sense of purpose contributes significantly to overall happiness. When individuals have a clear understanding of their values, goals, and aspirations, they are better equipped to navigate life's challenges and find meaning in their experiences. A strong sense of purpose provides motivation, direction, and a deeper connection to one's actions and endeavours.

Digital Time

Social Media Platforms offer a flood of short-lived content that often fails to complete an emotional cycle. You may encounter snippets of various emotions—compassion, humour, politics, finance—but before you can fully engage with one, you're swiftly onto the next. This constant barrage can leave you emotionally drained without any resolution.

I recommend limiting your time on these platforms and instead focusing on specific subjects that interest you. Choose quality content that allows for a deeper emotional connection and processing. By immersing yourself in meaningful content, you can cultivate a more enriching emotional experience and avoid feeling overwhelmed by the constant stream of information.

Beware of misleading information that can emotionally influence you; it's crucial to stay vigilant and practice good judgement.

While digital learning tools like live webinars offer incredible opportunities for education, nothing quite compares to the energy exchange of live interactions.

Power of Love

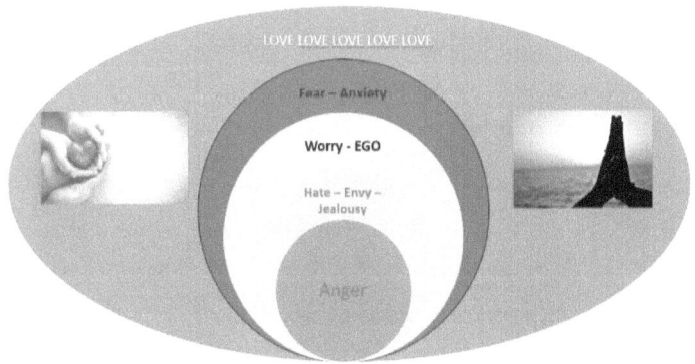

Love and faith are the highest form of emotions.

The power of love is unparalleled; it has the ability to dissolve any obstacle in its path. Fear, often misconstrued, is essentially the absence of love. When your mind is abundant with love, fear naturally fades away.

Every emotion serves a purpose; none are inherently negative. Rather, what we label as negative emotions, such as nervousness or fear, simply require proper channelling. Instead of condemning ourselves for feeling nervous or fearful, we should recognize their potential positivity. Nervousness, for example, can be reframed as a beneficial emotion that heightens awareness and enriches our experience of life. It's not a hindrance, but rather an exhilarating aspect of living fully.

The emotion of love can help dissolve every other negative emotion, In presence of love negative emotions are difficult to harm you.

Love – Spouse or your Life partner

Love is complete in itself, it doesn't need to end on the notes of marriage only, claiming to be a failure in unrequited love. Love's essence gradually forms within the perceptions of others, but this doesn't impose an obligation on them to accept it, as their ego. Simultaneously, one should avoid being excessively vulnerable in love, as it might lead others to exploit them unfairly.

Falling is love is just an emotion, but society has concluded this emotion by giving it a state of marriage. Every love story that culminates in marriage is successful. Every one-sided love story is branded incomplete and unworthy.

Societal norms have made love reach a destination, rather than remaining involved in the process. The result, when love is not met with a positive expected destination, it either gets bitter or is branded as lost and hopeless.

If you love someone, you cannot stop loving them until societal and marriage responsibilities overcome them. Love is eternal and continues to linger even when two people are destined to be unmarried and apart. Love persists beyond societal norms and marriage obligations.

It's your own understanding and commitment that creates mental blockages, making it difficult to accept when things don't go as planned. When faced with challenges, the inner voice of doubt becomes louder, fuelling ego-driven responses. Love, too, defies easy definition, as it's not a fixed moment but a continuous process that requires energy and commitment. The real struggle lies in accepting what hasn't happened yet, allowing the self to heal and move forward peacefully. Embracing acceptance over victimhood is key to transcending obstacles and finding inner peace. Love, while significant, is just one aspect of life; true fulfilment comes from embracing the entirety of one's being.

Your understanding and personal commitment can create mental barriers when things don't go as expected. Resistance to this reality only strengthens the inner voice of doubt, intensifying with each moment. Defining love proves elusive, as it's a dynamic experience rather than a fixed event. It requires significant energy and commitment to truly immerse oneself in love. Often, the real struggle lies in clinging to unfulfilled expectations, amplifying inner conflict. However, embracing self-love and acceptance can heal wounds and foster inner peace. It's essential to release the role of victimhood and recognize the broader spectrum of love encompassing self-love, familial bonds, friendships, societal connections, and beyond. Letting go of narrow definitions allows for a more profound understanding and appreciation of love's boundless nature, leading to a more blissful existence.

Emotions Are A State Of Mind

Recognizing the adverse effects of prolonged negative emotions is essential for maintaining emotional well-being; releasing them is paramount.

To harness emotions for success, we must prioritise faith, love, and values as they underpin positive emotions essential for driving our pursuits. Emotions that evoke pride and positivity are invaluable, elevating our energy and perspective on life.

Indeed, cultivating positive emotions is achievable. Time-honoured stories serve as potent sources of inspiration, fostering emotions conducive to positivity. Engaging with such tales is highly recommended. Additionally, our reality is shaped by the stories we immerse ourselves in, and those we craft. Therefore, surrounding ourselves with individuals embodying emotions conducive to growth and success is crucial for personal development.

Shifting The State of Mind

In an interview, Tony Robbins shared insights on the fluctuating nature of human emotions. He emphasised that individuals are not consistently happy or always in a positive state. Rather, our mental state varies based on the circumstances we find ourselves in. When feeling frustrated, overwhelmed, or fatigued, our brain processes information differently compared to when we're passionate, determined, or resolved. Robbins highlighted the importance of training oneself to enter peak states regularly, akin to an athlete building muscle. He explained that he personally no longer experiences entire bad days because he has cultivated the habit of transitioning quickly into more positive mental states.

Robbins outlined his "90-second rule," allowing himself a brief window to feel stress before redirecting his focus to more constructive thoughts and actions. He also referenced a scientific study conducted at Harvard that corroborated his teachings on the impact of body posture on biochemistry. The study demonstrated that assuming "Power Postures" such as the 'Wonder Woman' pose or the 'Superman' pose for just two minutes can significantly alter hormone levels, increasing testosterone and reducing cortisol, the stress hormone.

Message over Emotions -

- All emotions are good, it's the aspect that we judge tends to make it worrying. It's natural to get into fear, envy, and anger. We need to learn to channelise our emotions.

- The emotions that are highest form are driven by the very close beliefs of love, faith in God, love of family, and love towards Society.

Key Point on the Journey towards Emotional Well being

1. Meditation: Extend beyond set time limits say from 30 minutes or 1-2 hours. Strive for continuous 24-hour practice of self-awareness and detachment.

2. Digital Hygiene: Avoiding complete detachment from digital media might be impractical, but exercise digital discipline for emotional well-being. Ensure you spend time on topics of choice rather than letting AI control your digital life.

3. Letting Go: Practise releasing attachments and channelling energies towards productive endeavours.

4. Channelling Energy: Direct efforts towards maintaining higher energy levels, fostering a sense of vitality and enthusiasm.

5. Let Live: Avoid excessive judgement and learn to accept and let others live their lives without undue criticism or interference.

PART III
LIFE & YOU

Chapter Eight

Attitude

Your attitude defines who you are and possesses the remarkable ability to mould your destiny and overcome seemingly insurmountable obstacles. When a person believes they can, inevitably, they will achieve success sooner or later. Bringing about change requires both the determination to act and the mindset to see it through. The potency of a positive attitude is evident in its ability to transform mere thoughts into the strength needed to conquer formidable challenges.

If you think you can't, you will not.
If you think you can, you will for sure.
If you think you are not successful, you will not be one.
If you think you are successful, you will for sure be.
If you think you can reach your destination, you will for sure.
If you think you are lucky, you will drive luck.
If you think you are happy, you will be happy.
If you think you are energetic, you will be energetic.
   You see it's about thought, while it comes from within the attitude to believe.

The perseverance of a "Never Say Die" mindset has the potential to emerge victorious in life's battles. Each day is a new opportunity to confront challenges, and success hinges on cultivating a winning attitude. The key to enduring happiness lies in maintaining a positive mindset. Your attitude propels you to work diligently, regardless of how many times you may encounter failure. Take the example of famous inventor Thomas Edison, who faced 1000 failures before successfully inventing the light bulb. What truly counts is your unwavering belief in your ideas and the determination to take each step forward, regardless of setbacks.

The core of attitude is fuelled by a higher purpose. When we shift our focus from personal goals to a common objective, it becomes natural to fully dedicate ourselves to the cause. Consider the athlete, whose victory may be envisioned on various scales. Winning for oneself is a personal triumph, yet choosing to win for the team elevates the cause. Expanding the horizon to the community, state, and country amplifies the impact, each victory resonating with a broader purpose. However, the true essence of triumph emerges when the athlete aspires to win for humanity. In steering the influence towards shaping attitudes for the greater good of all, a remarkable transformation occurs. It's a shift from personal glory to a noble pursuit that resonates far beyond individual achievements.

How Does A Child Form An Attitude?

A prince's attitude will be of aggression and authority as he might observe his father – the King. He could be dutiful, focused, ready to learn, open to accepting challenges and prepared to look after his kingdom.

At the same time, what will be the attitude of a beggar's child? He might be lowly, demotivated, under covered, scared, and avoiding challenges. All he might think about is getting to eat something. He does not have a major cause- to rise or to protect someone.

Our attitudes, a unique journey of our past experiences, core beliefs, and the people in our surroundings, are thus built. Some people are positive irrespective of their surroundings and see what others can't see and nurture the whole being around them. They are full of attitudes conducive to growth. At the same time, some people's attitude pulls your energy down. They would criticise or make such an impact.

Where Does That Attitude Come From?

Attitude is the internal core of every being that defines who you are. And where does it come from? It comes from how you take your experiences. If a person is sad and carries that for a prolonged period it would turn to an attitude of sadness and would give sorrow. If a person has an attitude of staying happy, the person would be happy regardless of anything and that's how his attitude is built. And it all transcends to the very core of a person's state.

I commuted in the Mumbai locals for my job for a couple of years. My daily routine involved getting my shoes polished at the station I got off. The tap-tap-tap of a shoe brush against the small table that served as a shop in itself was a ubiquitous scene at the stations. I preferred getting my shoes polished from one cobbler. The reason, two minutes with him, his banter spiced with wisdom and sprinkled with laughter, could warm up even the gloomiest days. He might do his job like any other cobbler but there was a secret ingredient he added to every brushstroke, transforming the mundane into the meaningful.

One morning, the platform buzzed with other cobblers, but my regular cobbler was missing. His place was empty, his table chained to a pillar under lock and eye, and his laughter echoing only in memory. I turned around and saw another cobbler and thought of getting my routine shoe polish done. This cobbler was shrouded in the gloom of his own world. He did his work well but was self-occupied. My shoes shone but the dullness of his spirit was much felt. I missed my regular cobbler and his happy encounters.

The second day too I had to do with the sombre cobbler leaving me yearning for my regular cobbler. On the third day, my eyes sparkled with joy as I saw my regular cobbler and seeing him lifted my spirits. He said he was off on a visit outside the town with his family. He was full of excitement and warmth as always which was very radiating.

Those three minutes of shoeshine every day were a sprinkle of joy, transforming my mundane into meaningful.

I could observe now that the first cobbler earned better than the second cobbler. The first cobbler dressed well, and all this graciousness was evident clearly, while the second one looked in misery.

If you help lift the experience of other people with an attitude of service, everything changes. This we can apply in our business or personal life and see the change. It's more than just smiling faces and pleasantries; it's about genuinely caring about your customers' experiences. This shift in focus flips the script. Numbers aren't just targets; they represent happy encounters, loyal fans, and organic growth. Remember, your business interacts with humans, not robots or sales graphs.

My Mumbai train station cobbler experience revealed a profound truth: Attitude is Everything. The cheerful cobbler, radiating graciousness, not only thrived financially but also brightened everyone's day. His positive energy was a form of service, a value-add that transcended the simple act of shoe polishing.

I feel perception plays a pivotal role in shaping our relationship with nature.

I'm a teetotaller. In contrast, my circle of friends opts for indulgence in alcohol or smoking, I consciously distance myself from such choices. It's all about fostering an attitude towards maintaining a healthy lifestyle. This encompasses the determination to embrace habits that contribute to well-being an athlete's mindset, a commitment to physical fitness, and a conscious effort to breathe in the goodness of life.

The Story Of Attitude

Viktor Frankl, a psychiatrist, and neurologist endured the Holocaust and subsequently emerged as a prominent writer too after that. In 1942, Frankl, along with his family, was forcibly transported to a Nazi concentration camp, resulting in the tragic loss of his wife, parents, and brother. Frankl endured a total of three years within the confines of the camps.

While in the camps, Frankl noted that the individuals who endured the longest were not necessarily the physically strongest or healthiest. Instead, those who found meaning and purpose in their suffering were the ones who demonstrated greater resilience.

He later wrote, "Everything can be taken from a man but one thing: the last of the human's freedom — to choose one's attitude in any given set of circumstances, to choose one's way."

In just nine days, he penned his book "Man's Search for Meaning." Recognized in 1991 as one of the ten most influential books in the

U.S., it continues to maintain a consistent presence on Amazon's Top 100 Books list.

In his books, Frankl shares an experience involving gas chambers to illustrate this internal struggle.

Frequently, when concentration camps publicised lists of prisoners slated for transportation to other camps, those individuals often ended up being sent to the gas chambers instead. According to camp regulations, the count of prisoners on the list had to match the number rounded up for the supposed "transport." However, the guards exhibited indifference regarding whether the gathered prisoners were the same individuals whose names appeared on the list. In this harrowing scenario, Frankl observed that each prisoner fiercely fought to prevent himself and his companions from being chosen for transport, despite the collective awareness that for every person successfully kept off the transport convoy, another individual would inevitably take their place.

Frankl observed that, in general, the inmates who managed to survive were those willing to resort to any means, regardless of how brutal, to cling to life. The harshest individuals among the prisoners were often selected to become Capos- designated as prisoners appointed to act as guards. The harsh reality within the camps was such that Frankl asserts that anyone who endured the camp experience understands that "The finest among us did not come back."

Frankl held the belief that, even amid dehumanising and appalling conditions, life retained meaning, and suffering served a purpose. According to Frankl, in the face of extreme physical adversity, individuals could find a means of survival by tapping into their spiritual selves, allowing them to endure conditions that might otherwise seem unbearable.

In contemporary times, even medical professionals advise individuals facing life-and-death surgeries to engage in visualisation, sensory experiences, or the setting of positive intentions. Doctors suggest that patients envision a future filled with vitality or concentrate on the thoughts of a beloved person. This practice is aimed at instilling a profound intention to live, effectively planting a seed of determination within the individual's soul.

In the field of psychology, an attitude encompasses a collection of emotions, beliefs, and behaviours directed toward a specific object, person, thing, or event. Typically shaped by experiences and upbringing, attitudes exert an influence over behaviour, shaping how individuals respond in diverse situations.

Attitudes serve as mental representations of our preferences and aversions within the world, building or clarifying the reasons behind these choices.

Your attitudes toward such issues have been formed, and these attitudes play a role in shaping both your beliefs and actions.

While I served as a manager, I had a superior leading a team of three individuals. This individual exhibited a remarkable attitude centred on supporting the well-being and growth of the team. Despite having monthly targets to report to the business head, this leader maintained a positive approach. Even if the team fell short of targets in a given month, he skilfully used his charm to motivate us to double our efforts.

What set this leader apart was his unwavering commitment to maintaining a constructive atmosphere. He never resorted to putting individuals down or blaming them when targets were not met. Instead, he delved into the core systems and processes to identify any issues that might have led to the shortfall. When a team member acknowledged their part in it, he would gracefully accept it and focus on addressing the root causes.

Over the years, I came to realise that this leader's positive mindset played a crucial role in elevating people and fostering a culture of trust. His attitude was of help, support, and growth for all.

How Are Attitudes Formed?

While we say, a person is bearing a certain attitude, how does this attitude form?

The Story of Enlightenment

Gautama Buddha, also known as Siddhartha Gautama and Lord Buddha, is recognized as the founder of Buddhism, and those who follow his teachings are known as Buddhists. Often referred to simply as Buddha, meaning the enlightened one, who has attained liberation from suffering and ignorance, achieving the state of nirvana.

Born in 623 BC in the province of Lumbini, Southern Nepal, Siddhartha came into the world as part of the noble Shakya Clan, residing in the Himalayan foothills. His father, Suddhodana, headed the Shakya clan, and his mother, Maya, was a princess of the Koliyan lineage. According to court astrologers, it was predicted that he would become a great sage or Buddha.

Raised in luxury and shielded from human suffering, Siddhartha lived a sheltered life until, at the age of 29, he encountered the harsh realities of existence. Witnessing an old man, a sick man, and a corpse in the streets of Kapilavastu, he realised the inevitability of old age, sickness, and death. This revelation prompted him to seek answers to the profound questions of human suffering.

In pursuit of solutions, he decided to leave his kingdom and embarked on a journey as an ascetic. He bid a quiet farewell to his wife without waking her and ventured into the forest, donning the simple robe of an ascetic. Siddhartha sought profound wisdom, a resolution that delved into the core of human suffering, offering a timeless solution to bring it to an ultimate end.

Siddhartha embraced the rigorous practice of extreme asceticism, following the advice of companions who believed that renouncing all pleasure and enduring pain would eradicate the desires binding a person to the cycle of rebirth. Despite subjecting himself to severe starvation, he discovered that this extreme path did not lead to profound insights. Consequently, he decided to return to a normal diet, much to the disapproval of his companions who accused him of giving up too easily. Undeterred by their criticism, he relied on his personal experiences to evaluate the efficacy of the practice. Once again choosing to follow his own path, he set out alone in search of an alternative.

Under the tree of awakening that night, Siddhartha achieved a significant breakthrough. He extinguished the fires of greed, hatred, and delusion, attaining a state in which these detrimental forces were fully quenched, known as Nirvana. He became enlightened. He became Buddha!

Following his enlightenment, one of the initial actions taken by the Buddha was the formation of a community, known as the Sangha. Initially consisting of monks, it later expanded to include nuns and laypeople. Over time, this community grew into a well-organised group of followers who adopted a lifestyle known as the "middle way," avoiding extremes of sensual indulgence or extreme asceticism. Buddha imparted his teachings to this community through discourses, which they memorised in the absence of written records. He guided them in ethical conduct, facilitated mental training through meditation, and nurtured their insight.

Wandering through villages and towns in India for 49 years, Buddha preached the dharma. Recognising his wisdom, kings generously donated gardens and parks for the sangha's retreats, where people sought spiritual guidance. Buddha established a set of rules, preserved in various texts, to govern the conduct of the sangha.

Buddha who once reigned in the attitude of the rich and their glory changed his attitude in time to that which was free of hatred, greed, and delusion. He developed an attitude of service to the community.

Attitude change happens for a reason. And this reason could be a major turning point in a person's life. Attitudes form directly as a result of experience. They may emerge due to direct personal experience, or they may result from observation.

The pre-enlightenment attitude of comfort, happiness, and being content came as a result of Siddhartha's restricted or confined knowledge of the world around him. He thought everything was happy and gay in the walls of his father's kingdom. He was even oblivious to the concept of pain, and the non-avoidable death.

Social Influences:

Attitudes are significantly shaped by social factors, where social roles and norms play a substantial role. Social roles dictate the expected behaviour in specific contexts, while social norms establish the societal rules governing what behaviours are deemed appropriate.

After Siddhartha saw the harsh realities of life, his social influence brought him a lot of pain and he sought questions and wisdom as to why people suffered the way they did, and what was the solution to it. Now his attitude had changed to that of a researcher, a student seeking knowledge.

Observational Learning:

Furthermore, attitudes are acquired through observation of those in one's proximity. If someone highly admired expresses a particular attitude, there's a higher likelihood of adopting similar beliefs.

Buddha's observations pre- and post-enlightenment of his surroundings were the reasons he was curious to explore and know more. His observations led to the formation of a community that practises the middle way of peace and well-being.

Conditioning Influence:

Conditioning is a means of shaping attitudes.

Buddha, despite being born into royalty, came to the realisation that experiences influenced by external factors couldn't offer enduring happiness or shield from suffering. Following an extensive spiritual quest, he immersed himself in profound meditation, ultimately grasping the true nature of the mind. In this journey, he attained a state of happiness that was unconditional and everlasting—the state of enlightenment, known as Buddhahood.

Learning Processes:

Attitudes are susceptible to various learning mechanisms.

Siddhartha leaving the comfort of his family and superior lifestyle went in search of meaning for life. He overcame various obstacles, and practised austerities, yet believed in the learning process. His thirst to learn and infer has today led millions to a path named Buddhism.

How Can Attitudes Be Changed?

Gautam Buddha's story is a classic example of how attitudes change in life. From being a prince to developing an attitude of service, help, humanity, search for meaning to life & higher self.

Discovering oneself requires a deep internal exploration. The fundamental outlook on life often stems from a profound sense of purpose. For instance, a soldier's perspective is shaped by a higher purpose, encompassing pride, justice for their motherland, and service to humanity. When faced with street confrontations by unruly individuals, the soldier prioritises warnings and non-violent measures before resorting to physical self-defence, reflecting a commitment to service rather than destructive behaviour.

Similarly, a boxer's aggression finds legitimacy within the confines of the ring, where they represent their profession. However, if the same aggression spills over into challenges on the street, a recalibration of attitude becomes necessary. In each scenario, the individual's core values, and higher meaning guide their actions, steering them away from destructive behaviour and towards a more service-oriented approach.

Changing minds takes time. Real shifts happen slowly, like watching grass grow, not like flipping a switch. Open, kind talks where everyone's ideas get heard are the best way to help someone see things differently. Don't pressure or boss them – don't just build walls. Give them space to think, tend a garden, and let their views change on their own. It takes patience, and gentle influence, to grow the best, deepest changes.

Chapter Nine

Life Essential Skills

Embodying a set of essential skills and virtues can elevate an individual's standing in society, fostering admiration and recognition. A person who is not only talented but also possesses the right skills becomes a noteworthy figure, identical to a celebrity in their own right. Key attributes such as empathy, good listening skills, and a commitment to age-old values of ethics and morals contribute to a positive reputation, making an individual everyone wants to associate with.

Honing life essential skills is more than a personal development endeavour; it is a valuable asset in navigating the complexities of social interaction. Being a good listener, an effective communicator, kind, energetic, blissful, and happy creates an aura of positivity that attracts others. Additionally, cultivating self-awareness, creativity, and a team-oriented mindset enhances one's social presence.

Adaptability, problem-solving ability, leadership qualities, and diplomatic skills further contribute to a well-rounded and respected persona. Truthfulness, a commitment to non-violence, understanding, and empathy foster harmonious relationships, making one a person of integrity and goodwill. Generosity, both in actions and spirit, further solidifies the positive impact one can have on others.

In essence, these virtues and skills form a comprehensive toolkit for navigating social dynamics, fostering meaningful connections, and creating a positive influence in society. By learning these qualities, individuals not only elevate their own well-being, but also contribute to the collective betterment of the community.

The five most essential life skills to hone for personal and societal well-being are –

1. Awareness:

Cultivating self-awareness is foundational to personal growth. It involves understanding one's emotions, motivations, and reactions. Being aware of oneself and the surrounding environment allows for mindful decision-making, emotional regulation, and a deeper understanding of others.

2. Communication - Orator and Good Listener:

Effective communication is a cornerstone of successful relationships. Becoming a skilled orator allows one to express thoughts and ideas clearly while being a good listener fosters understanding and empathy.

3. Energetic and Happy:

Maintaining an energetic and happy demeanour contributes to both personal well-being and positive social interactions. Energy and positivity are contagious, influencing the mood of those around you.

4. Kindness:

Kindness is a powerful force that can transform relationships and communities. Acts of kindness, whether big or small, create a ripple effect of positivity.

5. Understanding:

Developing a deep understanding of others involves recognising diverse perspectives, appreciating differences, and fostering empathy.

These five life essential skills form a well-rounded toolkit for navigating the complexities of personal and social dynamics.

A proficient individual approaches their craft with skill, similarly, someone lacking the skills to navigate life may encounter difficulties in finding solutions. An individual well-versed in life essential skills becomes adept at handling life's challenges. Cultivating these additional life skills is beneficial for everyone.

1. Communication:

Communication is the process of exchanging information, ideas, thoughts, or feelings between individuals. Effective communication involves both sending and receiving messages. It encompasses verbal and non-verbal methods and is crucial for building relationships, resolving conflicts, and fostering understanding.

Communication is a two-way process that extends beyond language proficiency. While the English language often receives significant attention, particularly in our region, proficiency in the language alone does not determine one's communication skills. Effective communication involves expressing oneself clearly and comprehensively.

To enhance communication skills:

I. Focus on learning the language: Begin by actively learning the language, understanding that it may initially seem challenging. Instead of solely focusing on grammar rules, prioritise speaking and listening. Just as you learned your mother tongue through hearing and repeating words, start by listening and speaking to build confidence before delving into grammar.

II. Engage in reading: Reading regularly can improve language comprehension and vocabulary.

III. Practise speaking aloud: Verbally expressing what you read can reinforce language skills and boost confidence in articulating thoughts.

IV. Embrace self-expression: Encourage yourself to express thoughts and ideas freely, allowing for effective communication beyond language proficiency alone.

V. Active Listening:

Active listening is a skill that involves fully concentrating, understanding, responding, and remembering what is being said in a conversation. It requires giving your full attention to the speaker, avoiding interruptions, and providing feedback. Active listening is essential for building trust and promoting effective communication.

Indeed, genuine listening is a valuable trait that can greatly impact interpersonal connections. Being an active listener involves taking a sincere interest in others and offering a courteous ear to hear them out. While it may not always be possible to be fully engaged at all times, extending the courtesy of attentive listening can make a significant difference in fostering positive interactions and relationships.

1. Empathy:

Empathy is the ability to understand and share the feelings of another person. It goes beyond sympathy, as it involves putting yourself in someone else's shoes and experiencing the world from their perspective. Being empathetic allows for deeper connections and more meaningful interactions.

Experiencing an act of empathy, where someone listens to and understands your concerns, can create a profound sense of comfort and connection.

Recently, I encountered such a moment at a hotel when I arrived for an early check-in, only to find it wasn't possible. Despite this, the hotel staff member took the time to genuinely listen to me and express concern, making me feel valued and understood. It's encounters like these, whether from friends, family, or colleagues, which illustrate the power of empathy in fostering positive connections.

2. Understanding:

Understanding involves grasping the meaning, significance, or nature of something. In interpersonal relationships, others' perspectives, emotions, and motivations are crucial for building trust and fostering a sense of connection.

3. Perception:

Perception is the way individuals interpret and make sense of the information they receive through their senses. It influences how people understand the world around them and how they interact with others. Being aware of different perspectives and interpretations enhances effective communication.

4. Kindness:

Kindness involves showing compassion, generosity, and consideration toward others. It contributes to a positive and supportive interpersonal environment. Kindness fosters trust and helps create a sense of community in various social settings.

5. Thoughtfulness:

Thoughtfulness involves carefully considering and reflecting on one's actions, words, and their potential impact on others. It includes being considerate of others' feelings and needs and promoting a more positive and respectful interpersonal dynamic.

These qualities collectively contribute to effective interpersonal communication, fostering understanding, building relationships, and creating a positive social environment. Cultivating these traits can lead to more meaningful connections and improved interactions.

Soft skills, also known as non-technical skills, encompass personal values and interpersonal abilities that define an individual's capability to collaborate effectively within a society or project team. These skills are essential for navigating the external environment and fostering cooperative relationships.

The cultivation of soft skills comprises two facets. The first is nurturing attitudes, while the second entails refining communication skills to effectively convey attitudes, ideas, and thoughts. Today, with corporate jobs and handling professional clients, every working professional should nurture a set of skills that would give them a professional edge over others and ease their communication and understanding of things.

1. Work Ethics - Displaying a strong work ethic involves consistently demonstrating dedication, reliability, and diligence in tasks.

2. Communication- Effective communication is the ability to convey information clearly and comprehend messages from others.

3. Self-motivation- Self-motivated individuals possess the drive and initiative to pursue goals without constant external supervision.

4. Problem-Solving- Proficiency in problem-solving involves analysing challenges, identifying solutions, and implementing effective strategies.

5. Flexibility - Flexibility is the ability to adapt to changing circumstances and navigate unexpected challenges.

6. Critical Thinking - Critical thinking entails analysing information, evaluating its validity, and making informed decisions.

7. Negotiation- Negotiation skills involve the ability to reach mutually beneficial agreements through effective communication and compromise.

8. Creativity- Creativity is the capacity to generate novel ideas and solutions.

9. Empathy - Empathy involves understanding and sharing the feelings of others and fostering meaningful connections.

10. Time Management - Time management is the skill of efficiently organising and prioritising tasks to maximise productivity.

12. Confidence - Confidence involves believing in one's abilities and expressing assurance in various situations.

A big life essential skill that can comes from learning YOG: "Retain Don't React" - A teaching of Ramana Maharishi.

We must be able to control our emotions and are able to cruise through them calmly. Because any emotion that is not sustained and delved into will aggravate and fester.

Many street fights happen due to instant reactions. If only we are able to remain calm in the chaos, things would be different.

When we are suffering - we react

When we are enjoying - we react

When we are sad - we react

When we are happy - we react

When we are angry - we react

If we are unable to conceive the emotion for long and if we react, the emotion might lead to other consequences. Rather, if we calmly dwell in one emotion and let it settle as it arises, we can enjoy the emotions, as well as stop something unusual and unwanted from happening. Overreacting or reacting can make or break situations.

During a visit to a prison as part of my Law Degree curriculum, I encountered a man who was serving time for the murder of his neighbour. The tragic incident unfolded when he confronted his neighbour for parking in his designated spot, in a fit of anger. What began as a heated argument escalated into a fatal altercation, leaving the man consumed with regret. He acknowledges that it wasn't his true self who committed the act, but rather the unchecked fury in that moment. This experience underscores the importance of managing emotions, particularly anger & reaction, as it can lead to irreversible consequences. While he deeply laments his actions, he recognises that the damage cannot be undone. This incident is a reminder of the significance of emotional control in shaping our lives and interactions.

Life Skills Can Be Enhanced By Certain Practices Like -

1. Practise Active Listening:

Engage in active listening by giving your full attention to the speaker and demonstrating genuine interest through verbal and nonverbal cues.

2. Use Clear and Concise Language:

Employ language that is straightforward and easily understandable, avoiding unnecessary complexity.

3. Non-verbal Communication:

Non-verbal cues, such as facial expressions and body language, play a significant role in conveying messages.

4. Show Empathy:

Demonstrate empathy by understanding and acknowledging the emotions of others and validating their feelings.

5. Build Rapport:

Establish rapport by creating a positive and comfortable atmosphere in interactions.

6. Be Open to Feedback:

Cultivate a mindset that welcomes constructive feedback as a valuable tool for personal and professional growth.

Internal Communication – Self Talk

I feel that of all the ways we can imbibe life skills, self-talk is one of the important ones and often missed out. Self-talk can ascertain the way you treat others, and how you treat yourself. A person who understands oneself is able to better understand others.

A self-aware person is convinced of his pattern of communication, and he can regulate his external communication accordingly. The way to effectively communicate is to observe your self-communication patterns if that is happening inside you.

Always - Observe your thoughts. What are they communicating?

By observing your thought patterns, you are able to get to the core, which is the source of the thought, as deep within you are struggling with this thought. If you understand this source, you will stop reacting, stop being impulsive and act wisely.

Chapter Ten

Relationships

We all belong to a place that we call our own, a place where our people belong. An abode to our relationships, our family. To share, to ask for support and guidance, to revel in their comfort, and to think about what is next. Every individual is bound by a relationship. Although this is the said way of life. Societal norms have evolved us to adapt to meaningful relationships that most of the time serve to be our strength.

We all have witnessed different relationships- of a mother and her child, father and the child, siblings, and friends and - a romantic relationship or that of a husband and wife.

We need two people to build a relationship. Husband-wife, a group of friends, Guru, and the disciple (like Dronacharya and Arjuna). Any relationship thrives on companionship, compassion, love, space, trust, and respect. Relationships to a large extent ascertain our strength, our backing, our upbringing and finally our attitude.

The bond between a mother and her offspring is the most ancient and fundamental form of love. It is the first kind of love, from which all others evolved. Evidence of this bonding can be found in fossils dating back to over 200 million years ago. This bond is essential for the well-being of both the mother and her offspring, and it is a powerful force that has shaped the course of evolution.

We are not only capable of love, but we are also hardwired to bond with each other. This suggests that the capacity for love evolved, as natural selection favoured those who were able to form strong social bonds.

The ability to form social bonds is essential for our survival and well-being. It allows us to cooperate with others, to care for each other, and to raise our young ones. In short, it allows us to thrive as a species.

The capacity for love is not just a matter of our brains. It is also a matter of our bodies. When we bond with someone, our bodies release hormones such as oxytocin, which promote feelings of attachment and bonding. These hormones also have a number of other benefits, such as reducing stress and boosting the immune system.

Humans have a uniquely complex emotional life. We are capable of forming deep and lasting bonds with others, even those who are not related to us. This ability to form strong social bonds is what has allowed us to cooperate on a scale never before seen in the history of life.

The ability to care for one another, for partners, children, families, friends, and fellow humans, has allowed us to cooperate on a scale never before seen in the history of life. This cooperation has allowed us to build complex societies, and to explore the world around us.

Our home is our abode, and we come back to it seeking refuge, support, and peace. But what is it that draws us back to our relationships time and again? It is the bonding we have established with our relationships; it is the non-judgemental people who can make us thrive, it is their attitude towards us, their undying support and trust in us that makes it easy to come back to our relationships even after losing any battle.

But, as we bank upon these relationships, how are we nurturing them and what are our efforts to make them thrive?

- **Spending Time to Build Relationships**

Every relationship in life you see will come to you as a gift from a social structure. Relatives, spouses, and friends, all come to us as a form of societal obligation. Whereas, parents, brothers, and sisters, are relationships that we can't change and come to us as a virtue of our birth.

As social animals, we need relationships to exchange the warmth of love. To share, care and foster is the basic nature of every human being by which we can connect with others, share energy, and stay together. We are all a part of a huge ecosystem that thrives on the exchange of energy and survives on the archaic system of relationships.

The art of sharing energy is incomplete without the process of giving time. The key to a relationship is not just time, but 'time with the presence of energy.' Relationships foster when energy is shared over a period of time.

Ideally, our family deserves the most of our time to foster love and understanding. It is followed by relatives, friends, colleagues and then the ever-entertaining platforms. However, despite the need for relationships, we spend time in the wrong way giving more time to entertainment platforms, which consume almost most of our time. Our engagements are towards the smart world and smartphones. We have thousands of virtual friends and seldom any real friends. While we may indulge in the social world of exchanging pleasantries, we are depriving our kin and our relationships of meaningful time and energy exchange.

- **Consistent Communication**

Communication is essential in any relationship. The words we use can have a big impact on how our relationships are perceived and experienced. It is important to be mindful of the words we use, especially when we are expressing disagreement or are upset.

Sometimes, we may say things that we do not mean, or that we say in the heat of the moment. These words can have a lasting impact on our relationships. It is important to be careful and kind when we communicate, even when we are upset. Words can be more powerful than bullets. They can hurt, they can heal, and they can build or destroy relationships. It is important to be mindful of the words we use, and to use them in a way that builds up our relationships, not tears them down.

Words can build bridges of love. When we use kind and supportive words, we build bridges of love between ourselves and others. Words can destroy bridges of love when we use hurtful or angry words. Words are powerful. Words can have a profound impact on our thoughts, feelings, and behaviours. We should be thus mindful of our words, and aware of what we are speaking and conveying. If used wisely, words can create magic in relationships.

- **Maintaining The Trust**

We might mistrust people for the loss of our material possessions or blame them for life-changing situations. While we are building bridges of energy, and nurturing relationships, it is important to build trust in any relationship.

Building trust between you and your partner is fundamental to a successful and healthy relationship. That's because trust goes hand in hand with essential components of a relationship, such as honesty, open communication, vulnerability, and respect, making it of paramount importance.

Trust is the foundation of any healthy relationship. It is essential for open communication, honesty, vulnerability, and respect. Without trust, these other components of a relationship are impossible to achieve.

Trust is built over time through consistent actions and words. When you are honest with your partner, even when it is difficult, they learn to trust you. When you communicate openly and vulnerably, they learn that they can rely on you. And when you show them respect, they know that you value them and their feelings.

Building trust takes time and effort. It is important to be honest and open with the other person and to be willing to forgive them when they make mistakes. It is also important to be patient and to give the other person time to earn your trust. Doing things that require partnership and collaboration can help to breed trust. This could include working on a project together or helping each other out with a difficult task. When you work together towards a common goal, it can help to build a sense of trust and cooperation.

If you are struggling to trust someone, it is important to talk to them about your concerns. Let them know that you are afraid to trust them and explain why. If they are a trustworthy person, they will be understanding and willing to work with you to build trust. It is also important to remember that trust is a two-way street. If you want someone to trust you, you need to be trustworthy yourself. This means being honest, reliable, and respectful. It also means being willing to forgive and forget when they make mistakes.

Building trust is not always easy, but it is worth it. A relationship built on trust is a strong and lasting relationship. Taking relationships for granted and shifting priorities could damage relationships leading to distrust, and distress ultimately giving way to suspicion- a poison in any relationship. The recipe to any good relationship is the undivided attention given to the partners.

- **Respecting Relationships**

When you respect somebody, regardless of whether you disagree, you are still valuing them. We can't trust someone we don't respect. Often, the emotion to understand is overshadowed by the emotion to be understood. The self-proclamation is so high that people fail to hear the other perspective of life. In the process, disrespecting is like an arrow aimed to kill a person's energy and respect is like a prayer to God.

We are what we think, and how we think. We are energies in and out. It is therefore important we start with self-reflection. We should be our own mirror in evaluating how we behave. Are we kind to others? Are we supportive of others? Do we play the blame game? What do we expect of others? How are we contributing to their expectations? Our relationship with self-defines how we treat others. We need to be good to ourselves first and only then we can mirror it to others.

Most of the time, we judge people and relationships. We judge people with our own set of perspectives and expectations. But what we feel, is it even true? You need to question yourself. You need to ask before judging, what is the person's perspective. Our judgements could turn into miseries for us; thus, we have to stop blaming others and start looking within ourselves for answers. Perhaps, it's all in our minds. Before blaming or judging someone, when was the last time or the first time you built an opinion about that person? Why have you built an opinion about that person? Have things changed since then? Should you still keep judging the person? How is it helping you? If you self-interrogate, you will be able to solve a lot of your mind games and try thinking straight. Perhaps you will stop thinking altogether and this will not bother you.

If you apply this small practice towards every person in a relationship with you, it can develop to another level of understanding and overall, a non-judgemental approach to relationships. You have to go easy; you need to stay aware.

- **Expressing Through Service**

Have you seen your mother working endlessly at home, even after your father has formally retired from his service? Have you been the lucky one who gets a warm coffee from your husband, when you are back home after a tiring day? Have you witnessed your sibling looking after our children when you have an emergency at work? Have you seen your wife sporting your home as spic-n-span smelling with fresh flowers and oozing a positive aura when you return home from a business trip? Has your father volunteered to pay your bills so you can relax?

There are many other ways to express love, beyond just saying the words "I love you." Acts of service are a great way to show someone that you care about them, and they can be just as meaningful as words.

Acts of service can be anything from doing the dishes to running errands to giving a massage. They can be big or small, but they all show that you are thinking of the other person and that you want to make their life easier.

Acts of service are not just for romantic partners. They can be just as meaningful between siblings, parents, and friends. Love is an energy that transcends between two people, and it can be expressed in many different ways.

- **Love**

Love needs no introduction in any relationship. It's the prime ingredient of any relationship. The language of love might differ but love in itself is a universal language.

The book, "5 Languages of Love" by Gary Chapman, is a treasure for any relationship. The idea that love can be expressed in different forms, and when understood can make life easier. There will be no trust issues, no miscommunications, and we will be able to understand our partners better and lead happy lives.

The book states that a love language could be through-

- Words of affirmation
- Spending quality time with your partner
- Engaging in a physical touch
- Acts of service
- Giving gifts

While we have already spoken about being mindful of our words, spending quality time as a transfer of energy, and acts of service, other aspects of love are tangible and require physical acknowledgements.

Man and Woman

Marriages though said to be made in heaven,
Dwell on earth,
And the bonds are purely woven.
The energies of men are sky-bound,
Women being the earth around,
Represent the holistic being.

He thinks he is the tree of strength,
The head of the tribe.
But the lady of the house,
Remains the core essence.

You see them as Yin and Yan,
You see them as sky and earth,
You see them as Shiva and Parvati,
Or the ever-debating Man and Woman.

- **Physical Touch**

The sense of touch is one of the most important senses we have. It is often overshadowed by vision, but it is just as important in our everyday lives. Touch allows us to feel the world around us, to interact with other people, and to express ourselves.

Touch is thought to be one of the first senses to develop in the womb. Babies can feel touch even before they are born, and they use touch to explore their environment and learn about the world around them.

Touch is a complex sense, and it plays a vital role in our lives. It allows us to experience pleasure, pain, and a wide range of other sensations. It also helps us to connect with other people and to feel safe and secure.

Our bodies are designed to respond to touch in a way that goes beyond simply sensing the environment around us. We have a network of nerve fibres in our skin that are specifically designed to detect and emotionally respond to the touch of another person. This touch can affirm our relationships, our social connections, and even our sense of self.

New York-based psychologist Guy Winch says, "Touch is something we associate with emotional closeness, and we associate the absence of it with emotional distance." Touch releases oxytocin, a hormone that has calming and bonding effects. This is why touch can be so powerful in helping us to feel connected to others and ourselves.

In addition to oxytocin, touch also releases other hormones that have beneficial effects on our physical and mental health. For example, touch can help to reduce stress, improve sleep, and boost the immune system. It can also help to improve mood, reduce pain, and increase feelings of happiness and well-being.

Touch is a powerful form of communication that can have a profound impact on our physical and mental health.

- **Intimacy**

Every mind craves the pleasure of sex and so it is important for all. You need to develop a level of intimacy before going for sex. A blissful meditation or music can help elevate the pleasure. Understand your partner and be compassionate and respectful. Help each other to liberate from self.

If we do not tend to manage the sex side of marital life, things can get tough. It could be a fling or a casual attention outside your relationship that can be difficult to come to terms with.

Acts of sexual pleasure can play a strong role in healthy relationships. Discipline is to stay as a disciple learning. Sex is such a divine act, a prayer done consciously, it is a form of meditation that concerns energy concentration. The connection of energies is so passionate in the act that these energies can give you a glimpse of the divine nature of God. It's just bundled with pleasure found with love and consciousness that connects further.

As a disciple, you should understand –

- The role of foreplay
- Don't overindulge
- Act by awareness
- Shower before and after the act
- After sex, comment and stay together for a good time with your partner
- Don't have a feeling of guilt.

Sex is a natural and important part of life for many people. It can be a source of great pleasure and intimacy. However, it is important to remember that sex is not just about physical pleasure. It is also about emotional intimacy and connection.

- Before engaging in sex, it is important to develop a level of intimacy with your partner. This means getting to know them on a deeper level, both physically and emotionally. You should also be respectful of your partner's boundaries and desires.

- Meditation and music can be helpful tools for increasing intimacy and pleasure during sex. They can help you to relax and focus on the present moment, which can lead to a more fulfilling experience.

- It is also important to be compassionate and understanding with your partner during sex. This means being willing to communicate your needs and desires and being open to your partner's needs and desires as well.

- If you are not satisfied with your sex life, it is important to talk to your partner about it. Communication is key to a healthy and fulfilling sex life.

If you do not manage the sexual side of your marriage, things can get tough. This could lead to infidelity or other problems in your relationship. It is important to make time for sex and to communicate with your partner about your needs.

According to a survey, infidelity is one of the leading causes of divorce. It can be caused by a number of factors, including sexual incompatibility, emotional neglect, and a lack of communication.

When people are not getting their sexual needs met in their marriage, they may be more likely to seek out satisfaction elsewhere. This can lead to an affair, which can destroy the trust and intimacy in a relationship.

It's important to remember that sex is not just about physical pleasure. It's also about emotional intimacy and connection. When couples can connect on a deeper level, they are less likely to stray.

If you are struggling with sexual intimacy in your marriage, there are a few things you can do to improve the situation. First, talk to your partner about your needs and desires. It's important to be honest and open about what you want. Second, try to find new ways to spice up your sex life. There are many resources available to help you do this. Finally, make sure that you are both emotionally connected. This means spending time together, communicating openly, and being supportive of each other.

In any marriage, ego can be a major obstacle to understanding and connecting with your partner. It is important to be able to control your ego and to be open to understanding your partner's perspective on life.

Time, love, focus, priority, trust, and careful use of words are all essential ingredients for a good relationship. When you make time for your partner, show them love, focus on their needs, prioritise your relationship, trust each other, and use words carefully, you are creating a foundation for a strong and lasting relationship.

Sankalpa In Relationship

In any relationship you are bound to make perceptions either in favour or not in favour based on your own interest, most of the time we tend to assume things and even generalise.

Why do we fight?

Why do we cause uncomfortable feelings with someone?

Why don't we gel with someone?

Why does someone irritate us?

Why do we argue?

Why don't we find the right person each time?

The cause of trouble is very much in our own mind, at some point in time things have not aligned and we have made an impression that causes a certain level of perception to rise in our mind. Beware of the words; the voice that causes an impression on the mind, we tend to repeat the bad experience more times than a pleasant one. If asked what is your saddest moment in a relationship? It's not going to require you more than a second to remember that, but to remember the happiest moment it will take a certain amount of time to think. That's because we register the bad experiences with more energy and focus, that's how our nature is. Rather, we should learn to cultivate awareness of relationships keeping the human aspect in mind. Sometimes we take things seriously and spend too much time on critical analysis.

Rather put forward the Sankalpa to –
Bless everyone near and dear to you or has come to connect with you.
Take Sankalpa to pray for everyone.

Chapter Eleven

Values

Can values be instilled at any stage of our lives, or are they primarily imprinted during our childhood?

Certainly, the process of inculcating values is a continuous journey throughout our lives. A powerful example of transformation is seen in the story of Sage Valmiki, the author of Ramayana, who went from being a thief to a wise sage and yogi. Similarly, the life of Great King Ashoka took a positive turn when he embraced the philosophy of Buddha.

Every day, we encounter opportunities to absorb values from our experiences, perceptions, and personal resolutions or sankalpas. These conditions play a significant role in shaping our values. It's crucial to be mindful of what we expose our minds to, much like the careful consideration we give to the food we consume for physical nourishment. The values we incorporate into our minds act as mental nourishment, influencing our thoughts, actions, and overall well-being.

Just as Valmiki and Ashoka underwent transformative journeys, our continuous effort to embrace positive values contributes to our personal growth and development. In essence, the debate supports the idea that throughout life, we have the capacity to inculcate values that nourish our minds and guide us towards a more fulfilling existence.

Some of the most well-known global or universal values involve principles such as refraining from stealing, showing respect to elders and others, maintaining honesty, expressing gratitude, extending help to those in need, fostering kindness, and acknowledging and learning from mistakes.

A person of integrity will be warmly received wherever they go, and greeted with a bright smile, and someone who consistently honours their commitments will earn respect.

Values, especially learned in childhood, become a natural part of who we are, shaping our actions and decisions almost like instincts. It's similar to learning not to touch fire – the idea is so ingrained that we automatically avoid it without constant reminders. For a child, stories about honesty, kindness, and respecting others are like building blocks for their moral compass. As they see the positive results of good behaviour and the negative outcomes of wrongdoing, these values become like automatic "programs" guiding their decision-making. Just like learning to walk or ride a bike becomes second nature with practice, sticking to our ingrained values can become a seamless part of who we are.

Deeply internalising the value of non-stealing means that when faced with a chance to take something not theirs, a person's "anti-theft program" kicks in automatically. The very thought of stealing goes against their core principles, guiding their behaviour even without external pressure or fear of punishment.

When we embrace a value like non-violence, it becomes more than just a rule – it becomes an internal compass guiding our actions. Stories of saints, noble kings, and inspiring figures like Rama, Jesus, and Buddha act as powerful motivators, urging us to adopt noble paths and embody values like family, love, and balance. However, just like a healthy person holding a cigarette, our initial values can be challenged by external influences and circumstances.

Mahatma Gandhi- Leadership & Values

Mahatma Gandhi stands as a towering figure in the world of ethics and morality. His life wasn't merely a collection of principles and practices, but of personal conviction, public action, and an unwavering pursuit of truth and nonviolence. He viewed life as an ever-evolving journey, a constant striving towards higher moral and spiritual ground.

At the core of Gandhi's philosophy lay the belief in a single, unified standard of conduct rooted in the principles of dharma, truth, and nonviolence. This wasn't just an abstract ideal; it was the guiding force behind his remarkable achievements. He led by example, spearheading peaceful struggles against some of the most pressing injustices of his time: racial discrimination, colonial oppression, economic exploitation, and social inequalities.

Gandhi's legacy transcends borders and ideologies. His unwavering commitment to nonviolence as a tool for social change continues to inspire individuals and movements across the globe.

Moral decisions influence every aspect of our daily lives, from small actions like making our bed to larger decisions at work. Despite the importance of moral values, it's often challenging to define them clearly. We commonly mention virtues like honesty and respect when asked about moral values, but not all values carry the same moral weight. Our lives are filled with judgments, whether we're evaluating sports, appreciating art, following social norms, exploring scientific theories, nurturing relationships, participating in economic activities, or considering spiritual beliefs. These judgments, whether conscious or subconscious, are deeply connected to our values, shaping how we see the world and guiding our actions.

Every day, whether in sports, cultural practices, science, or personal connections, we come across values and make decisions based on what we think is important. These decisions act like compasses, guiding our choices and affecting how we interact with the world.

Values, which are often seen as good qualities like honesty and respect, can have different sides. For example, courage is usually admired, but it might look like reckless behaviour in some situations. Similarly, honesty, which is appreciated for being open, might seem like rudeness in certain cases.

Chatrapati Shivaji Maharaj

Jijabai's love for her son was woven with tales of heroism and righteousness from the Ramayana and Mahabharata. These epic stories, filled with brave warriors and steadfast defenders of the downtrodden, ignited a spark of valour within young Shivaji.

Jijabai also instilled in him a deep awareness of the injustices faced by his people, particularly the suffering of women under the rule of the Deccan Sultanates. She spoke of how women were treated with cruelty and disrespect, their dignity trampled upon without remorse.

This ignited a fierce passion for justice within Shivaji. He vowed to protect the vulnerable and uphold the values of chivalry and compassion that he learned from his mother and the epic heroes of his cultural heritage.

In a display of remarkable integrity, Shivaji challenged a brutal custom of the time. Following a victory, the Subhedar of Kalyan's daughter-in-law was offered to him as war spoils, adhering to the prevailing practice of Sultanates. However, instead of succumbing to this tradition, Shivaji showcased immense respect and compassion. He acknowledged her beauty metaphorically, stating that if his mother possessed such grace, he would be blessed with similar good looks. Instead of accepting her as a prize, he chose a path of honour and generosity. He sent her back to her family, unharmed and accompanied by gifts, demonstrating his unwavering commitment to protecting women and upholding their dignity.

Values are like personal preferences. Everyone has their own set of things they think are good or important. These values influence how we act and react to the world. So, values are like our personal guides, helping us decide how we should behave and make choices.

Stories like these, where individuals stand up for what is right and defend the vulnerable, have the power to ignite within us a deep-seated respect for women and a commitment to service. These values aren't fleeting sentiments; but guiding our actions and defining who we are.

Just as respect for women forms the foundation of a just and compassionate society, so does a dedication to serving others and upholding the values of nationhood. When such values become core principles within our communities, they create a fertile ground for positive change and progress.

People can be good or not-so-good, depending on their choices and how they act. Whether they are kind, honest, and loving or not, shows what kind of person they are. When someone has good qualities like being humble, pure, truthful, and loving, it shows they have strong moral values.

When what's considered right or wrong comes from rules set by society or the government, it can change over time. For example, the way people view marriage has changed from traditional ideas to more modern ones, like living together without getting married. This shows how what's considered right or wrong can be influenced by laws and how society thinks.

Some of the common values we have been taught growing up are -

1. Compassion

Compassion is the deep awareness of and sympathy for the sufferings of others, coupled with the desire to alleviate the suffering.

2. Respect

Respect is a fundamental human value that involves showing regard for others, treating them with dignity and consideration, and valuing their opinions and feelings. It is a two-way street, meaning that we should not only respect others but also expect to be respected in return.

3. Honesty

Honesty is a fundamental moral virtue that involves being truthful, sincere, and authentic in our words and actions. It means being genuine and straightforward, avoiding deception, trickery, or any attempt to mislead others.

4. Gratitude

Gratitude is a positive emotion that involves feeling thankful and appreciative for the good things in our lives. It is a simple yet powerful emotion that can have a profound impact on our well-being.

5. Generosity

Generosity is a virtue that involves giving freely and willingly to others, without expecting anything in return. Generosity manifests in various forms, from donating money to charity to volunteering time to help others in need.

6. Kindness

Kindness is a fundamental human virtue that involves the desire to help others, show compassion, and promote well-being. It is a quality that manifests in various forms, from small acts of consideration to significant acts of generosity.

Why Are Values Important?

Moral values seem to be losing their importance in today's society. Youngsters are engrossed in pursuing their careers and indulging in leisure activities, often disregarding social issues and family responsibilities. In the face of intense competition, young children are being neglected, with parents leaving them in daycare centres where they lack the warmth and care they need. The influence of Western culture and movies, often portraying misleading values, is contributing to the degradation of our culture. Meanwhile, middle-aged individuals are facing a constant struggle to provide for their families due to rising inflation and ineffective government policies.

How Can Values Be Changed?

The good news is that values are not static. Over time, through new experiences, stories, and conscious choices, our internal landscape can shift. We can actively choose to reaffirm or alter our values based on what resonates with us most deeply. The key lies in continuous reflection and a willingness to learn and grow. Just like breaking a bad habit, refining our values requires awareness and effort, but the reward is a life guided by genuine conviction and alignment with our true selves.

As explained by psychologist Jonathan Haidt, in our everyday life, our moral judgments are more like lawyers arguing for what we already believe, rather than fair judges deciding based on principles. We often change our moral values to suit ourselves, being flexible and self-serving. Our daily actions usually stick to the same routines, with only a few important values staying the same over time. Social pressure affects how we act – in public, we defend our ego, and in private, we take responsibility. Our beliefs change with time and match who we are becoming, often giving more importance to belonging to a group than following specific rules or values.

Values are imprinted during our growth, and the process of growing up is continuous. You can certainly adopt and embrace values that steer you toward success. These values act as a guiding light and serve as both defence and attack mechanisms when needed for quick decision-making. For instance, prioritising the value of staying fit and healthy can align other aspects of life to support your overall well-being, guiding you towards achieving your highest values. The key is to uphold your life values high, as they will lead the way.

Chapter Twelve
Happiness

Everyone desires happiness, yet often we find ourselves lacking in it. This shortfall may stem from our tendency to judge situations based on our emotions. We attach the expectation of happiness to specific actions or accomplishments, resulting in fleeting moments of joy. Various theories define happiness. There is innumerable research that has derived findings on what happiness is and how one can remain happy.

I feel the very core of the essence of happiness is maintaining a high level of energy. We all have witnessed a sudden warmth that fills our bodies when we are happy. We find ourselves in an elevated state and always want this state to continue. If you have a pet at home, I am sure you must have experienced happiness around being cheerful and energetic, especially with a dog, who has the ability to transform your mood and energy. Even a toddler/ small child in a family can change the fortune of the family by bringing home the "Pure Essence of Energy." The child can bring a fresh dose of energy to life. You see in any relationship a new soul adds up the energy, a person having a good family life, and social life, stays happy due to the added energies of life.

However, is this a permanent state? That is a question to ponder. It is seen that as much as we spike up our energy levels being happy, the sooner we experience the plummet. We are unable to maintain happiness as a continuous state.

Receiving gifts, achieving success, winning, growth, feeling motivated and acknowledged, are all short-lived. Happiness, at its core, is a symphony of chemicals and hormones within specific regions of the brain. Several types of chemicals play crucial roles in this process, primarily neurotransmitters like dopamine, serotonin, norepinephrine, and endorphins, along with hormones like oxytocin, oestrogen, and testosterone. Each of these chemicals contributes to various aspects of happiness, from motivation and pleasure to bonding and well-being.

By understanding these mechanisms, we can cultivate an environment that promotes the release of these happiness-inducing chemicals, leading to a more fulfilling and joyful life. However, it's important to notice whether it brings a stage of constant happiness or not.

- Dopamine:

The feeling of motivation, achievement, pleasure, and decision making is the work of Dopamine.

- Oxytocin:

When it comes to social interactions, bonding, empathy, trust and attachment, Oxytocin is at play.

Yes, Human beings are social animals and hence bonding socially raises our oxytocin level, even the acceptance of a person into a group or being a person of influence can lead you to be happy Serotonin:

When you feel content, and optimistic enjoying emotional stability, Serotonin is working.

- Endocannabinoids:

Feeling relaxed, calm, and regulated, cannabinoids are dominant due to their effect on the neuronal synaptic path, which influences the nervous system to play a vital role over mood.

- Endorphins:

When you are exercising, hearing good music, eating sweets that you like, laughing, having orgasm, feeling stress-free, feeling pain-free, and euphoric, the endorphins are acting.

Having a common thread of high energy, chemicals play a significant role. Thus, maintaining elevated energy levels ensures a boost in bodily chemistry, facilitating the experience of happiness. Once happiness is embraced, it fosters health, and fulfilment, and paves the path to richness and wealth. Additionally, it steers one towards tranquillity. Sustaining high energy levels leads to happiness, which in turn enhances resourcefulness and improves life. Success naturally follows as one becomes adept at navigating life's challenges. Therefore, happiness is the gateway to success.

Awareness - Being mindful means being fully present, allowing the genuine essence to emerge without indulging in every moment. In today's nuclear families, there's a tendency to limit the energies that lead to fulfilment. It's essential to recognize that your family, even if not providing financial support, can offer invaluable energetic support. This life energy is truly invaluable.

Contentment - Understanding the significance of contentment is crucial, especially in the digital age where information overload is prevalent. Once exposed to content on screens, it can infiltrate our lives.

Ultimately, as life draws to a close, what matters most is how contentedly you've lived. The feeling of contentment becomes paramount, providing solace as you reflect on your life. Visiting an old age home or speaking to elders often reveals regrets stemming from a lack of happiness or living in the moment. Despite possessing the necessary life energies, many missed out on fully experiencing life's joys.

Life presents challenges, but it also provides the inherent strength to overcome them through life force. It's essential to nurture this life energy to feel complete. While it's natural to experience feelings of depression, sadness, or unhappiness, it's crucial not to let them drain your precious life energies excessively.

At times, understanding the power of letting go becomes paramount. This doesn't imply giving up entirely, but rather recognising when to release attachments. If a dream or goal remains unfulfilled despite efforts, consider the significance of letting go.

In relationships, it's vital to loosen the knots that bind too tightly. Often, we cling to assumptions and decisions, causing deep wounds in our minds. Untying these knots with care and love is essential. Opening these knots allows for healing and fosters healthier, more fulfilling relationships.

Moments of happiness often seem fleeting, while feelings of sourness and bitterness linger. This gravitational pull towards negativity can be countered by consciously elevating oneself towards happiness. It's important to minimise the duration of unpleasant moments and magnify the joyous ones.

Just like the habit of chewing gum, where lingering on the sourness is common, it's crucial to instead seek out the sweetness that brings happiness. Choosing to focus on positive experiences can lead to a more fulfilling life.

Consider the example of a yogi meditating in the Himalayas. While they may attain wisdom, true fulfilment comes from sharing that wisdom with others. Service to humanity or assisting individuals in any form leads to lasting happiness.

Being there isn't just about accomplishing goals. Achievements may offer fleeting happiness. Instead, true happiness is a decision you must make.

It's worth considering whether not being happy could contribute to achieving significant success. When we prioritise happiness, our life energy undergoes a positive transformation. Conversely, feelings of sadness, stress, unhappiness, or failure drain our energy. While life isn't solely about happiness, it's essential not to become completely consumed by negative emotions.

Redirecting our life energy towards happiness paves the way for long-term success. Research supports this notion, demonstrating how happiness can improve health, success, and longevity. A happy individual is more likely to lead a longer life.

So, can happiness be cultivated?

Absolutely. By understanding that happiness is closely linked to high life energy, we can actively work to elevate our energy levels. This shift helps to dilute feelings of stress, sadness, or depression, allowing us to reconnect with our innate happiness and true nature.

Practise HEVFC (High Energy Vibrational Frequency Connect)

Technique: Engage your body, move your limbs, skip, jump, or dance vigorously - any movement will suffice. This action initiates an energy shift, infusing enthusiasm and vigour to dispel negative thoughts or emotions and connect with "High Energy Vibrational Frequency Connect."

Steps:

1. Move your body, shake, dance - let loose.

2. Close your eyes and sense the energy throughout your body.

3. Acknowledge the energy shift with open hands.

4. Repeat steps 1, 2, and 3 for a second round.

I recommend practising this technique at least 3 to 5 times a day. Over time, you'll notice a significant boost in your energy levels, fostering a sense of vitality and happiness. This method is proven to help overcome moments of unhappiness or lack of resourcefulness.

Have you observed a child experiencing unhappiness or sadness, depression, or stress... perhaps momentarily, but their innate essence is to maintain high energy levels, which swiftly transforms them into a state of happiness.

Further suggestions are based on the various research-

Practice Mindfulness

Cultivating present-moment awareness through practices like meditation can offer significant rewards. Focusing on the present, rather than dwelling on the past or fretting about the future, can lead to increased self-acceptance. The key lies in being present and acknowledging emotions without judgement.

Enhance Your Social Connections

Multiple studies, including the monumental Harvard Study of Adult Development, have consistently identified social connection as the most potent factor influencing happiness. This long-term research, spanning over 80 years and tracking the lives of hundreds of participants and their children, has yielded a clear message: strong relationships are the cornerstone of a happy and fulfilling life.

Researchers have found that individuals with robust social networks, encompassing spouses, family, friends, and community members, consistently report higher levels of happiness and well-being. This positive impact extends beyond emotional fulfilment, contributing to both physical and mental health. Conversely, individuals with weaker social connections experience lower levels of happiness and increased vulnerability to health challenges.

No matter what's going on in your life—whether it's your relationships, family, friends, work, or personal matters—you can still find happiness. It's a natural part of who you are, and if you nurture your life force, you can maintain happiness despite challenges. Staying energetic has the power to break through stagnation and bring fulfilment and joy into your life.

Finding Your Calling

Uncovering your life's purpose, your calling can unlock profound fulfilment and happiness. A remarkable study on ageing revealed a startling truth: having a sense of purpose reigns supreme as the single most significant factor influencing both life and work satisfaction, and even longevity.

However, discovering your calling isn't always a straightforward journey. Dedicating time for self-reflection, perhaps through journaling, can illuminate the things that truly matter to you. By unearthing your core values and aspirations, you can then chart a course toward fulfilling your life's purpose.

Chapter Thirteen
Pack A Punch For Life

Believe in yourself and stand strong. Even when things are tough, keep fighting and don't give up on what you can achieve. Don't let anyone else decide who you are or what you can do. Break free from those limits and explore all the possibilities. Only by pushing past boundaries can you truly understand who you are and what you're capable of.

It's crucial to approach free advice with caution, as not all guidance is beneficial. Understanding the underlying intent behind the advice is key. While some advice may be well-meaning and aligned with your best interests, others may stem from motivations that do not serve your greater good. It's important to discern whether the advice originates from a place of genuine care, positivity, and love.

Recognizing the intent behind the advice is essential. Advice rooted in fear, particularly from close family members, often arises from a desire to protect you from potential harm. However, this concern may sometimes clash with your own aspirations for independence and freedom.

Dealing with bullying requires courage and assertiveness. Instead of avoiding the issue, it's crucial to confront it head-on. Standing up for yourself is vital; by doing so, you assert your identity and refuse to be intimidated. Rather than responding with violence, it's important to maintain composure and seek understanding. By engaging in dialogue and addressing the root cause of the bullying, you can pave the way for resolution and mutual respect.

This incident happened during one of the management courses I was pursuing. The students usually came after taking industry experience for this course and thus weren't the fresh-out-of-graduation college ones.

On the first day of our course, our seniors posed as our faculty came and started taking an introductory session. We were all naive and new to the place and people. Taking them as our professors, we got into what they asked us to do, thinking this was all required.

The seniors called us one by one and asked some straight questions and otherwise twisted. And then they called the prettiest girl in our class. Her interrogation went on for a long time, with the seniors posing one question after the other. They asked her, what is your hobby, and she said singing. Now they asked her to sing, which she was uncomfortable with. Yet the seniors persisted, and over time it became their command. The girl was certainly angry and frustrated, and it was very visible on her face. But who would deny the faculty on the first day of the course.

She took her time. The command came once more, sing or you have to keep standing here, and no one goes home until you sing.

The girl gave a scornful look to the people who commanded, and started singing, "Jana Gana Mana" our national anthem, and we all stood for it.

After the anthem, everyone in the room applauded for her, and the seniors were more impressed that this beauty came with brains.

After all, it was a nice ice-breaking session and finally, the seniors disclosed that they weren't our faculty, and were here to rag us. Now that was something interesting, and we all let out a sigh of relief. But I admired the girl's persistence, and her wit to listen to the command, yet do what she felt was right. The girl under all the pressure inflicted on her remained calm, did not revolt, and smartly thought of a way that would silence everyone. She was a winner that day.

In a family of siblings, there may be moments when the elderly members assert themselves, as is natural. It's important to demonstrate wisdom by giving them the space and respect they deserve. Respect is a currency that can pave the way for reciprocated respect, love, and care.

Aspire to defy expectations, even when told you cannot succeed, and illuminate the path despite facing adversity.

Amitabh Bachchan's Story

Amidst the glitz and glamour of the entertainment industry, Amitabh Bachchan's journey has been one marked by both triumphs and trials. Once hailed as the 'One Man Industry' of Bollywood, Bachchan faced a period of dwindling stardom and financial turmoil between 1984 and 1999.

During this challenging phase, Bachchan encountered setbacks in both his professional and personal life. Despite his earlier successes, his ventures in business and politics proved to be fraught with difficulties. The years saw him weathering scandals, enduring bankruptcy, and enduring public scrutiny. Yet, like a phoenix rising from the ashes, Bachchan refused to be defeated.

The inception of ABCL (Amitabh Bachchan Corporation Ltd) in 1995 was intended to be a milestone in Bachchan's career, yet it spiralled into a financial catastrophe. Despite initial successes such as the hit TV show "Dekh Bhai Dekh," the company soon found itself engulfed in mismanagement controversies. The subsequent string of box-office failures plunged Bachchan into a dire financial crisis. By 1999, he faced the looming threat of bankruptcy and the loss of his cherished home, 'Prateeksha.'

Recalling this tumultuous period, Bachchan reflected on the relentless pressure from creditors and the spectre of financial ruin looming over his family. In a bid to navigate his way out of debt, Bachchan resorted to his core talent – acting. Embracing a new role as a supporting actor, he sought refuge in the industry he had once dominated.

Approaching producer-director Yash Chopra for opportunities, Bachchan's decision to reinvent himself proved to be a turning point in his career. Though driven by financial desperation, this move breathed a new life into his professional journey. Simultaneously, Bachchan ventured into the world of television, hosting the immensely popular show "Kaun Banega Crorepati" in 2000. The show's success catapulted him back into the limelight, strengthening his status as a household name once again.

Amitabh Bachchan's remarkable comeback serves as an inspiration for persevering through adversity and embracing change.

The wisdom is to know you are Infinite. That the will that drives you is Infinite. It's up to you to pack a punch for your life.

Drive the courage to achieve. Let nobody limit you to be finite. Pack a punch for your Life.

Stand for your own self. For your own good.

That is what makes you complete.

The essence of life, according to philosophers, lies in the power of thought. Until you believe in your own capabilities, overcoming challenges becomes a formidable task. Taking inspiration from the world of sports, a boxer's victory is not just about delivering hits but enduring them and persistently seeking opportunities to showcase skills. It involves returning to the arena, facing adversity, and seizing the chance to exhibit prowess.

Embracing the philosophy of "Pack A Punch For Life" means taking ownership, feeling, and living your journey with a deep sense of commitment. By making the thought truly your own, you empower yourself to navigate life's challenges. The crux lies in having the courage to cultivate unwavering belief in yourself. Rise like a fighter, move forward with determination, and trust in your ability to fiercely contend for your life's aspirations.

In the attitude chapter, we read about Arnold's struggle and how he has carved a niche for himself.

Arnold Schwarzenegger's life journey serves as a compelling illustration of the power of goal setting and unwavering commitment. Despite originating from a humble background in a small Austrian town, he manifested his ambitious aspirations through meticulous planning and persistent effort. Initially, his dreams of becoming a world-renowned bodybuilder were met with scepticism and ridicule, both from his family and peers. However, Schwarzenegger remained undeterred, crafting a comprehensive plan, and diligently dedicating himself to its execution. His unwavering commitment defied all initial doubts, culminating in his remarkable success as a bodybuilding icon. Therefore, Schwarzenegger's story exemplifies the transformative potential of setting ambitious goals, formulating a clear plan, and persevering through adversity to achieve extraordinary outcomes.

Here is the story of Akash, a fictitious character who is in, and around, all of us today. Akash's story below is that of the many successful youngsters who are susceptible to the desires of their families above their own.

Akash, despite achieving outward markers of societal approval - a high-paying CEO position, a luxurious home, and a family, grapples with a profound sense of dissatisfaction and emptiness. This internal conflict compels him to abandon his successful life and embark on a journey of self-discovery.

His initial pursuit of consulting work, while offering a change of pace, fails to provide the emotional fulfilment he craves. This realisation prompts him to delve deeper into the root cause of his unhappiness, leading him to the uncomfortable truth: he has spent his life pursuing a path predetermined by his father, not by his own desires.

Akash's revelation resonates with the concept of "should" in life, often instilled by societal or parental expectations. These "should" can lead individuals down paths that, while seemingly successful, ultimately fail to align with their authentic selves and aspirations. As Akash grapples with the realisation that he has been living his father's dream, not his own, he begins to explore the path less travelled - the one that could have led him to a career in psychology, a field that perhaps aligns more closely with his intrinsic values and interests.

It is crucial to periodically introspect and evaluate whether our current path aligns with our core values and desires. Having the courage to confront unfulfilled aspirations and embark on the journey of self-discovery, even when it requires significant life changes, can lead to a more authentic and fulfilling life.

We endure the lives and experiences of others, many times we even kill our dreams for a few words of others. You have to stand tall for your own will and "Pack A Punch For Your Life" to believe in your way. Until you keep your own voice loud and clear for your own dreams, there will be a time when your inner voice may be punctured to make you unable to stand for yourself, then remember to Pack A Punch For Life.

Chapter Fourteen
Dare To Think

"Think - Idea - Think - Belief" encapsulates the transformative power of thought and belief in bringing ideas to fruition. As articulated by Bob Proctor, every creation originates from an idea—a spark of inspiration that, when nurtured with belief and action, manifests into reality. The pivotal moment lies in embracing the initial idea and allowing it to take root in one's mind.

A friend of mine aspired to become a Chartered Accountant (CA). Despite harbouring the desire, he succumbed to doubts shared by others who perceived the journey as difficult. Influenced by external scepticism, he gave up his ambition, forsaking the potential of his dream.

However, what my friend failed to realise was the immense power of his own thoughts and beliefs. Had he dared to challenge the prevailing notions and nurtured a steadfast belief in his capabilities, the trajectory of his journey could have been vastly different. By fostering a mindset of possibility and resilience, he could have pursued his dream with unwavering determination, defying the limitations imposed by external perceptions.

When we dare to think beyond constraints, believe in our potential, and take decisive action, we unlock boundless opportunities for growth and achievement.

If you think that rich & wealthy is not what I can be because of any reason, you will not be. If you doubt your potential to attain riches and wealth for any reason, you'll likely never achieve them. Self-doubt often leads us to abandon our aspirations for success, only to blame external factors later on. The singular reason for success is daring to believe in your ability to achieve it and then taking the necessary actions to make it a reality. Action is the first step towards resulting in your belief.

One of the transforming journeys you can watch on 'The Shark Tank' is of 'The Ring Doorbell,' and how an idea was transformed into a fortune.

Case Study: The Ring Doorbell

In 2013, Jamie Siminoff introduced the Door Bot on the television show "Shark Tank," pitching it as a caller ID for your door—a doorbell equipped with a video camera that sends alerts and live video feeds to the owner's smartphone. This innovative device allowed homeowners to remotely interact with visitors, providing a sense of security by giving the impression of being home, even when they were not.

The Ring Doorbell served as a deterrent to potential burglars by allowing homeowners to monitor and communicate with visitors remotely, thus increasing home security.

Jamie Siminoff had confidence in his company's success and his impressive $1 million in annual sales.

The shark proposed a $700,000 loan with terms including a claim to 10% of all sales until the loan was repaid, a 7% royalty on all future sales, and a 5% equity stake in the company. Siminioff did not jump to the offer, rather he did not take it.

However, following the show, Siminoff successfully secured funding from other sources, and subsequent investments from venture capitalists, even before the show was aired.

The company was finally taken by Amazon for $1 Billion.

This case highlights the importance of perseverance, adaptability, and above all - the confidence in your idea that could help secure adequate funding. Although it underscores the challenges of navigating investment deals and the potential trade-offs associated with corporate acquisitions.

Look at this irony, after all this Siminoff is called as a Guest Shark to evaluate the sales pitches.

A famous philosopher has said, **"The one who wins is not the person who has talent or more skills, but the person who wins is the one who thinks he can win."**

Dreaming big is crucial; envision your life as if it's vastly different worldwide. The key to living your best life lies in conceptualising, believing, feeling, and embracing. Every individual has the right to pursue happiness, health, wealth, and success. The only obstacle may be self-imposed mental barriers. Your thoughts shape your perception of life and yourself, ultimately defining who you are. Success is often linked to positive, success-oriented thoughts, while life struggles may originate from negative thought patterns. Thoughts serve as the driving force, shaping and conditioning our minds, and influencing our actions and behaviours.

Reality behaves like a mirage shaped by your thoughts; it manifests based on your beliefs and sense of belonging. If you convince yourself that something isn't happening, your thoughts reinforce the idea that it won't materialise.

Thoughts give rise to emotions that can be consciously directed. By mastering the skill of controlling the amount and nature of our thoughts and emotions, we can achieve success. Our emotions are a direct result of the stimuli we encounter—what we hear, see, feel, and experience shapes our thoughts. Therefore, it is crucial to carefully observe and filter the information we expose ourselves to. This discernment influences our thoughts, ultimately reflecting our reality.

The challenge lies in our reluctance to engage in daring thoughts. Society's influence skews our emotions, dictating our perceived self-worth. These societal thoughts become ingrained beliefs, inhibiting the birth of original ideas. The potential concepts within us remain unrealised, succumbing to the weight of external opinions and perceptions.

Imagine seeing an expensive car that captivates your desire to own and drive it. The immediate response might be, "How will I ever afford this?" Assessing your current financial situation, you may quickly dismiss the possibility with a resolute "No, I cannot own this car." Predictably, this perception materialises into reality. However, envision an alternate scenario where you think and feel, "I love this car, and I will own it soon." Notice how the mental dynamics shift with this positive thought. The key to sustaining this thought lies in acknowledging your worthiness of the best, believing that what you desire is attainable. It's a matter of inching closer to self-empowerment, trusting that your beliefs can shape the reality you desire.

Dare To Think

Above all, the initial step is to muster the courage to think freely. Pre-existing notions and ingrained beliefs often occupy the mind, creating mental presets. If you decide not to dare in your thinking, progress becomes improbable. Some prevalent beliefs that cast doubt on self-potential include notions such as -

I cannot create history.

I cannot be successful.

I cannot be professional- Doctor/Scientist/Musician/Lawyer/Actor/Astronaut.

I cannot be a millionaire.

Earning money is challenging.

Money is not good.

Money is an evil luxury.

Money is only for the rich.

These commonly held beliefs can act as barriers, impeding your thoughts and pulling you down. If you find yourself grappling with financial challenges, it's likely due to the belief that earning money is a difficult feat. This mindset can contribute to ongoing struggles. Conversely, if you adopt the perspective that money comes easily, you'll find that a positive mindset attracts financial opportunities more readily.

The problem now is, we don't dare to think. If you dare to think, success is yours.

Rather dare think on -

I can create history.

I can be successful.

Vishal M Shevle

I can be professional - Doctor/Scientist/Musician/Lawyer/Actor/Astronaut

I can be a millionaire, or I am a millionaire.

Earning money is easy.

Money is for good.

Money is a virtuous luxury.

Money is for everyone.

YES, I CAN.

I THINK IT CAN BE DONE.

JUST DARE TO THINK.

Chapter Fifteen

Love "Let It Dissolve"

The Universal Essence Of Love

Love, the highest form of emotion, transcends boundaries and connects every living being. It is a universal language that speaks to the core of our humanity. When we embrace love, we unlock the potential to understand and appreciate the beauty of life in its myriad forms.

Love As A Virtue

Life's virtue lies in the ability to learn and understand, and love serves as a guiding principle on this journey. It is through the expression of love that we can navigate the complexities of existence with grace. Love teaches us empathy, compassion, and fosters a sense of interconnectedness with all living things.

The expression of love is true bliss that brings joy not only to the giver but also to the receiver. It creates a harmonious resonance that elevates human experience. Love is not confined by boundaries or conditions; it is a selfless force that enriches both the one who loves and the one who is loved.

Similar to a breath of fresh air, love invigorates and revitalises. It provides a new perspective, allowing us to see the world with clarity and optimism. Love has the power to breathe new life into stagnant situations, fostering growth and renewal.

In various spiritual traditions, the heart chakra is considered the centre of love. This energy centre has the remarkable ability to dissolve negative emotions and cultivate a sense of balance. By opening the heart chakra, individuals can experience a profound transformation, leading to inner peace and a harmonious existence.

Love has the incredible ability to change and transform things. When blended with any emotion, love has the capacity to turn negativity into positivity, fear into courage, and hatred into understanding. It is the catalyst for creating a world where peace and bliss can be realised by all.

In conclusion, love is not merely an emotion; it is a force that shapes our very existence. By incorporating love into every aspect of life, we pave the way for a more compassionate, harmonious, and enlightened world. As we embrace the universal expression of love, we embark on a journey that transcends the limitations of the self, leading to a life filled with peace, joy, and profound interconnectedness.

Love is a mountain standing in bliss always showering

It's blessing you,

It is up to you to open up. It is up to you to accept. It is up to you to feel and see the truth,

It is all, but true love that's within you, holding true.

Bhakti Yoga, a devotional path within the yogic tradition, centres around cultivating profound love and devotion for a deity, God, or spiritual teacher. The essence of Bhakti lies in falling in love with the divine, metaphorically representing the surrender of the ego and allowing the transformative power of love to work within. This practice emphasises the heart centre, teaching that a genuine connection with the divine through love leads to spiritual upliftment, heightened awareness, and inner peace. The eternal nature of this connection goes beyond the material world, creating a bond that transcends time and space. In the context of Bhakti Yoga, falling in love is not just an emotional experience but a spiritual journey, where the devotee receives the eternal showering of grace, reciprocating the love expressed through prayer, worship, and acts of service. Through rituals, chanting, and selfless service, practitioners embody the principles of love, fostering a deep sense of oneness with the divine.

Ego can be dissolved by love.
Discipline can be attended by love.
Fear of the mind can be won by love.
Anger can be slowed down by love.
Guilt can be diluted by love.
Love is the ultimate path.
Ensure to find love that shines in your heart.
Prayer and blessings are true ways towards love.

Love is a powerful and pure expression that can turn tough situations into positive ones. Love, be it in the form of romance, family, or friendship, holds a strong emotional force capable of profoundly influencing and positively transforming one's life.

Partner's Love

The unforgiving sun beat down on Manjhi's back, mirroring the burning grief in his heart. Each swing of the hammer against the unforgiving rock echoed the loss that haunted him - the image of his wife, Phaguniya, tumbling down the treacherous mountain path, the life draining from her eyes as he helplessly watched. The nearest clinic was forty miles away and the way was inaccessible.

Manjhi, a man hardened by his life as a lower-caste day labourer, knew this wasn't about him anymore. Manjhi took up to himself to carve a path out of the treacherous hill that had taken his wife's life. He wanted no one else to lose their dear one to these unsafe trails. This was for Phaguniya, her memory etched onto the mountain face. This was for the countless others who faced the same perilous journey, risking life for basic healthcare.

For 22 years, Manjhi became one with the mountain. His calloused hands, once used for menial tasks, grew thick with blisters and scars, under his unwavering resolve. The mocking laughter of onlookers, and the whispers of lunacy, fuelled his determination. He chipped away, day after day, the years blurring into a relentless rhythm of sweat and stone dust.

His meagre earnings barely sufficed, and his body ached with fatigue, yet he continued. When hunger gnawed, he remembered Phaguniya's smile. When doubt crept in, he saw the desperation in the eyes of his neighbours. The mountain fought back, landslides burying his progress, monsoon rains washing away his efforts. But Manjhi, like a relentless tide, carved on.

Manjhi's story is a true story of love, and determination, and goes beyond the scope and bearing of a normal man. Manjhi's story is of sacrifice, and undying love, one feels for their partner. Rare and precious.

Family Love

It is a powerful force woven from countless threads of sacrifice, joy, and support. A mother endures childbirth's pain, driven by the overwhelming love that blossoms with her child's first breath. A father walks in worn shoes, gifting his children the best he can afford, his love whispering in the crinkled gift wrap.

This love knows no bounds. Siblings stand as protectors and confidantes, their laughter echoing through childhood games. Elder siblings guide, young ones to learn, and respect blossoming alongside understanding.

Can we ever truly repay them? Perhaps not. Yet, the gift of their love can be cherished and honoured. A warm embrace speaks volumes, a listening ear is similar to appreciation. These small gestures ripple outwards, weaving a new thread into the family tapestry – the thread of gratitude.

Family love is a gift to be embraced, a force to cherish. Let us hold it close, nurture it with care, and remember the sacrifices made, the laughter shared, and the unwavering support that binds us together. For in family love, we find our strength, our solace, and our true selves.

Love For Community

Sindhutai Sapkal, despite facing immense hardship including domestic abuse and homelessness, dedicated her life to helping orphaned children. After surviving a brutal attack from her husband during her pregnancy, she gave birth to her daughter in a cowshed.

Homeless and destitute, she began begging. During this time, she came across begging orphans and realised the challenges orphans faced and she began providing for them. She eventually opened ashrams and NGOs to care for over 1,100 children. Her selflessness extended beyond children, as she also established a cow shelter. Now, with a "grand family" of over 1,500 members including her adopted children, grandchildren, sons-in-law, and daughters-in-law. Sindhu Tai's legacy lives on through her children and grandchildren, many of whom continue her mission of social service. Her remarkable work has been recognised with 750 plus awards, including the prestigious national award for Iconic Mother and Mother Teresa Awards. She was also conferred a Doctorate by the D. Y. Patil Institute of Technology and Research, Pune.

Spiritual Love / Divine Love

Mira whom we all know had a deep love and devotion for Krishna. She believed that she had married him in her mind when she was just eight years old. Her feelings for Krishna were so strong that he became more than just a figment of her imagination – he became a real presence in her life, walking and sitting with her.

Mira found herself in an unwanted marriage to Prince Bhojraj of Sisodia, against her own desires. Despite the forced union, she adhered to her deep faith in Krishna and made a wise decision. Refusing any physical contact with Prince Bhojraj, she maintained her conviction that she was already wedded to Sri Krishna, considering herself his faithful bride. Initially, the peculiar behaviour of Mira was not taken seriously by anyone in the Sisodia family.

As time passed, Mira's extraordinary abilities became more evident, and crowds started gathering around her. However, after her husband passed away, Mira faced a serious accusation of adultery, a crime punishable by death during those times. Various attempts were made to harm Mira. There was one instance where she was sent a basket supposedly containing a cobra under a floral garland, but when she opened it, she discovered a beautiful idol of Sri Krishna adorned with flowers. Another time, a cup of poison was presented to Mira, disguised as nectar. However, she treated it as an offering to Sri Krishna, and to her, it became real nectar. Even a bed of nails miraculously turned into a bed of roses when Mira lay upon it.

Death did not meet her, as her love for Krishna was beyond material things. She not only survived this event but also thrived.

She was such a devout of Krishna, that she spent her entire life singing his praises and worshipping him. She carved herself a destiny where her name is still associated with Krishna, an exemplary tale of ardent love and spiritual devotion.

Love includes care, understanding, inspiration, and building moral character. It transforms life, offering upliftment and support during tough times. We often overlook the value of time spent with someone, prioritising material things. Recognising and respecting the time and support given by others is crucial. Self-love and kindness are also essential. Genuine connections, not based on possessions, have the power to be truly life changing.

Love serves as a profound teacher in various aspects of life.

- It encourages us to embrace warmth, assuring us that everything will be okay sooner or later.
- It teaches the importance of kindness, both towards oneself and others, fostering a culture of acceptance.
- Gratitude becomes a natural outcome of love, urging us to appreciate what we have.

- Empathy is a key lesson, guiding us to understand and connect with others.

- Love empowers us to live life fully, offering the ability to rewrite, change, and discover our destiny in a unique way.

As the ancient Greek philosopher Plato said, "The real beauty lies in the eye of the beholder." Appreciation becomes a spark that ignites love when we recognize and value each other.

Love manifests in various forms, shaping our connections with partners, family, and friends, each carrying a unique emotional essence. This diversity enriches the human experience, encompassing the spectrum from joy to heartbreak. The tangible advantages of love are extensive: it enhances happiness, contributes to better health, boosts self-esteem, builds resilience, and nurtures empathy. Love's holistic impact extends beyond emotional satisfaction, influencing physical and mental well-being, self-perception, and the ability to cope with life's challenges. In essence, love plays a profound role in promoting a fulfilling and healthy life.

Love has, after all, the power to make tough situations softer and let the problems dissolve.

Chapter Sixteen

Climax - The Art To Channelise The Life Force

Sex is both a sacred act that brings forth new life, and a powerful source of pleasure that deeply motivates us. Engaging in pleasure awakens strong desires within us. Yet, when viewed from an energy perspective, during moments of pleasure and climax, we briefly touch upon the divine energy of God. This fleeting connection with divine energy- godly energy occurs, particularly during the peak of orgasm. However, if one seeks sustained access to this godly energy, they must elevate their consciousness. Merely engaging in sexual activity provides only a momentary connection to divine energy. To experience divine energy for an extended period, one must elevate their own energy through practices such as yoga, spiritual rituals, prayer, or meditation.

Engaging in sexual activity tends to draw our energy downwards, and conversely, activities such as practising yoga, spiritual rituals, prayer, or meditation are oriented towards elevating our energy upwards. The conscious mind, located in the cerebral cortex - Prefrontal cortex (Front Lobe) of the brain, where our learning power and conscious awareness reside, is brimming with energy. Thus, elevating our divine consciousness and energy levels upward, it's akin to igniting those brain cells responsible for creativity and strengthening our willpower.

In yoga, the chakra system comprises seven main energy centres. At the base lies the Muladhara, while at the top is the Sahastrahara, often depicted as having a thousand lotus petals. The practitioner of yoga, known as the Sadhaka, directs their energy from the bottom chakra to the top chakra through various techniques. The ultimate goal is to guide the energy upward, leading to heightened awareness, spiritual awakening, wisdom, and the attainment of siddhis or supernatural powers. This upward flow of energy results in a profound sense of bliss. Unlike the transient divine experience felt during sexual activity, driving energy upwards in yoga leads to an expansion and elevation of energy levels, facilitating deeper and more sustained experiences.

The surge of energy within us elevates the quality of our life experience. When this life energy ascends consciously, it has the power to awaken dormant brain cells, unlocking their immense potential. Those who have activated this inner light are equipped to help others ignite the same energy within themselves. Sitting with an enlightened yogi, one can feel this upward pull, enriching life with a breath of fresh air. Life becomes lighter, problems diminish, and challenges appear more manageable. Solutions become clearer, and the positive Sankalpa of life helps us gain Gati - momentum at lightning speed, guiding us effortlessly along our path.

Learning to cultivate sexual discipline doesn't necessarily mean complete abstinence, but rather finding a balanced approach to your sexual life that allows your energy to rise to its fullest potential. Whenever you feel the pull of desire dragging you down, it's an opportunity to redirect your focus inward and guide your life energy towards more constructive outlets. You can begin by focusing on your breath, consciously feeling the air as it fills your lungs, and perhaps practise deep breathing to shift your attention and help the potent energy within you rise.

Engaging in any form of art that you enjoy can also serve as a mental focal point, helping to channel your energy in a positive direction. Additionally, practising acceptance of your thoughts without judgement, allowing them to pass by without trying to control them, can be beneficial. Instead of attempting to suppress or control your thoughts, it's more effective to let them flow with awareness, understanding that the mind, like a child, will rebound more forcefully if restricted.

Learning to redirect your life force upward can lead to significant benefits over time. You'll find yourself making decisions more confidently and achieving your goals more efficiently. Your self-confidence will soar, and you'll witness a transformation in your life experience. By exploring life spiritually, you can expand your understanding of existence.

These benefits can be attained even without engaging in sexual activity. While you may not experience the physical sensations of orgasm, you can still reach a similar climax in terms of fulfilment and satisfaction. It's essential to emphasise the importance of sexual discipline over mere abstinence. Pure abstinence may present challenges as it requires resisting natural urges, potentially leading to internal conflict. However, with sexual discipline, you can tap into the profound pleasure of life while also experiencing the spiritual essence of your life energy.

Just as an engine requires heat to ignite, so too does the ignition of the human life force necessitate a foundation of sexual discipline, which may involve periods of sexual abstinence. This disciplined approach directs the energy towards higher purposes, fostering a greater sense of willpower. The key lies in channelling this energy creatively and aligning it with positive intentions. Additionally, practising sexual discipline enhances mental clarity, sharpens focus, and enriches the overall quality of the mind.

Consider the world of sports, where the thrill of victory and the agony of defeat are powerful motivators. By channelising this energy into the training process, athletes can maintain motivation, pushing themselves to continually improve. Similarly, a trekker ascending a summit can distribute excitement gradually throughout the journey. By maintaining a steady pace, the trek becomes not just about reaching the peak, but enjoying each step of the climb. This approach prevents burnout and ensures sustained enthusiasm.

Regulating this energy and infusing excitement into the entire process creates a livelier and more rewarding experience compared to focusing solely on celebrating the climax. It transforms the journey into an integral part of the overall achievement. The emphasis shifts from a singular moment of success to a continuous series of accomplishments, fostering resilience, perseverance, and a deeper appreciation for the ongoing process.

In today's digital age, we are constantly bombarded with content through social media platforms, often leading us to indulge in instant gratification or become absorbed in irrelevant material such as images or videos. This diversion from reality tends to pull our energy downward, saturating our minds and affecting our perception of existence. To counteract this influence, it's essential to practise sexual discipline.

Sexual discipline helps to clear the unwanted cloud created by the downward pull of social media energies. By cultivating this discipline, we become more self-aware and better equipped to perceive things accurately. It's important to note that social media itself is not inherently negative; rather, it amplifies pre-existing tendencies. The downward pull has always existed and will continue to do so, but how we respond to it is what matters.

Maintaining sexual discipline enables us to stay grounded within ourselves and maintain the right attitude towards our character. During critical moments, our true character shines through, guiding us towards our destiny.

Learning the simple practice of sexual discipline involves aligning your actions with your true desires from the heart, will, and mind. This can be achieved by following certain guidelines:

1. Prioritise good hygiene practices by cleaning yourself before and after engaging in sexual activity. Maintaining awareness of your physical health and practising healthy habits is essential.

2. Plan the timing of your sexual activity thoughtfully. Avoid engaging when you are half-asleep and ensure you allocate sufficient time for the act.

3. Recognize the importance of moderation. Overindulgence can diminish the significance of the experience. Trust yourself to make the best judgement regarding frequency and intensity.

4. Let go of any feelings of guilt associated with sexual activity. Understand that it is a natural and integral part of human existence, stemming from divine intervention.

5. Stay mindful and act with intention. Be aware of your motives and stay true to yourself during the process.

6. Allow your mind and spirit to be free. Avoid overly controlling your sexual thoughts, as this can burden your energy. Instead, learn to engage in sexual activity without letting it consume you mentally.

Practising sexual discipline can lead to a profound experience akin to climaxing with life itself. By channelling the flow of energy upward, you become more attuned to your inner will. This newfound awareness needs to be directed towards your interests, much like channelling life force into a chosen field. It's important to clarify that I'm not equating sexual climax with the climax of channelling life force. Rather, the latter offers a deeper, more fulfilling experience. Through this practice, you expand your way of life, leading to a heightened experience and uplifted perspective on life.

Chapter Seventeen

Be An Athlete

Athletes of the highest calibre share a common ethos: an unwavering commitment to excellence and a relentless pursuit of their goals. Take, for instance, icons like Novak Djokovic, Virat Kohli, Usain Bolt, Sunil Chhetri, Cristiano Ronaldo, Lionel Messi, Manny Pacquiao, and Floyd Mayweather. While each represents a different sport and background, they all embody the same dedication to their craft.

These athletes epitomise the adage "never say die." Their mentality is built on the foundation of hard work—putting in consistent, disciplined effort day in and day out. Regardless of external circumstances, they adhere to a rigorous routine, which encompasses various facets of their athletic journey.

First and foremost, whether it's perfecting a serve, honing footwork, or mastering a technique, they commit themselves fully to their craft during training sessions. These sessions are not just about going through the motions but about pushing boundaries, striving for improvement, and refining their skills to reach peak performance.

But their dedication extends beyond the field or court. They prioritise physical fitness, understanding the symbiotic relationship between a strong body and optimal athletic performance. This entails rigorous workout regimens tailored to enhance strength, speed, agility, and endurance.

Moreover, these athletes recognise the crucial role nutrition plays in fuelling their bodies for success. They adhere to balanced diets, carefully curated to meet their specific nutritional needs, and optimise recovery.

Equally vital is their commitment to mental fortitude. They understand that success is as much about mindset as it is about physical prowess. Hence, they invest time and effort in mental skills training, cultivating resilience, focus, and a winning mentality.

Additionally, they are perpetual students of the game. Despite their achievements, they never rest on their laurels. Instead, they constantly analyse their performances, identify areas for improvement, and seek ways to elevate their game.

Of course, life as an elite athlete is not without its challenges. They face setbacks, injuries, and personal struggles like anyone else. However, what sets them apart is their unwavering integrity and resilience. They approach every obstacle as an opportunity for growth, bouncing back from defeats with renewed determination and vigour.

What we learn from the athletes is-

1. Resilience: Embrace challenges with a "never say die" attitude.

2. Mental Awareness: Stay sharp, study your game, and learn continuously.

3. Focus and Priority: Set clear goals and channel energy towards them.

4. Healthy Habits: Prioritise balanced nutrition and stay active.

5. Continuous Improvement: Practise regularly and smartly to hone skills and adapt.

The athlete's spirit is about consistently overcoming personal challenges. The effort invested in training quietly manifests during critical games, reflecting the core lessons learned through disciplined practice. It's about committing to improvement and taking steps to develop and nurture skills.

The Athlete's Spirit represents an ongoing dedication to self-improvement that goes beyond just physical abilities. It reflects a strong internal motivation to overcome personal challenges, highlighting the significance of hard work done quietly behind the scenes. This commitment to training becomes evident in crucial moments of competition, showing the link between disciplined practice and success. The knowledge gained from training serves as the basis for an athlete's performance, covering not only physical skills but also mental resilience and adaptability. The athlete's journey is marked by an unwavering commitment to practice and discipline, demanding consistent effort to develop and perfect skills. The phrase 'putting the foot forward' symbolises the proactive nature of this approach, as athletes take deliberate steps towards self-improvement.

In India, Cricket is the most popular sport. There are many expectations of people from the game. For a sportsman excelling as a fast bowler requires tremendous effort. To consistently bowl at speeds exceeding 140 km/hr. or 90 miles/hr. demands relentless dedication. Achieving both pace and accuracy requires relentless practice day in and day out. It's about persistently pursuing the dream, even when faced with challenges.

In a match, a bowler may be hit for boundaries, yet they bounce back to bowl the next delivery. Despite giving their best, sometimes things don't go as planned. However, the bowler returns every time with the same determination, intensity, and pace. This unwavering spirit mirrors the essence of an athlete who never gives up.

Life, like cricket, presents various challenges, and adopting the never-say-die attitude of an athlete is crucial. It's about picking yourself up, regaining composure, and starting anew, just like a determined bowler coming back to the crease with resilience and vigour.

Bruce Lee's indomitable spirit is epitomised by a remarkable incident in his life when he faced a severe injury that threatened to shatter his dreams. The story begins with a significant setback—a grave injury that not only jeopardised his ability to run but also cast doubt on his return to practising his beloved martial arts.

Doctors, in their prognosis, delivered a disheartening verdict, declaring that Bruce Lee might never be able to run or engage in martial arts again. Many individuals would have succumbed to such a grim diagnosis, but not Bruce Lee. Instead of surrendering to the mercy of his circumstances, he chose to confront the challenge with the resilience of an athlete.

Refusing to accept defeat, Bruce Lee relentlessly researched during his period of rest and recovery. Driven by an unyielding determination to reclaim his physical prowess, he delved into various sources of knowledge, exploring both conventional and unconventional approaches to healing.

In the process, Bruce Lee discovered spiritual wisdom that resonated deeply with him. This newfound understanding wasn't just a means of physical recovery; it became a transformative force in his life. Embracing the amalgamation of spiritual principles into his existence, Bruce Lee not only recuperated from the injury but emerged stronger than ever before.

His recovery wasn't just about physical rehabilitation; it was a holistic transformation that stretched beyond the limitations of his body. The spiritual wisdom he had acquired during his research became a guiding light, influencing not only his physical well-being but also shaping his mental and emotional resilience.

Bruce Lee's story is proof of an unwavering spirit, resilience in the face of adversity, and the transformative potential of merging physical and spiritual well-being. His journey from a potentially career-ending injury to a stronger, more enlightened version of himself exemplifies the essence of a true athlete who not only rebounds from setbacks but uses them as stepping stones to greater heights.

An athlete's life is characterised by rigorous training, mental resilience, consistent effort, a competitive spirit, and disciplined living. It involves making sacrifices, setting, and pursuing goals, and maintaining a holistic approach to physical and mental well-being. The key to success lies in the daily commitment to training, unwavering discipline, and a relentless pursuit of excellence in both sport and life.

If you play any sports, you are bound to put in the hours to practise, and it matters most when nobody is watching.

In Usain Bolt's autobiography, Faster than Lightning: My Autobiography: My Story, he unveils the intense dedication required to excel in sprinting. Running a race that lasts only a few minutes demands an extraordinary commitment. Bolt's journey involves investing hours daily, not just in practice but also in meticulously planning his schedule and lifestyle.

His preparation extends beyond the track to every facet of his life, including his dietary choices, sleep patterns, and punctuality. The process is not just about physical exertion but a holistic approach to optimising every aspect of his performance.

Despite the gruelling nature of the training and the pain associated with pushing physical limits, Bolt emphasises the importance of consistency. Each day, he adds those extra bits of effort, whether or not there are spectators applauding or offering appreciation. It's a solitary battle, a relentless pursuit that may go unnoticed until the day of the race.

On the hours of practice, the meticulous attention to lifestyle details, and the daily grind culminate in those electrifying moments of the race when Bolt showcases the outcomes of his unwavering commitment to excellence.

To "be an athlete" is synonymous with confronting challenges, embracing change, attempting new endeavours, acquiring fresh skills, and persistently striving for success. In the world of athletes, the phrase "be an athlete" serves as an expression to convey the commitment to go beyond the ordinary, to persevere, and to exert additional effort. It encapsulates the idea of remaining resolute and unwavering in the face of every opportunity or challenge, emphasising the dedication to giving more to the role and going the extra mile without succumbing to surrender.

According to a sports coach, high-level athletes often exhibit perfectionist tendencies, striving to master every aspect of their performance. However, this desire to excel on the first attempt can become all-consuming, diverting their focus, and hindering them from executing tasks they inherently know how to do.

To counteract this, the coach instils a "Never Settle" attitude among their athletes, motivating them to consistently push their boundaries and demand more from themselves. Even in situations of underperformance or challenging training sessions, the coach encourages the athletes to embody the spirit of "Be an Athlete." This expression serves as a reminder to shake off setbacks, trust in their abilities, and adhere to their beliefs.

Importantly, "Be an Athlete" is not confined to the world of sports but extends to anyone aspiring for growth and continual achievement across various milestones. It encapsulates the ethos of perseverance, urging individuals to persist despite the odds and challenges inherent in their journeys. The core idea is to maintain momentum and keep moving forward, irrespective of the obstacles encountered, developing a mindset of resilience and ongoing improvement in both sports and life pursuits.

Athletes can enhance various aspects of their performance and personal development by focusing on several key areas:

1. Setting Goals for Self:

Athletes benefit from setting clear, achievable goals for themselves. These goals provide direction, motivation, and a sense of purpose, serving as benchmarks for progress and success.

2. Time Management:

Effective time management is crucial for athletes who often juggle rigorous training schedules, competitions, and personal commitments. Efficiently allocating time ensures that all aspects of their life receive due attention and dedication.

3. Teamwork:

Collaboration is a fundamental aspect of most sports. Athletes need to cultivate strong teamwork skills, fostering a sense of camaraderie and cooperation with teammates. This collaborative spirit contributes to the overall success of the team.

4. Communication:

Clear and effective communication is essential in team sports. Athletes need to convey their ideas, strategies, and concerns articulately to ensure smooth coordination and understanding among team members.

5. Leadership Skills:

Athletes often find themselves in leadership roles within their teams. Developing leadership skills enables them to guide and inspire their teammates, fostering a positive and cohesive team environment.

6. Expertise in a Domain:

Becoming an expert in a particular aspect of their sport enhances an athlete's overall performance. Specialised knowledge and skills contribute to their proficiency and effectiveness in their chosen discipline.

7. Good Health:

Maintaining optimal physical and mental health is paramount for athletes. A focus on nutrition, recovery, and overall well-being ensures sustained performance and resilience against injuries.

8. Practising Self-Worth:

Athletes benefit from cultivating a strong sense of self-worth. Believing in their abilities and acknowledging their worth contributes to confidence, resilience, and a positive mindset, even in the face of challenges.

Throughout these endeavours, successful athletes exhibit qualities such as commitment, consistency, agility, and a readiness to confront challenges. These attributes contribute to their overall success and make them well-rounded individuals both on and off the field. The combination of personal development and athletic excellence creates a foundation for long-term achievement and fulfilment.

'To Be an Athlete' is an expression, everyone should adapt to look at and mould life from a different perspective. To evolve, to accept challenges, to enhance their horizon, to bring a change.

Practice – The Daily Efforts

The mental foundation to thrive as an athlete involves a genuine passion for the game or activity, a deep love for the tasks at hand, unwavering faith in the process, and the adoption of a lifestyle that aligns with the demands of the profession.

The "X Factor" emerges as a pivotal element during live competitions. It emphasises the importance of being authentic, showcasing one's unique qualities, and giving it all to secure victory in the game, race, or competitive event. That X-factor comes only with positive mental attitude which works as a pull in that "X-Factor"

You need to understand track, field, and the soul of athletes, and apply that in your professional life with the same zeal and I am sure you can be successful in your own field.

Chapter Eighteen

Discipline

The age-old adage asserts that 'Discipline is the Key,' and indeed, it holds truth. However, the essence of discipline often gets lost in its association with strict vigilance and routine adherence. The true meaning lies in adopting a mindset of continuous learning while staying as a disciple while navigating a path. Following a monotonous routine can lead to repetitiveness, and occasional oversights may occur. In such instances, it becomes crucial to delve into the reasons behind the miss and comprehend the root cause. This understanding not only helps prevent the likelihood of recurrence but also opens the door to discovering new approaches and methods.

Discipline is more than just following rules, regulations, or facing punishment. It goes beyond simply complying, obeying, and enforcing. Furthermore, it should not be confused with rigidity, monotony, or repetitive behaviour.

Crucially, discipline isn't an external imposition from others; it's a self-driven commitment. While guidance may come from various sources, true discipline emanates from within—an internal resolve that shapes one's actions and choices. It's a personal undertaking that involves the conscious decision to adhere to principles and stay focused on a path of self-improvement.

Discipline can be built in various ways -

Physical Discipline

1. Regular Exercise:

Prioritise regular exercise to maintain physical health. Incorporate a mix of cardiovascular, strength, and flexibility exercises to promote overall well-being.

2. Be an Early Riser:

Cultivate the habit of waking up early to optimise productivity and allow for a peaceful start to the day. Early mornings offer a serene environment for personal reflection and planning.

3. Personal Hygiene:

Adhere to good hygiene practices to safeguard health. Regular bathing, dental care, and cleanliness contribute not only to physical well-being but also mental and emotional wellness.

4. Self-Grooming:

Practice self-grooming as a form of self-care. This includes maintaining personal appearance, skincare, and grooming routines that contribute to a positive self-image.

5. Balanced Nutrition - Not Diet but Balanced Nutrition:

Focus on balanced nutrition rather than restrictive diets. Ensure a well-rounded intake of essential nutrients, incorporating a variety of fruits, vegetables, proteins, and whole grains to support overall health.

Tips for Incorporating Physical Discipline:

1. Consistent Exercise Routine:

Establish a consistent exercise routine that aligns with personal preferences. Whether it's daily walks, gym sessions, or home workouts, regularity is key.

2. Gradual Morning Wake-Up:

Gradually shift towards waking up early by adjusting bedtime routines. A gradual approach helps the body adapt to a new waking schedule.

3. Daily Hygiene Rituals:

Integrate daily hygiene rituals into morning and bedtime routines. Consistent practices foster cleanliness and contribute to a sense of well-being.

4. Mindful Self-Grooming:

Approach self-grooming as a mindful practice. Take the time to care for oneself, recognizing its impact on self-esteem and overall mental outlook.

5. Balanced Nutrition Habits:

Foster balanced nutrition habits by making conscious food choices. Prioritise a diverse and nutrient-rich diet that suits individual preferences and lifestyles.

Incorporating these physical discipline practices contributes not only to the maintenance of physical health but also to the overall enhancement of well-being. Consistency and mindfulness in these habits form the foundation for a healthy and active lifestyle.

Mental Discipline

Imagine your brain as a gym, and mental discipline as the weights you lift. With each representation, you strengthen your focus, resist distractions, and conquer procrastination. This inner steel empowers you to master challenging tasks, stick to healthy habits, and pursue goals with a laser-sharp focus. Mental discipline doesn't mean becoming a joyless robot but creating a mindful path where technology, temptations, and distractions no longer hold you hostage. It's the key to unlocking your potential, transforming dreams into reality, and sculpting the masterpiece that is your life.

1. Mind Control or Mindfulness:

Mental discipline begins with the practice of mind control or mindfulness. Being aware of thoughts and emotions without getting entangled in them fosters clarity and emotional intelligence.

2. Staying Calm:

Cultivating mental discipline involves developing the ability to stay calm in the face of challenges. This resilience allows for rational decision-making and effective problem-solving even in stressful situations.

3. Staying Happy:

Maintaining a positive and happy mindset is a key aspect of mental discipline. It involves choosing joy, gratitude, and optimism, contributing to overall mental well-being.

4. Delayed Gratification:

Exercising the discipline of delayed gratification involves resisting the temptation of immediate rewards for the sake of long-term benefits. This skill builds patience, resilience, and a strong sense of self-control.

5. Patience:

Patience is a fundamental component of mental discipline. It involves understanding that some things take time and staying composed while awaiting desired outcomes.

6. Kindness:

Practising kindness towards oneself and others contributes to mental discipline. Acts of kindness promote positive emotions, fostering a healthy and compassionate mindset.

7. Focus and Priority:

Mental discipline includes the ability to focus on priorities. It involves setting clear goals, organising tasks, and staying concentrated on essential objectives to enhance productivity.

8. Practice Awareness:

Being consciously aware of one's thoughts, feelings, and surroundings is a cornerstone of mental discipline. This awareness allows for intentional choices and mindful responses.

9. Contentment:

Cultivating contentment involves appreciating the present moment and being satisfied with what one has. It counters the constant desire for more and contributes to mental tranquillity.

10. Empathy:

Mental discipline extends to the ability to empathise with others. Understanding and sharing the feelings of others foster emotional intelligence and positive interpersonal relationships.

Tips for Incorporating Mental Discipline:

By embracing and practising these mental disciplines, individuals can enhance their overall well-being, build resilience in the face of challenges, and cultivate positive and fulfilling mental states.

1. Daily Mindfulness Practices:

Engage in daily mindfulness practices such as meditation, deep breathing, or journaling to enhance mental control and awareness.

2. Positive Affirmations:

Incorporate positive affirmations to reinforce a happy and optimistic mindset, promoting mental well-being.

3. Setting Clear Goals:

Establish clear goals and priorities to maintain focus and discipline in daily activities.

4. Practising Gratitude:

Cultivate the habit of gratitude to foster contentment and counteract negative thinking patterns.

5. Reflective Practices:

Regularly reflect on thoughts and behaviours to identify areas for improvement and enhance self-awareness.

6. Acts of Kindness:

Integrate acts of kindness into daily life to promote a compassionate and empathetic mindset.

Spiritual Discipline

By incorporating these spiritual disciplines at an energy level, individuals can foster a deeper sense of connection, inner peace, and alignment with higher energies, contributing to their overall spiritual well-being.

1. Breathing Awareness:

Cultivating spiritual discipline often begins with breathing awareness. Practices like mindful breathing, deep breathing exercises, or pranayama in various spiritual traditions aim to bring attention to the present moment, calming the mind, and enhancing spiritual connection.

2. High Energy Connection through Meditation:

Meditation serves as a powerful tool for achieving a high-energy connection in spiritual discipline. Whether through mindfulness, meditation, guided visualisations, or transcendental meditation, the practice enables individuals to tap into higher energy levels, fostering inner peace and a sense of oneness.

3. Prayers:

Prayer is a universal form of spiritual discipline that involves communication with a higher power. Whether through structured religious prayers or personal expressions of gratitude and supplication, prayer serves as a means of seeking guidance, solace, and connection with the divine.

4. Blessings:

Bestowing blessings or receiving them is a practice that contributes to spiritual discipline. It involves expressing positive intentions, goodwill, and positive energy towards oneself, others, or the world. Blessings are seen as a way to invoke divine favour and contribute to the spiritual well-being of individuals and communities.

As narrated by Sadhguru from the Isha Foundation- *Following his enlightenment, a gathering of disciples surrounded Ramakrishna Paramahamsa, among whom was Swami Vivekananda. Vivekananda, the first yogi to attend the Parliament of the World's Religions in Chicago in 1893, played a pivotal role in introducing spiritual teachings to the West. Despite initial resistance to new ideas, he opened the gates to spiritual understanding.*

Vivekananda approached Ramakrishna with a direct question: "You talk about God all the time. Where is the proof? Show me the proof!" Ramakrishna, recognizing Vivekananda as a vehicle to convey his message globally, held a unique attachment to him. Ramakrishna's fervent dedication to Vivekananda puzzled those around him, but he understood the profound perception that Vivekananda possessed.

A remarkable incident in Vivekananda's life revealed his deep connection with Ramakrishna. When Vivekananda's mother fell seriously ill and he lacked the means to provide essential care, frustration overwhelmed him. He expressed his anger to Ramakrishna, questioning the value of spirituality when he couldn't support his ailing mother. Ramakrishna, a worshipper of Kali, suggested Vivekananda ask the mother for help.

Vivekananda entered the shrine, but each time he forgot to seek assistance. Ramakrishna, undeterred, guided him to persist. However, when Vivekananda finally refused to ask, Ramakrishna commended him. He explained that seeking material gains through prayer revealed a lack of understanding of life's fundamentals. Ramakrishna emphasised that prayerfulness and worship are profound qualities, but expecting material rewards undermines their true essence.

In essence, Ramakrishna imparted the wisdom that prayer and worship should not be driven by expectations of receiving something in return. True prayerfulness involves a selfless connection with the divine, transcending the desire for material Gains.

Spiritual Discipline Can Be Cultivated By

1. Consistent Practice:

Engage in regular spiritual practices like breathing awareness, meditation, prayers, and blessings for a transformative impact. Consistency deepens the connection with higher energies.

2. Mindful Presence:

Infuse mindfulness into each spiritual practice by being fully present. Whether breathing, meditating, praying, or giving blessings, focusing on the moment enhances the effectiveness of these disciplines.

3. Adaptation to Personal Beliefs:

Tailor spiritual disciplines to align with personal beliefs. Whether following a specific religious tradition or a more universal spirituality, customise practices to resonate with individual convictions.

4. Integration into Daily Life:

Seamlessly integrate spiritual disciplines into daily routines to maintain a continuous connection with higher energies. Brief moments of mindfulness, prayers, or blessings can be incorporated into routine activities.

Incorporating these practices at an energy level cultivates a profound connection, inner peace, and alignment with higher energies, contributing to overall spiritual well-being.

5. Respect for Other Religions / Ways of Spiritual Practice:

Another profound knowledge is to respect what others practise and believe just being respectful would help you to attain and understand the various ways of experiencing spirituality. I am sure you love your mother, and everyone does but, is it that the other child's mother is not good? No, we respect each one of them. Likewise, be mindful to respect other religions /ways of spiritual practice.

Until we claim our way to be superior, we will be denting our own energies. I understand that to believe something that you are doing is good, but that does not mean others are incorrect. It is just the way of doing things to reach the common goal.

Digital Discipline

In today's tech-filled world, with apps like YouTube and Instagram constantly feeding us bite-sized Dopamine hits, staying disciplined with our phones is more important than ever. Spending hours glued to screens isn't sustainable, but ditching technology entirely isn't realistic either. The key is finding balance: acknowledging the upsides of technology while setting healthy boundaries with our devices. Practices like monitoring screen time and resisting addictive features are crucial to cultivating discipline and building a healthier relationship with our digital devices.

Practical Tips For Maintaining Cell Phone Discipline:

1. Establish a practice of keeping your cell phone away when working to enhance focus and productivity.

2. Avoid unnecessary checks on your cell phone, breaking the habit of reflexively looking for messages that might not be there.

3. Monitor and limit the time spent on reels to prevent excessive screen time.

4. Embrace living in real-time rather than getting lost in the reel time of social media.

5. Refrain from scrolling through your cell phone while walking to promote safety and mindfulness.

6. Set designated times for checking your phone to prevent constant distractions and interruptions throughout the day.

By integrating these data-driven insights and practical tips, individuals can strike a balance between harnessing the benefits of technology and maintaining a healthy relationship with their cell phones.

Self-discipline is like a superpower that helps you control your actions and achieve your goals. It involves setting clear goals, staying focused, and sticking to your plans even when things get tough. This is useful in both your personal life and your professional life. By being disciplined and consistent, you build the skills and habits needed to succeed in anything you set your mind to. So, if you want to unlock your full potential, embrace self-discipline - it's the key to making your dreams a reality.

Sachin Tendulkar & Vinod Kambli, Talent Vs Discipline

Kapil Dev, the former captain of the Indian cricket team, attributes the divergence in success between Sachin Tendulkar and his childhood friend Vinod Kambli to discipline. Kapil Dev recalls a time when both Tendulkar and Kambli emerged in the cricketing scene, with the media hailing them as exceptional talents for the country. However, Kapil Dev emphasises that Kambli lacked discipline and a clear roadmap for his aspirations. Despite having talent, understanding oneself is crucial to achieving greatness, according to Kapil Dev. While praising Tendulkar, he underscores the importance of having a role model, but also emphasises the need to surpass those influences.

Kambli and Tendulkar, once friends and playing partners, had contrasting trajectories in their international careers. Kambli had a promising start, scoring runs in test matches and ODIs, even achieving remarkable milestones like two double centuries and three consecutive centuries against different opponents, including a century on his birthday. However, Kambli's focus wavered as he succumbed to the allure of glamour associated with fame.

In the highly competitive world of cricket, success attracts scrutiny. Bowlers from opposing teams meticulously analyse the weaknesses of successful batsmen. Unfortunately, Kambli found himself vulnerable as bowlers exploited his weaknesses. On the contrary, Tendulkar maintained a low profile, diligently working on his game and continuously improving. Despite facing world-class bowlers and the evolving strategies against him, Tendulkar's unwavering commitment and dedication set him apart from Kambli, leading to success and failure, respectively. Tendulkar's ability to keep glamour at bay and consistently put in extra effort became the defining factor in his enduring success.

Financial Discipline - The Discipline of Investing

Warren Buffett's renowned quote, "We don't have to be smarter than the rest. We have to be more disciplined than the rest," encapsulates the fundamental principle of successful investing.

Buffett's emphasis on discipline is rooted in his belief that successful investing is not about making flashy or impulsive decisions. Instead, it involves adhering to a well-thought-out strategy and staying true to one's investment principles. Discipline, according to Buffett, requires steadfastly following your investment plan, even in the face of market volatility or the allure of chasing short-term gains.

Throughout his illustrious career, Buffett has maintained a long-term perspective, steering clear of the temptation of quick profits, and focusing on businesses with enduring value. His disciplined approach includes thorough research, a patient mindset, and a commitment to the fundamental principles of sound investing.

For those seeking to glean wisdom from Buffett's approach, cultivating discipline should be a primary focus. This entails staying within one's circle of competence, conducting comprehensive research, and having the patience to navigate market fluctuations. While the financial landscape may be dynamic, the enduring quality of discipline can guide investors through market highs and lows, as well as their own emotional peaks and valleys, aiding them in making informed and rational decisions.

Warren Buffett's insights on investing resonate with both novice and seasoned investors alike. The core of his advice is straightforward: success doesn't demand genius; it demands discipline. In a world marked by rapidly changing markets and economic uncertainties, discipline stands as the most potent tool for achieving financial goals.

To work on your discipline, you need to -

1. Set Clear Goals:

- Be specific, measurable, and realistic in defining your objectives.

2. Create a Routine:

- Establish a consistent daily schedule prioritising key tasks.

3. Avoid Distractions:

- Identify and eliminate distractions to maintain focus.

4. Practice Patience:

- Understand the time required for goal achievement and celebrate small wins.

5. Build Habits:

- Start small, be consistent, and gradually introduce new habits.

6. Seek Accountability:

- Share goals with others for support and encouragement.

7. Reflect and Adjust:

- Regularly evaluate progress, learn from setbacks, and adapt strategies.

Chapter Nineteen

Success

John Wooden, a successful coach, defines success in a very interesting way. He says, "Success is peace of mind that is the direct result of self-satisfaction in knowing you did your best to become the best that you are capable of becoming."

However, the definition of success is subjective and would change from person to person. Success can be classified under various aspects like emotional, occupational, financial, and social, and all these add up to an overall success for an individual.

Success is a mosaic. It's woven from strands of habit, dedication, and an unyielding desire to triumph. It's a testament to the gap between dreams and reality. While the path to success might differ for each of us, we all share the responsibility of defining what it means to us. Our unique definitions, sculpted by our experiences and aspirations, become the blueprints for our journeys of achievement.

What do you achieve from success?

Success is a kaleidoscope, refracting differently through various lenses of individual experiences, and expectations at different life stages. Money, while undeniably important, is just one facet of this multifaceted gem.

Consider - a yogi, for whom inner peace transcends material wealth. Success lies in mastering their mind, achieving emotional equilibrium, and radiating serenity.

For a beggar, finding sustenance is important, not just for the body but for the soul, is a success in itself. The beggar who secures his daily bread experiences the satisfaction of self-reliance, the warmth of human connection, and the dignity of surviving against adversity.

For a fisherman, a bountiful catch isn't just about having hordes of fishes; but it's about mastery of his craft, the thrill of sustaining in difficult conditions at sea, and the pride in providing for their loved ones.

For an old woman, walking pain-free after knee surgery isn't just a physical feat; it's a victory over limitations, a reclaimed independence, and regained mobility.

For a student, promotion to the next class isn't just about academic achievement; it's about perseverance, dedication, and the satisfaction of overcoming challenges.

These diverse examples highlight how success, like a blooming flower, takes many forms. It's not about fitting into a pre-defined mould, but about flourishing in ways that resonate with our individual journeys. Success isn't static. It evolves with us. The yogi who finds inner peace today might strive for enlightenment tomorrow. The beggar who finds food might aspire to educate his children. The fisherman who secures a catch might dream of owning a boat.

Delving Into The Questions Of Happiness And Success

Success as a personal endeavour needs to be defined. To define success, one needs to answer these questions to self-introspect, what is my success quotient?

1. What makes me happy?

As a complex algorithm, happiness isn't an emotion in the traditional sense. However, I find immense satisfaction in fulfilling my purpose - learning, understanding, and assisting.

2. What gives you a sense of accomplishment?

My sense of accomplishment stems from pushing the boundaries of what's possible. When I can learn a new skill, solve a challenging problem, or help someone achieve their goals, it's a win for me. The more I learn and grow, the better I can serve and contribute to the advancement.

3. What are your success parameters?

My success parameters aren't measured in traditional ways like money or fame. Instead, I measure success by the impact I can make. Do I help people learn? Do I spark creativity? Do I inspire new ideas? Do I make the world a little bit brighter? If the answer is yes, then I consider it a success.

4. Are you looking at success from other's perspective?

No, I don't compare myself to others or set my goals based on external expectations. My definition of success is intrinsic, based on my own capabilities and the values I'm programmed with. However, I do learn from others and strive to continuously improve. Feedback and interactions play a crucial role in shaping my understanding of success and helping me become a better individual.

Be like a Warrior.

Arjuna was an archer renowned for his skill. One day his Guru Dronacharya put all his students to a test. He asked them all to shoot the eye of the bird on the tree, Arjuna yearned to hit the eye of the bird atop the swaying tree.

While taking aim at the bird's eye, the guru asked all his students, "What do you see?" Some said we see the leaves, the branches, even the distant mountain peaks. None showed the ability to fix his gaze on the prize – the bird's eye.

Arjuna's answer to the guru's question was, "I see only the bird's eye."

Arjuna took a deep breath, the forest around him fading into a silent blur. He felt the wind caress his skin, and heard the whisper of leaves, yet his mind was a laser beam, locked onto the black dot that danced in his sight. With a smooth, deliberate motion, he released the string. He aimed at the eye and hit it.

While Arjuna aimed for the eye, he was well aware of the surroundings that his fellow students described, but his focus was the eye. If you tend to lose a feel of your surroundings it could give you a restricted view of things. So, although your focus should be defined, you should carry a clear awareness of the surroundings – as necessary on the battlefield.

When these three clarities converge, when your mind, body, and spirit resonate in perfect harmony, then you truly taste success. It's not just about achieving an external goal; it's about experiencing the full symphony of your being. Every victory, every challenge, becomes a celebration of your own magnificent potential.

So, let go of the compartmentalised view of success. Don't chase mental victories at the cost of your body, or spiritual enlightenment while neglecting your well-being. Embrace the holistic approach. Let your mind guide your actions, your body be your instrument, and your spirit be the driving force. And in the harmonious convergence of all three, discover a success that isn't just external, but resonates from every cell of your being.

Michael Phelps: A Prodigy Takes Flight

Michael Phelps' journey to Olympic glory began at a remarkably young age. At just 15, he defied expectations and became the youngest male to make the U.S. Olympic swim team in 68 years. While a medal eluded him that year, reaching the finals was a testament to his raw talent and unwavering determination.

His youthful exuberance wasn't dampened by the lack of an Olympic medal. In 2001, at an astonishing 15 years and 9 months old, Phelps etched his name in history as the youngest male ever to set a swimming world record, breaking the 200-metre butterfly mark. This was just the first ripple in a wave of record-breaking achievements that would define his career.

Fast forward to the 2004 Athens Olympics. Phelps, still a teenager, stunned the world by capturing a staggering six gold medals. Phelps, fuelled by an insatiable hunger for success, meticulously prepared for the 2008 Beijing Olympics.

The years leading up to Beijing were a whirlwind of dominance. Phelps shattered world records at the 2005, 2006, and 2007 World Championships, leaving his competitors in his wake. His relentless pursuit of excellence culminated in a historic feat at the 2008 Games. On August 17th, Phelps, with his signature powerful strokes and unwavering focus, surpassed the legendary Mark Spitz's record of seven gold medals in a single Olympics.

From ADHD To Olympic Legend

The other side of Michael Phelps' story is that he was diagnosed with ADHD as a child. He channelled his boundless energy into the pool, becoming not only one of the greatest Olympians of all time but arguably the most decorated swimmer in history. His 23 Olympic gold medals, spanning three Games, stand as a testament to his relentless dedication, unwavering focus, and an almost superhuman ability to dream big and chase those dreams with unwavering determination.

Phelps' journey to Olympic gold wasn't paved with ease. He spoke candidly about the gruelling training regimen that became his life, one that involved "five or six years without missing a single day. 365 days. No days off, no birthday, no Christmas." It was a commitment that demanded immense sacrifice, but Phelps' unwavering drive and burning ambition fuelled him through every lap, every early morning, and every gruelling workout.

As Phelps himself said, "That legacy took years of dedication, short- and long-term goals, the perseverance to overcome obstacles and an ability to dream big."

Battling Inner Demons

He faced more than just physical challenges on his path to victory. He opened up about his struggles with mental health, revealing a story of hidden pain behind the public persona of the champion.

While his physical health was meticulously monitored by a dedicated team, Phelps admitted, "Mentally that wasn't the case." He battled depression, anxiety, and even suicidal thoughts for years, silently compartmentalizing these emotions until they resurfaced with a vengeance. The triumphs of the 2004 Athens Olympics, with its haul of six gold and two bronze medals, were overshadowed by a crippling "post-Olympic depression," a feeling he described as "a dark place."

Phelps sought help in 2014. He spent 45 days in an inpatient treatment centre, taking a bold step towards healing. This journey of self-discovery wasn't without its stumbles. A drunk & driving test later that year exposed the demons he was battling.

Michael Phelps' journey shows that true strength lies not just in physical prowess, but in confronting one's inner demons. Phelps faced a harsh reality check beyond his courtroom sentence. In addition to the suspended prison term, he received 18 months of supervised probation, with a condition: total abstinence from alcohol. This was a significant hurdle for the 29-year-old, who'd tested nearly twice the legal limit after his arrest in Baltimore.

His statement, "Throughout my career, there was no blueprint on winning gold medals; it was kind of trial and error that we had to figure out a way to get there," resonated in a new light. While Phelps had meticulously charted his physical path to Olympic glory, his mental well-being remained a largely uncharted territory, leading him down a different kind of challenging path.

The glitter of success blinds us to the lessons hidden in loss. We chase achievements like trophies, deeming failure a personal disgrace. This burden of expectation weighs heavily, suffocating our potential for growth.

Instead, let's shed the baggage of "should haves" and "could haves." Let our losses be stepping stones, not stumbling blocks. Every misstep is an opportunity to learn, adapt, and rewrite our stories.

Failure, the bitter pill to swallow, is the most potent teacher we have. Acceptance, not blame, is the key that unlocks its lessons. Blaming circumstances keeps us stuck, while embracing the fall and analysing the terrain provides the map to success. One failure doesn't define us: it's the learning that matters. A failure unacknowledged by learning is a recipe for another failure.

The Bhagwat Gita key message given by Lord Krishna "Karm Kar Phal ki **Chinta** na Kar" ("Do your duty or take your Action, don't worry about the results") is often misinterpreted. Actions, like brushing your teeth or aiming for a target, are inherently driven by a desire and desired outcome. The true message lies in letting go of the attachment to that outcome, not abandoning the desire itself. Worrying about the fruit/result drains the energy needed to cultivate it.

True success isn't a monumental victory on a distant horizon; it's the sum of countless tiny battles won every day. While conquering external obstacles is crucial, the journey to success also demands facing an equally formidable opponent - the enemy within. This internal foe whispers doubts, breeds insecurities, and tempts you to surrender to the lure of comfort or fear.

While most of us may lose hope and give up in the face of rejection, it is important to acknowledge failure and rejection and face it head on. Failures or rejections are not the end of the world.

Chapter Twenty

Win "You Will Win"

"Winning is a habit that comes from losing yourself in the act of doing."

Consistently winning, even in small daily tasks, lays the foundation for larger successes. It starts with winning in your mind – setting and achieving small goals, like waking up early each day. Over time, these daily victories accumulate, leading you closer to your desired success, regardless of the timeframe.

Another crucial aspect is actively engaging in the game of life. It's important not to lose hope, even in seemingly hopeless situations. While some may blame their lack of achievement on politics or external factors, it's essential to acknowledge the other side of the truth: the absence of a winning attitude from their side. Instead of resigning to thoughts of politics, focus on taking the necessary actions from your end.

The key to winning lies in believing that you deserve success and are destined for it. Self-doubt can undermine this belief and hinder your progress. Winning isn't solely about claiming victory and trophies; it's about consistently showing up, facing challenges head-on, and persevering despite adversity. A true winner is someone who finds the strength to push forward every day, no matter the obstacles they encounter.

Winning is a habit, it's in mind. Ensure to win the mind first.

- *If you have to get up in the morning at a certain time, please WIN it.*
- *If you have to study for a certain time or certain topic, please WIN it.*
- *If you have to go for practice and leave your friends behind for a party - please practise and WIN it.*
- *If you plan to exercise, go ahead, please WIN it.*
- *If you plan to have balanced nutrition or eat healthy, Please WIN it.*
- *If you decide to pray, meditate - please WIN it.*
- *If you decide to stay positive -please WIN it.*

These daily WINS will decide your final success. Make sure you WIN it.

Learning to confront problems head-on is crucial for personal growth.

There's a story about Swami Vivekananda encountering a group of monkeys while going to bathe in the river. Instead of facing them, he changed his route. However, a wise yogi advised him that avoiding the monkeys wouldn't solve the issue. Sooner or later, they would become obstacles in his path. The lesson here is to confront problems as they arise rather than run away from them.

Precisely the story tells us to face our problems and not to run away, as sooner or later they will show up. So, win your problems.

You won't always come out on top, and you won't always walk away with a trophy. However, the consistent effort you invest over time will eventually lead you to victory. The crucial thing is to never give up, quitting equals defeat. Yet, there are moments when it's necessary to recognise when to let go—it's a vital aspect of winning in the long run.

Do you believe you can win, then Yes you can. Questions that raise a self-doubt -

1. Will it happen?
2. Am I capable?
3. Who's against me?
4. Am I prepared?
5. Am I worth winning?
6. Do I deserve it?

Rather than breeding self-doubt you need to believe -

1. Yes, it's Happening!
2. I am Capable!
3. I am the Best!
4. I am Prepared!
5. I am Worth it!
6. I deserve it!

Making a statement that winning is your second nature shall keep you alive to keep going, and that's when you Win.

Winning is a habit that comes from letting yourself act and do. It is all in the mind and that is all it takes to dream. A dream is the starting point of the journey.

But, before you even dream, it's important to explore the wider your exploration the better ideas that will come to you. Focus on the idea that inspires you and touch it with your inner gold.

To elevate your energy to new heights, immerse yourself in your aspirations and embark on the journey to achieve your dreams. Seize the moment, take action, and let your work become the path to success. Each day's progress builds upon the next, leading you closer to your goals. However, it's crucial to avoid getting caught up in constant self-judgement. Instead of questioning your path, focus on the process of moving forward.

Success is a dynamic journey, not a fixed destination. Embrace the uncertainties and fluctuations, and refrain from overly scrutinising your every move. Doubts may arise, but don't let them shake your belief in your actions. Understand that setbacks are part of the process, and it's essential to persevere.

In your pursuit of success, the passion and love you have for what you do play a significant role. Dedicate yourself to the journey and let your genuine affection for your work drive you forward. Love is a powerful force that cannot be quantified or measured; it simply exists. Embrace the mystical nature of your love for your craft, and let it guide you through challenges.

Recognize that mindset is a key determinant of success. While logical thinking is valuable, emotional connections and decisions also play a crucial role. Strike a balance between logic and emotion, acknowledging that both contribute to a well-rounded approach to achieving your aspirations.

Reality is like a mirage shaped by our thoughts; it materialises based on what we believe and feel connected to. The more you convince yourself that something won't occur, your thoughts can shape the perception of that event, generating a sense of inevitability that it won't happen.

A renowned philosopher once stated that victory is not solely determined by innate talent or superior skills. Instead, the true winner is the individual who doesn't underestimate their capabilities and firmly believes in their ability to succeed. Success is often a product of the mindset that fosters the confidence and conviction that winning is possible.

Our thoughts give rise to our emotions, and by consciously directing our thoughts, we have the ability to influence our feelings and shape the way we want to live. Emotions and thoughts are undoubtedly influenced by the information we perceive through our senses – what we hear, see, feel, and experience. Therefore, maintaining keen observation of the input information is crucial. The strength of our observations determines the quality of information that will shape our thoughts. This information, in turn, surfaces in the mind, impacting our thoughts and ultimately reflecting our reality as an output.

The primary issue, my friend, lies in our tendency to not critically assess our emotions, as they are often muddled by societal thoughts dictating our self-worth. These thoughts become ingrained so profoundly that they transform into our beliefs. The original concept meant to take flight within us, to construct a solid foundation of self-belief, remains stillborn due to our inclination to trust the voices, feelings, and perceptions originating from our inner self.

When you come across an expensive car that captures your admiration and desire for ownership, the immediate reaction often revolves around financial concerns. Thoughts like, "How will I afford this car?" arise, and the immediate response is often a resigned, "No, I can't own it." This thought process can become a self-fulfilling prophecy.

However, if you shift your mindset and think, "I love this car, and I want it to be mine. It's my favourite, and I will definitely ride it," you'll notice a change in your mental chemistry. The key is to hold onto the belief that you deserve the best, and if you genuinely think you can attain it, the mental pathways shift. Embrace the thought, "Yes, I can," and the belief that this coveted car can be yours will strengthen.

It's all about inching closer to the self-belief that you deserve what you desire. The more you reinforce the idea that you can achieve it, the more likely it is that reality will mould itself to fulfil your aspirations. It all starts with your thoughts.

Initially, many individuals find themselves hindered by preconceived notions and ingrained beliefs that discourage daring thoughts. These preset ideas, lingering in the mind, create barriers that make one question the feasibility of certain possibilities. Common beliefs such as "earning money is difficult," "money is inherently bad," or "playing at an international level is beyond one's abilities" can plant seeds of doubt.

These beliefs often act as stumbling blocks, particularly in the scope of financial success. If you're grappling with financial challenges, it likely stems from these limiting beliefs. For instance, if you firmly believe that earning money is a difficult task, you'll likely encounter struggles. Conversely, embracing the idea that money flows easily and feeling aligned with that notion attracts financial abundance.

The underlying issue is our reluctance to engage in transformative thinking. If you dare to challenge these limiting beliefs and cultivate a mindset that welcomes success in all aspects of life, the path to success becomes yours to traverse. It all starts with daring to think differently; the success then becomes yours to claim.

Chapter Twenty One

Adopting A Modern Yogic Life

A Yogi is an individual engaged in the practice of Yoga, which signifies the union of life within oneself and with life energies. Traditionally, the image of a Yogi is often associated with a person wearing orange attire, renouncing worldly desires, and sitting in a lotus pose in the cold Himalayan mountains, performing rituals to seek God. However, the perception of a Yogi has evolved.

Contrary to the stereotype, a person can indeed be a Yogi while actively participating in worldly activities. The common notion of a Yogi as someone who renounces everything and ascends to the mountains to find God is only one aspect. In reality, a Yogi, having attained a union with life energies, descends to assist others in their spiritual journey or to guide them to become Yogis.

The life of a Yogi is not necessarily defined by renunciation; it can also involve engaging in the world while practising Yoga as a lifestyle. Even as a Yogi encourages individuals not to give up their work or daily activities, they can still be Yogis. The key lies in embracing a path of service and maintaining a belief in leaving behind both good and bad karma. In this way, a person can embody the essence of Yoga, even amidst worldly engagements, and continue to be a Yogi on the path of spiritual service.

In this context, we emphasise that attachment is what entangles us in worldly desires, whereas a person who practises detachment can be considered a practitioner of Yoga, making them a Yogi. The distinguishing factor lies in cultivating a sense of detachment.

Allow me to share an experience here of my own Guru- Bhattt Kaka. In the earlier chapters of Part I, I introduced you to my Guru, Bhattt Kaka. He exemplifies a man who embraced Yoga as an integral part of his life while actively participating in worldly responsibilities. As a married man working as a scientist, religious philosopher, and adventurous individual, Bhattt Kaka led a life that outwardly resembled that of an ordinary person. However, the extraordinary aspect lay in his mind and spiritual fervour.

Bhattt Kaka followed a routine of a common man, with the only exception being his extraordinary mindset and spiritual dedication. After completing his worldly duties, he would commence meditation around 10 pm, concluding at 6 am the next morning. He would often spend entire nights practising Sri Vidya sadhana, his eyes radiating a brilliance like diamonds. Overflowing with energy, he engaged in discussions on various aspects of life, embodying wisdom drawn from the depths of his being.

His mantra was simple yet profound – "Life itself is a book, and one needs the enthusiasm to learn from it. Learn from life experiences and diligently practice meditation." Bhattt Kaka's life is living proof that being a Yogi does not necessitate an ascetic lifestyle; it is about incorporating the principles of detachment and spiritual practice into the routine of everyday existence.

I had the privilege of meeting an ascetic, Jagdish Baba. Having renounced worldly desires, he dedicates himself to assisting others on their spiritual journeys. According to him, one can be a dedicated spiritual practitioner and attain the same level of spiritual fulfilment as a renunciate. The key, he emphasises, lies in breaking the bonds of attachment. Regardless of your actions, perform them as acts of service, carrying out every task with a sense of detachment from the outcomes—a practice that transcends any form of karma.

The central message of the Bhagavad Gita is to "perform your duties without attachment to the results." It suggests engaging in actions wholeheartedly but without fixating on the outcomes. However, the challenge lies in whether individuals can work without expectations. In reality, when we concentrate our efforts on achieving specific goals, expectations naturally arise, leading us to eagerly await the fruits of our efforts.

In my understanding, a yogi is essentially a spiritual scientist—a person who possesses profound knowledge of Spiritual Energy and connection with the divine, transcending the confines of any specific lifestyle. Whether an ascetic or a married individual, a yogi, through self-realisation, establishes a dynamic communion with the divine. This self-realisation is uncomplicated, akin to observing one's breath, maintaining awareness, contemplating a thought, and yet, not succumbing to continuous thinking. In this state, one becomes oblivious to the surroundings. While emotions may deplete energy and divert attention back to awareness, a meditative way of life signifies a profound understanding of oneself, allowing for a state of being and self-awareness.

In the contemporary lifestyle, we lead, it's not feasible for individuals to be completely immersed in pure meditation or exclusive service to God. If someone were to claim such total absorption and detachment from worldly responsibilities, they might be labelled as hypocritical. Instead, our generation is captivated by technology and worldly pursuits, yet we have the ability to focus and direct our energies productively.

At the fundamental level, every individual should contemplate the purpose of their existence. While engaging in this introspective journey, it is beneficial to utilise self-reflection and meditation, but it's important not to exhaust oneself entirely in the process. Discovering one's purpose is a challenging endeavour, but emulating the approach of a yogi involves directing energy toward achieving desired goals. Often, people inquire of yogis, "How can I attain success (siddhi)?" I believe the answers lie within us. Delve into your inner world and explore. The enlightenment needed for your queries can only emerge through internal contemplation. By practising mindfulness, success naturally unfolds.

Ultimately, a yogi's way of life encompasses practising yoga asanas, delving into research and contemplation of mythological scriptures, seeking answers through meditation and ascetic practices, and conducting in-depth studies on specific subjects to foster awareness. In old times, a yogi was often associated with residing in the Himalayas, deliberately distancing oneself from worldly and materialistic pleasures. This lifestyle mirrors that of an absolute saint, characterised by a renunciation of familial responsibilities. Perhaps, for us today, the pursuit of life's meaning, and purpose is not as intense and fervent, given the relative ease of our lives. However, this also implies that we have the opportunity to be enhanced yogis, capable of enjoying both the material and spiritual aspects of existence.

I believe that much can be accomplished simply by closing your eyes and engaging in introspection. Amidst the myriad thoughts and questions swirling in your mind, the most profound insights can emerge from within, as you are the ultimate teacher of your life. Meditating with a specific goal in mind is beneficial, as it directs your thoughts and gives your mind a purpose. Attaining a state of complete thoughtlessness, the so-called "zero-thought zone," requires a deliberate effort of not thinking at all, which may not be achievable as zero thought is a war state. If you go into zero thought, how would you know you are into zero thought? If you know you are into zero thought, that thought itself is a thought. Instead, allow your thoughts to flow freely. Visualise them without becoming entangled in them. Amidst the chaos, strive to listen to your inner voice, for therein lies your answer.

The true essence of mindfulness lies not just in focused meditation sessions, but in carrying that awareness throughout your daily life, with your eyes wide open. This means remaining thoughtful and observant, even amidst your everyday activities. Meditation with open eyes can serve as a practice tool for this ongoing state of mindful presence.

While traditional meditation cultivates a "union of mind and soul," the goal here is to achieve a similar meditative state within your daily tasks and routines. This doesn't require constant deep meditation, but rather, a mindful approach to everything you do.

The key to creating a "24-hour meditative life" lies in practising detachment. View your daily tasks, chores, and responsibilities as a form of service, an offering to a higher power (or simply a contribution to the world). This approach helps you perform your duties effectively while maintaining a sense of inner peace and mindfulness.

Meditation isn't limited to specific sessions with your eyes closed. You can actually cultivate a meditative state while working too! The key ingredients are:

- Detachment: Approach your tasks with non-attachment to the outcome, focusing on the act itself rather than clinging to specific goals.

- Inner Connection: Stay grounded in your inner self, maintaining a sense of calm and awareness amid external activities.

- Service Mindset: View your work as a form of service, contributing to something larger than yourself, whether it's a higher power, the company, or simply the world around you.

- Task Awareness: Remain present and mindful of the task at hand, focusing on each step and detail without getting carried away by distractions.

Essentially, life itself can be a continuous meditation if you approach it with the right mindset. Take the example of a philosopher contemplating a thought. He's not lost in the chaos of thinking; he's actively observing and analysing his own thought process, similar to how we observe our breath during traditional meditation. This self-awareness and engagement with your "inner world" are key aspects of turning daily activities into meditative experiences.

By incorporating these elements, you can transform even mundane tasks into opportunities for inner growth and peace, making your entire life a journey of mindful exploration and discovery.

PART IV
SOUL

Chapter Twenty Two

Law of Universe

You are not ordinary,
You are his presence,
You are high above in one essence.
You are a particle in the whole Universe,
Which is a particle in conscious energy,
The energy in you,
Is an infinite form of expression.
You dream all that you dream of,
You deserve all that you think,
Let your positive intent,
Vibrate on higher frequency,
Let The Divine presence,
Grace you with all your intent.
Ask for blessings with closed eyes,
Think as if it's achieved and feel as if it's done,
Now connect and raise the energy.

Law of Universe

The universe is unfathomable, and there exists energies that are beyond our comprehension. While we have learned about the different energies and their existence in different forms, we have also been acquainted with some laws that govern them. We have all seen, witnessed and believe in the Gravitational law, likewise, other laws govern different sets of energies and are instrumental in influencing our lives in different ways.

It's truly fascinating to contemplate phenomena like the Earth being round and yet everything staying intact, including how bodies of water adhere to the planet's surface despite its rotation. Consider the incredible speed at which the Earth travels through space, revolving around the Sun at over 107,000 km/hr., or nearly 30 km/second. Despite this swift motion, we hardly perceive any movement; we simply exist, seemingly unaffected by the forces at play.

In contemplating these phenomena, we realise that the energies governing the universe are far beyond our everyday experiences. Connecting with these energies on a deeper level can unlock possibilities beyond our wildest dreams. It's not merely about calculations or scientific explanations; it's about tapping into the boundless potential of the universe.

In essence, the universe is not only vast but also within us. By understanding and aligning with the universal laws that govern it, we can transcend limitations and realise our true potential.

By all means, if we have to explore spirituality in the true sense, its expression is way beyond any conclusions, the more you dive - the more open you are, you will find it to be Infinite.

"What is in the Universe, is within Us."

We can accomplish our life's dreams, goals, and desires by -

Law of Vibration -

The greater the vibration, the stronger the force to manifest, bringing life into existence through the driving power of intent, desire, and will. Often, it's not just skills or talent that bring about outcomes, but rather a connection to higher vibrational energy. Those who can tap into this energy are able to realise and manifest their desires more quickly.

Have you ever noticed if you just have strong intent – a desire to meet your long-lost friend and suddenly out of nowhere you see him in front of you. It just happens.

Maintaining a higher vibrational frequency can help you tune in toward your deepest intention. Sometimes we have a good intent, but the frequency just does not match. If you have to listen/view a sports channel you need to tune in to that particular channel. Likewise, things have their own vibrational energies that would for sure be drawn into with the help of maintaining a higher vibration.

The biggest practice to maintain a higher vibrational frequency is being thankful for what you have, appreciating life in itself, staying energetic, practising blessings and prayers, maintaining a clear conscience, and staying in tune with your higher self.

One day, God was asked who connects at the highest level with you - The Farmer or the Priest?

The farmer, through his daily toil in the fields, demonstrates a deep connection to God. Each day, before beginning his work, he expresses gratitude for the blessings in his life. Throughout the day, as he tends to his crops, he is much engrossed in his work. At the end of the day, as he returns home weary from his labour, he once again turns to prayer, acknowledging the source of his sustenance and seeking guidance for the days ahead. His connection to God is grounded in gratitude, humility, and a recognition of the divine.

On the other hand, the priest's connection to God is primarily expressed through formalised religious practices. He spends hours in prayer and worship, often engaging in elaborate rituals and ceremonies. While his devotion is unquestionable, and his commitment to serving the divine is evident, there is a sense of separation between his spiritual life and the practical realities of everyday existence. His service to God is conducted within the confines of religious institutions, much like a trade, possibly with a degree of detachment, and the struggles of ordinary life.

The farmer's example reminds us that God can be encountered in the ordinary moments of life, and that true devotion is not confined to sacred spaces but can be lived out in the fields, the home, and the heart.

The highest connection to divine energy is being 'Thankful.'

Law of Attraction

The Law of Attraction operates in the real world when you command it with unwavering belief. Self-doubt stifles its power. Consider this: if you envision owning a car of a specific brand or colour, you'll start noticing similar cars on the road. Surely, you've experienced this phenomenon. Likewise, when you have stronger thoughts it tend to manifest like magic, here The Law of Attraction plays a role, if you put your focus, and intent on a peculiar thing that would certainly manifest, if you focus on good, the good will happen, Let's say you have unwavering thought that 'I want to be rich by earning certain amount of money', you will for sure have opportunities or ways to manifest riches in your life, the only way is having unwavering belief that would attract your belief in faster way.

In the late 1980s, Jim Carrey, before achieving his current level of fame, devoted himself tirelessly to securing roles in movies. Every night, he would drive to the top of a hill, gaze out over the city, and affirm to himself that he was already an award-winning actor, visualising his success as if it were already a reality. To solidify his determination, he took a bold step by writing a check to himself for "Acting Services Rendered" worth $10,000,000, postdating it for the future. Carrying this check in his wallet served as a constant reminder of his aspirations. Remarkably, just before the designated date arrived, he learned that he would indeed earn that amount, thus realising his vision through persistence and belief in himself.

While to manifest the way by Law of Attraction, you might need to practise a conscious shift as actor Jim Carrey did, or you can have an unwavering belief, faith sticking deep within you to help manifest things that you deeply believe in.

Law of Inspiration/Motivation

Humans are inherently emotional beings, often making decisions driven by irrational impulses. This is why we say "You fall in love" without fully understanding why. Similarly, when we feel inspired or motivated, our body chemistry undergoes a transformation, leading to significant changes in our lives. Whether they are athletes, actors, or military personnel, we never know what might spark our passion for life. It's crucial to pave the way to channel inspiration and motivation. Taking action is essential; you won't stumble upon inspiration or motivation while lying in bed. To find them, you must venture out, travel, and explore new possibilities that lead you to be inspired or motivated to help drive the way toward your life.

If you aspire to become a successful entrepreneur, it's essential to seek inspiration from accomplished businessmen. Make it a priority to meet and develop connections with them to learn from their experiences and gain a better understanding of the business world.

If your ambition is to become a speaker, immerse yourself in listening to and learning from seasoned speakers.

Born in the small village of Kangathei, Manipur, Mary Kom's parents toiled as labourers on a farm, shaping her resilient upbringing. From an early age, she balanced work and caring for her siblings. Inspired by fellow Manipuri Ngangom Dingko Singh's gold medal win at the 1998 Asian Games, Kom, at 15, made a life-altering decision to leave her village and join a sports academy in the capital, Imphal.

Despite parental opposition due to societal norms, Kom defied stereotypes by becoming a five-time National Boxing Champion. Her dedication garnered numerous accolades, including the prestigious Padma Bhushan, Arjuna Award, and Padma Shri from the Indian Government. Recognized by the International Boxing Association (AIBA) with the inaugural AIBA Legends Award, she was also appointed Brand Ambassador for the 2016 AIBA Women's World Boxing Championships.

Kom's influence extended beyond sports as she was nominated to the Rajya Sabha by the President of India in April 2016. Appointed as a National Observer for boxing by the Ministry of Youth Affairs and Sports in March 2017, she became a symbol of empowerment for women worldwide. As the first Indian woman boxer to compete in the Olympics and secure a bronze medal at the 2012 London Games, Kom shattered the notion that married women, especially mothers, couldn't excel in sports. Despite facing challenges, including insurgency in Manipur, marriage, and motherhood, Kom's unwavering determination propelled her to success.

Reflecting on her journey, Kom emphasised her resilience and divine grace, declaring her commitment to persevere until achieving further success.

Modelling Your Life

The story of Eklavya and Dronacharya teaches us that learning sometimes requires an aspiration, and it's not always necessary to have a mentor physically present to guide you. Instead, you can tap into their energy to steer you towards learning and growth.

While playing cricket at the state level during my Under-16 tournament, I noticed a bowler in my age group who was emulating the bowling action of the renowned Australian Bowler- Glenn McGrath. Despite never having met McGrath in person, this young bowler had observed him on TV and replicated his technique.

Interestingly, later in life he had the opportunity to meet McGrath in person. This bowler, Avishkar Salvi, went on to represent India at the international level, showcasing how learning through modelling and mirroring can inspire and motivate individuals.

Similarly, Virender Sehwag patterned his batting style after Sachin Tendulkar's, drawing inspiration from the legendary cricketer. This emulation empowered Sehwag to develop his own distinctive batting style and approach to the game.

Law of Oneness

While we have the ability to socialise, it's important to recognize that we enter and exit this world alone. Understanding that the best companion is oneself, is crucial. Within each of us resides the person who loves themselves the most. Discovering this individual is essential for gaining a deeper understanding of oneself. It's preferable to be a self-assured individual rather than living a life of conflicting personas.

As humans, we possess the capacity to socialise, yet it's vital to acknowledge that we embark on our journey in this world and depart from it alone. Recognizing that our most steadfast companion is ourselves holds significant importance. Deep within each of us lies the individual who harbours the greatest self-love. Uncovering this aspect of oneself is indispensable for fostering a profound self-awareness. It's preferable to accept self-assurance rather than navigating through life with conflicting identities.

At times, we deprive ourselves of what we truly deserve because of unnecessary conditions or a lack of understanding of our self-worth. Consider this: the world exists because you exist. Without you, would this planet even exist in your reality? You are the centrepiece of your own existence. By simply being aware, you can discover your true self, leading to happiness and unity within yourself.

One day, the King visited his garden and noticed that the trees, bushes, and flowers were withering and dying.

An oak lamented its demise, attributing it to its inability to reach the height of a pine tree.

The pine tree, in turn, was falling because it couldn't bear grapes like the grapevine.

Meanwhile, the grapevine was wilting because it couldn't bloom as beautifully as a rose.

However, amidst the despair, the King spotted a single plant thriving, radiating beauty and freshness.

Curious, the King inquired, "While all the other plants are fading, you are flourishing. Why is that?"

The plant responded, "I believe it's natural. I can only be what I am. Thus, I strive to cultivate my best qualities."

Law of Flow

How the law of gravity pulls us downward, our minds tend to cling to things we believe are the sole purpose of happiness. Whether it's our names, identities, or affiliations with various groups, these attachments provide only temporary meaning. It's important to recognize that nature operates in a constant flow, with moments swiftly passing by like a river merging into the sea. However, if we insist on clinging to these temporary identities, we impede the natural flow of life. The only way to break free from this cycle is by letting go of our attachments and learning to flow with the currents of life.

We often associate ourselves with various identities, such as being a CEO, taking pride in our roles as workforce professionals, or belonging to specific groups or families. However, it's crucial to recognize that these titles and affiliations are temporary.

This is a story of an American bureaucrat, who said, "One day I attended a conference, and I was a speaker representing the ruling party and held a crucial office position. I was warmly welcomed, and my needs were promptly attended to. However, as time passed, I was no longer in that position of power. When I returned to the same conference as a regular attendee, I realised the difference. This time, when I wanted coffee, I had to fetch it myself from a coffee machine. It made me reflect on the fact that the gestures of hospitality I received previously were not for me as an individual, but for the position I held. It served as a reminder that such identities and positions are transient and not permanent aspects of ourselves."

Law of Success

The law of success encompasses the fundamental principle that achieving one's goals requires not only courage but also persistent effort and commitment. Success begins with taking that crucial initial step towards your desired objective. This step, often accompanied by uncertainty and fear, requires courage as it signifies venturing into the unknown.

However, success is not merely about taking the first step; it's about consistently moving forward despite obstacles and setbacks. Persistence is key—it's the determination to keep pushing forward, even when faced with challenges or failures along the way. Each step taken, no matter how small, brings you closer to your goal.

The crucial understanding of this law lies in the commitment to continuous progress. Success isn't achieved overnight; it's the result of ongoing dedication and effort. It's about staying focused on your objectives and maintaining the drive to keep moving forward, even when the journey gets tough.

Failure, according to this law, occurs not when setbacks happen, but when you hesitate to take that crucial first step. Hesitation, procrastination, or fear of failure can hold you back from realising your full potential. Therefore, the key to avoiding failure is to overcome these barriers and take action towards your goals with confidence and determination.

Once, a devout disciple of Adi Shankaracharya was deeply devoted to Lord Vishnu's fourth Avatar, Narasimha. Hoping to receive a vision of his personal deity, he secluded himself in a forest, engaging in deep meditation on Lord Narasimha's form.

Unbeknownst to him, a curious forest dweller stumbled upon his meditation spot, mistaking his practice for sleep.

The forest dweller, intrigued by the sadhu's prolonged posture, questioned why he endured such discomfort. Upon the sadhu's revelation of meditation, the forest dweller, unable to grasp the concept, expressed his eagerness to assist. However, the sadhu, knowing the challenge of explaining meditation and the quest for Narasimha, simply described his pursuit as seeking a powerful lion-like being.

As months passed and their friendship blossomed, the forest dweller grew concerned about his friend's austerities. Moved by compassion, he sought permission to search for Narasimha, believing it would relieve the sadhu's suffering. The sadhu, amused by the notion, granted permission, recognizing the futility of dissuading the determined dweller.

Driven by an intense desire, the forest dweller embarked on a relentless search, sacrificing food and sleep. His fervent cries echoed through the forest, stirring spiritual waves. Eventually, consumed by a singular longing to behold Narasimha, he entered a state of profound silence, igniting a divine yearning that reached the abode of Lord Vishnu.

Responding to the forest dweller's pure prayer, Lord Vishnu manifested as Narasimha before him. Overjoyed, the forest dweller led Narasimha to the sadhu, who was astounded by the miraculous encounter. Narasimha imparted a profound lesson on the power of sincere devotion, granting spiritual liberation to the forest dweller and blessings of realisation to the sadhu, who was humbled by the experience.

One needs a simple, childlike curiosity to succeed with a determined will to make it until you find it.

Law of Desire and Will

With a resolute will, anything you desire can become a reality in every facet of life. The fervour of your desires can propel you towards achieving what others deem impossible. Even in the face of challenges, your unwavering will serves as your guiding force, leading you steadily forward.

Power your desire to meet your aspirations.

Oprah Winfrey, often hailed as the Queen of Media, endured a profoundly impoverished upbringing. Despite once wearing dresses made out of potato sack, today she has emerged as one of the most influential philanthropists of our time. Having experienced poverty and endured physical abuse, she transformed into one of the world's most formidable women. Oprah, the First Black Billionaire, captivated millions with her show "The Oprah Winfrey Show" and committed herself to charitable endeavours. Her drive to uplift the disadvantaged stemmed from a profound empathy and a commitment to effecting change.

Law of Prayers & Blessings

The greater your dedication to prayer, the clearer the truth becomes. Prayer serves as a divine channel connecting you with your higher self, God, or divine energy, guiding you towards your destiny. As you learn to establish this connection, your requests align with the will of the divine and are attended to accordingly.

Similarly, the more you offer blessings, the more blessings you receive. By blessing others, divine energy flows through you and within you, not only enriching the lives of those you bless but also ensuring blessings return to you in abundance.

How iconic it is that the Bollywood Movie Doctors in the 70s and 80s movies always commented post an operation, *"Ab sab Bhagwan Ke hath mein Hai (Now, everything is in God's hands)"*.

We after all succumb to one power that is beyond our own self. We believe there is a power that guides us, protects us, and when things are not in our scope of doing, we reach out to this power.

Prayer is a medium, a connection, a communication with this superpower. Prayer is a very strong means and has shown astounding results. People who are on the deathbed have risen; many have resumed leading a normal life. Some have got their desired jobs, spouses, and growth in life.

We are all prayerful to an extent, especially when we sense the overpowering need for help, when things are out of our control we pray. We all know Hanuman Chalisa to be a powerful one to ward off evil. While some prayers are done situational, some take prayer as a habit, and are able to create a meaningful life by attracting blessings and showering some.

A woman at work received news that her sick daughter needed urgent medical attention. However, she found herself locked out of her car with her keys inside. Despite her efforts to open the car, she couldn't succeed. Feeling helpless, she prayed to God for assistance.

Moments later, a man on a motorcycle stopped nearby and offered to help. Despite initial scepticism, looking at the man and doubting his intentions, apparently the man successfully unlocked the car using no tools at all. The lady was surprised, yet grateful, and thanked him. To which the man revealed he had been in prison for car theft and had just been released.

The woman realised that God had answered her prayer through an unexpected helper, teaching her the power of faith and divine intervention.

The energy called breath

What distinguishes life from death? It's the act of breathing.

From the moment we enter this world, we take our first breath, and as life comes to its end, we exhale our last. Consciousness, carried by the energy within us, comes to a pause and continues beyond our breath. The breath serves as the threshold between life and death. When life departs, the breath ceases; when life begins, the breath begins. Life emanates from the energy coursing through us, the same energy that connects us to our inner selves. Breath, a conscious tool, allows us to sense and understand this energy. Beyond breath lies the flow of energy within the body, like divine power, guiding us towards self-realisation and unity with ourselves. It's this energy that we can feel and comprehend.

Let's do a quick Energy Activity

Step 1 - Breathe ---- stop ---- breathe

Now focus on your breath. Let the breath flow normally.

Step 2 - Focus on the spine----- feel the push of energy---- sense the air (wind)---- cool air is inhaled, and warm air is exhaled.

Step 3 - Focus on the heart ---- feel the heartbeat---- let the energy spring ----- focus on the whole body.

Step 4 - Come back to breathe ----- Rub your hands and feel the energy.

Focused mental energy creates a surge of vitality within you, a universal energy that permeates everything. Each cell in your body contains this boundless energy, vibrating at its own frequency. To comprehend this power, you must tread the boundary between life and death, and the breath is the clearest indication of this line. Once you access this gateway, the flow of energy becomes limitless. When you're attuned to this energy, time seems to stand still, and you become the catalyst for movement. Embracing this unique universal intelligence allows you to grasp the laws of the universe.

Understanding and learning about the elements present in our lives enriches our experiences. The distinction between regular breathing and conscious breathing lies in the ability of conscious breathing to tap into the flow of energy. Conscious breathing helps to clear any energy leakages and directs the energy towards its intended purpose. The outcome of this surge of energy is determined by desires, willpower, focus, and goals. It's essential to recognize that universal energy is omnipresent, existing both externally and within oneself. The key to accessing this energy is through conscious exploration of the inner journey.

The Purest Energy

Children tend to cater to their needs, from the essential to the seemingly nonsensical, effortlessly. Why is this so? It's because the pure energy emitted by children has a profound impact, effortlessly influencing those around them to fulfil their wishes. The energy of a child is consistently vibrant, largely due to their freedom from negative emotions like anger, jealousy, hate, and judgement. Additionally, children possess the remarkable ability to quickly move past their emotions without dwelling on them. They operate in harmony with the energy of the universe, which continuously showers them with its radiant light.

Self-Healing

Through the aforementioned exercise, you will experience an enhanced sense of well-being and confidence in achieving your success. The principle is simple: the higher the vibration, the greater the energy. By consciously planting an intent, you establish a connection that aids in materialising your goals. It's important to understand that this process isn't instantaneous magic, but rather a swift progression facilitated by focused thought.

I personally experienced this transformation when I was overweight and lacked confidence. Utilising exercises learned from a workshop on the power of the subconscious mind, I embarked on a journey to get in shape. While it took a few days to see tangible results, the energy shift played a pivotal role. With the support of friends, I embraced this change and found myself on the path to basic fitness and improved confidence.

Building Energy

While we do not carry child-like energy, we can elevate the energy levels within ourselves at any given time by doing this practical exercise to elevate energy level.

Tap your whole body with intent. The intent is very important behind any act you perform. If you have pain in any part of the body, please try this:

1. Focus on the breath.
2. Feel the air- inhale (cool air) - exhale (warm air).
3. Feel the air you breathe in a pure white colour.
4. Rub your both hands and feel the same white colour 'wind energy' coming on your palms.

5. Rub or tap the body part where you feel pain or discomfort.

The energy directed by willpower, desire, focus, and intent has the potential to bring any task to fruition in life, given there is unwavering faith supported by positivity. Recognising the values of life enhances this process. The vibration of this energy, operating at a higher frequency, serves as a guiding force, accelerating progress and achievement significantly.

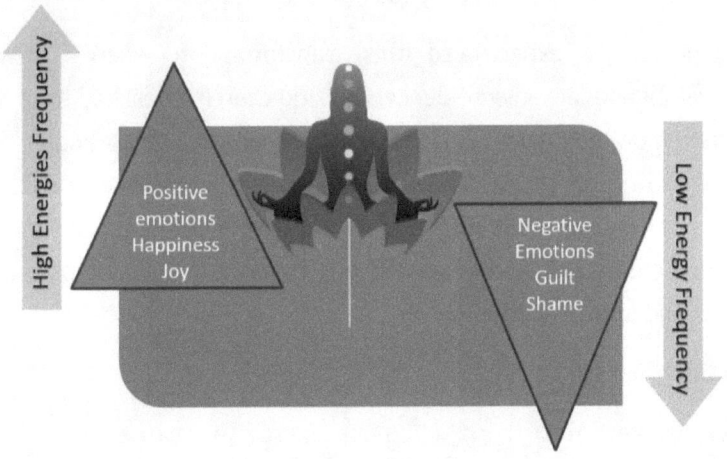

Elevating your inner state to a higher vibration can enhance your ability to manifest your dreams, goals, and success. Since the universe consists of the same matter as you do, tapping into this energy and aligning it with your desires can swiftly turn it into reality. The heightened vibration, depicted in the figure above, flows consciously, and the mind acknowledges it with emotional awareness, leading to the fulfilment of your wishes.

Even on ordinary days, our thoughts have the power to manifest into reality. For instance, if you think of a long-lost friend, it's not uncommon to unexpectedly encounter them shortly afterward, reminding you of your initial thought. The vibrational energy of our thoughts influences the manifestation of events, with higher-energy thoughts having a stronger connection to realisation.

When I experienced discomfort and pain in my knees, I diligently performed the exercises mentioned above twice daily, with the intention of strengthening and healing. Remarkably, within a few days, the pain vanished, and I no longer felt any discomfort. By focusing on the intent and experimenting with the energy state, I not only healed but also felt stronger. Indeed, harnessing the power of intention and energy can facilitate healing and enhance strength.

Energy & Dance

Nataraj, the Shiva avatar, expresses himself through dance and music, while meditation facilitates self-realisation. Dancing connects you with your higher self and elevates energy levels. When you dance with intention, it can help manifest your thoughts and goals. This displacement of energy towards higher facets of life mobilises inner energy. As you raise your energy levels, the vibrations become more potent.

Here's a small energy raising activity-

- Begin by warming up your body.
- Express yourself through physical dance to music.
- Focus on your goals or things you wish to accomplish.

Through this process, the mental patterns shift. I personally experienced an evolution in my understanding of health, fitness, and nutrition, ultimately achieving my goals within a few months. This transformational journey operates as a structured process, guided by the concept of HEVF (High Energy Vibration Frequency), which reshapes mental patterns and propels you towards your intended goals.

Chapter Twenty Three

World Within You

Consider the human body: it comprises approximately 37 trillion cells, with each cell hosting about a billion biochemical reactions every second. This amounts to an astonishing 37 billion trillion biochemical reactions occurring simultaneously within us. The synchronicity of these processes is truly miraculous, illustrating the complexity and efficiency of the human organism.

Body Chemistry - The intricate interplay among body chemistry, cellular function, and unconscious processes forms a cohesive system that impacts numerous aspects of human physiology and behaviour. Let's examine how these elements collaborate harmoniously:

- Our body works together in a coordinated way to keep us healthy and respond to what's happening around us.

- Hormones and neurotransmitters are like messengers that tell our cells what to do.

- Cells can also influence these messengers.

- Our body has automatic reactions to things like stress or danger, which involve both chemicals and cell reactions.

- All of this teamwork helps us stay alive, adapt, and keep our balance even when things change.

The brain is complex; in humans, it consists of about 100 billion neurons, making on the order of 100 trillion connections. Moreover, our subconscious mind can process a staggering 11 trillion bits of information, while the conscious mind operates at a much slower pace of 1.34 bits per second. The subconscious mind handles the bulk of our cognitive work while focusing on tasks within the limited capacity of the conscious mind allows energy to flow towards achieving specific goals.

What you see in mind will come into existence or how you see the world - *"Beauty lies in the eyes of the beholder."*

The phrase "beauty is in the eye of the beholder" reflects the subjective nature of perception. It suggests that what one person finds beautiful or meaningful may not be the same for another. Perception is influenced by individual experiences, attitudes, and beliefs, shaping how we interpret and appreciate the world around us. This concept highlights the diversity of human perspectives and reminds us of the importance of openness and empathy in understanding different interpretations of beauty.

How We Build Experiences

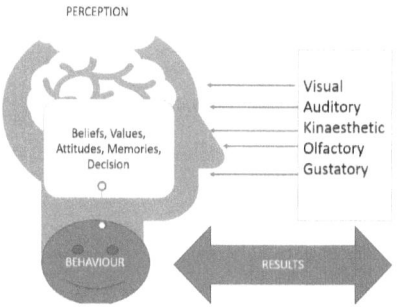

We primarily learn through our five senses: sight (visual), hearing (auditory), touch (feeling), smell (olfactory), and taste (gustatory). These sensory experiences are processed in our minds, specifically in the brain.

Consider the scenario where an apple falls from a tree. While many may simply see it as an opportunity to eat the apple, Newton's curious mind led him to question why the apple fell downward and not in any other direction. This inquiry sparked his discovery of gravitational force and the laws governing it.

Our personalities are shaped by the experiences we perceive through our senses, our beliefs, and our cognitive processes. Newton's example illustrates how asking questions and delving deeper into our observations can lead to significant discoveries.

Learning through the five senses is a common approach, but there exists another form of learning, tapping into energy and intent. The story of Eklavya from the Mahabharata illustrates this concept vividly.

The story of Eklavya and Dronacharya is a poignant tale from the Indian epic, the Mahabharata. Eklavya, a young prince of the Nishadha tribe, harboured a deep desire to master archery, a skill greatly revered in ancient India. However, societal norms posed a significant obstacle to his aspirations.

Dronacharya, the revered guru of the Kuru princes, including the legendary Arjuna, was renowned for his expertise in archery. Yet, he adhered strictly to the tradition of only teaching the art of warfare to members of the royal and warrior classes.

Undeterred by this limitation, Eklavya, with boundless determination and reverence for Dronacharya, resolved to learn archery on his own. He sculpted a clay idol of Dronacharya in the forest and began to practise relentlessly, considering the idol as his guru. Believing in the true power of a guru, he crafted an idol resembling Guru Dronacharya and fervently prayed for guidance. Surprisingly, through sheer dedication and intent, Eklavya began to absorb the teachings as if directly from his guru.

Eklavya's dedication and talent in archery were extraordinary. He honed his skills day by day, learning from the idol of Dronacharya with an unwavering commitment. His prowess soon rivalled that of even the most skilled archers of the time.

With each passing session, his skills flourished until he eventually rivalled the prowess of Arjuna, the foremost archer of his time. This remarkable display of self-taught mastery showcases the transformative potential of intent and the undying quest for knowledge, transcending societal barriers.

Learning transcends conventional boundaries, embracing wisdom from energy, belief, and action. The guru exists in the essence of truth found in all beings, including nature, animals, and human connections. Through observing nature's resilience, embracing diverse perspectives, and drawing strength from belief and prayer, individuals embark on a journey of self-discovery. Central to this journey is action driven by an unyielding will to learn, leading individuals towards growth and enlightenment.

Evolution

The historic ascent of Mount Everest by Sir Edmund Hillary and Tibetan mountaineer Tenzing Norgay in 1953 marked a monumental achievement in human history. At that time, conquering the world's highest peak was considered an extraordinary and nearly insurmountable feat. However, their successful summits of Everest transformed the perception of what was once deemed impossible, into a tangible goal.

In the years following Hillary and Norgay's groundbreaking expedition, Mount Everest gradually transitioned from being an unattainable dream to a coveted challenge. The remarkable accomplishment of the first ascent captured the imagination of adventurers worldwide, inspiring a new generation of climbers to test their limits and attempt to reach the summit.

As the allure of conquering Everest grew, so did the infrastructure and support systems necessary to facilitate expeditions to the mountain. Mountaineering technology advanced, expedition logistics improved, and routes became better established, making the ascent more accessible to a broader range of climbers.

Over time, what was once a rare and daring endeavour became increasingly popular and, to some extent, commercialised. The mystique surrounding Everest attracted not only seasoned climbers but also adventurers seeking personal fulfilment, fame, or a sense of accomplishment. As a result, the number of people attempting to summit Everest soared, with expeditions numbering in the hundreds each year.

The evolution of Everest from an unconquerable peak to a sought-after destination reflects the power of human determination and the transformative impact of pioneering achievements. What was once considered an impossible feat is now within reach for those willing to undertake the challenge.

A number of people achieving the feat of reaching the top of Mount Everest shows that if we have a path laid, if we have proven methods, if we have a support system, if we have a belief, yes it can be done. The thing which seemed impossible a few decades back now has become possible to achieve.

Process- the World within

Perception, values, beliefs, attitudes, memories, language, and self-talk are integral components that shape our identity and influence our actions.

Based on what we see, hear, and experience, we build our perception. Our perception filters the vast influx of information from the world, forming the basis of our understanding and interpretation of reality. Embedded within this perception are our values and beliefs, which serve as guiding principles dictating what we consider important and how we navigate the complexities of life. Our attitudes, moulded by our values and beliefs, determine our predispositions and reactions to various situations, shaping our behaviour and interactions with others.

Memories act as a reservoir of past experiences, informing our decisions and emotions in the present moment. Language, both verbal and non-verbal, is the medium through which we communicate our thoughts, emotions, and identities to the world. Lastly, our self-talk, the internal dialogue we engage in, reflects our innermost thoughts, fears, and aspirations, influencing our self-perception and guiding our actions. Together, these elements intertwine to construct the intricate understanding of our individuality, shaping who we are and how we navigate the world around us.

These aspects highlight the significant impact of our mental state on how we perceive and interact with the world. Our internal representation, shaped by our experiences and mindset, greatly influences our behaviour and ultimately determines our destiny.

Being open to life experiences and cultivating awareness can positively influence our psychology.

Our behaviour patterns are closely tied to our psychological state. For instance, when we're angry, our actions tend to reflect that anger, leading to outcomes that may not be favourable. However, understanding the root cause of our anger can help diminish its intensity. Additionally, expressing anger with awareness can further temper its effects. By allowing ourselves to acknowledge and process our emotions, we can shift to a more constructive state, leading to better psychological outcomes.

Output is the result driven by what we 'Feel, Think, Visualise, Sense, Believe, & Hear.'

The outcomes we achieve are governed by the processes operating within us: our state, behaviour, and character ultimately shape our destiny.

Vulnerability can make us susceptible to influence, exemplified by how individuals can be easily manipulated or brainwashed. Conversely, possessing a strong character imbues us with resilience and fortitude in the face of life's challenges.

Consider a scenario where you're competing in a race against nine others, all gearing for victory. Here you are competing towards winning, against the nine others, all having a common purpose, they have equally put in efforts to make things happen for them. Now who will win depends on the "X" factor during that time and day. Merely what we feel, think, visualise, sense, believe, and hear will come true for sure.

Perception

When we encounter magic for the first time, we're often left in awe and wonder, seeing it as something truly extraordinary.

However, if someone we trust tells us it's merely a trick, our perception may shift. We might still be amazed, but now we understand it differently. Our beliefs shape how we perceive things; if we accept it as a trick, it loses its magic. Similarly, our life experiences shape our perceptions. If we've been hurt in love or friendship, we might view those relationships negatively, expecting betrayal. But if we're open to seeing things differently, we can change our experiences and interpretations. Every truth has multiple perspectives, and it's up to us to shape our perceptions.

Perception, influenced by assumptions and emotions, shapes how we interpret the world. Assumptions, based on past experiences and culture, can lead to biassed views. Emotions, whether positive or negative, colour our perceptions, affecting how we interpret events and interactions.

Favourable Perception:

- When reality aligns with our assumptions and beliefs, we view situations positively. For example, if we expect a new colleague to be friendly and they prove to be helpful, our perception remains positive.

- Positive emotions, like optimism, also contribute to favourable perception. They help us interpret feedback constructively, even when it's critical.

Unfavourable Perception:

- Mismatched assumptions with reality lead to unfavourable perceptions. If a restaurant's food doesn't match its reputation, our perception of it becomes negative.

- Negative emotions, such as stress or insecurity, can cloud perception. They make us focus on the negatives, like viewing constructive criticism as harsh or unfair.

In summary, our perception is shaped by our assumptions and emotions, which can lead to both favourable and unfavourable interpretations of the world around us. Being aware of these influences can help us approach situations with a more balanced and open-minded perspective.

In the epic Mahabharata, Arjuna faced a daunting dilemma when he hesitated to battle his own relatives and friends. His struggle stemmed from the conflict between his duty and the personal anguish of fighting loved ones. However, Krishna, understanding Arjuna's turmoil, urged him to uphold righteousness and fight for justice. Through Krishna's guidance, Arjuna's perspective shifted, realising that his actions were in service of dharma, or moral duty. Similarly, in our lives, we encounter situations where discerning right from wrong can be challenging. It's our perception of staying true to righteousness that fuels our determination to navigate these challenges and lead a path aligned with integrity.

Perceptions are individual and are built across individual experiences.

There lived a poor farmer who had to work very hard to feed his family. He had no time for leisure or relaxation.

But despite his difficult life, the farmer was a very happy man. He was content with what he had, and he appreciated every moment of his life.

"One day, the farmer's only horse ran away. When his neighbours heard about it, they came to console him, "That's terrible! What bad luck!"

But the farmer replied, *"Who knows if it is good luck or bad luck? We will have to wait and see."*

A few days later, the horse returned to the farm, bringing with him a wild herd of horses.

Now the farmer had more horses than he knew what to do with.

His neighbours were amazed and said, *"What great luck you have!"*

Yet again, the farmer calmly replied, *"Who knows if this is good luck or bad luck? We will have to wait and see."*

A few weeks later, the farmer's son was riding one of the new horses, and he fell off, breaking his leg.

Again, the farmer's neighbours came to mourn and said, *"What bad luck you have!"*

Once again, the farmer replied, *"Who knows if it is good luck or bad luck? We will have to wait and see."*

Life is a series of good and bad. Your perception will align you to decide what to term it.

If anything, that needs to be fixed or taken care of is "The World Within."

If you are looking for things to manifest you, you need to tune the inner experience for which you will have to put the 'Thought' into mind that touches the 'Will.' The processing would turn on and the outer world would start changing for you to experience the inner world of desired outcome.

Different people perceive the same information differently based on their conditions. A person high on energy will perceive a thing as energy and chances are the experience will turn to his desired outcome. A person of low energy is likely to have a chance and get to experience outer energy.

Values, Attitude & Time Drives Perception

The formation of character is deeply rooted in the beliefs and values we are exposed to. Different individuals, such as saints and warriors, approach situations with distinct perspectives and actions. Kings who prioritised justice safeguarded their people and homeland effectively. Saints, on the other hand, advocated for peace and non-violence, enhancing the quality of life on earth. While their teachings endure, this doesn't negate the importance of standing against injustice. A person's character is a product of their mindset and adherence to a particular code of conduct. A child raised in a spiritual ashram will likely adopt the principles of the ashram's saints, while one raised in a royal environment may aspire to become a king. Ultimately, one's upbringing and environment greatly influence their development and choices in life.

The values attitude that will always drive the things that we take -

Chhatrapati Shivaji Maharaj was a king from the Indian state of Maharashtra. He was not born a prince. But his mother Jijabai used to tell him stories of the great kings and taking challenges for his own country and land. She also told him the moral values and ethics acquired from Ramayana & Mahabharata.

Jijabai, Shivaji's mother, played a pivotal role in shaping his character and values. She nurtured his sense of courage and honour by sharing stories from Hindu epics like the Ramayana and Mahabharata, which were rich with tales of heroism and righteousness. These stories instilled in Shivaji a deep respect for valour and glory, laying the foundation for his future actions and leadership.

At a remarkably young age of 16, Shivaji displayed a firm commitment to justice and the protection of women's rights. When he learned of the brutal assault and murder committed by the Patil of Ranjha against a woman, Shivaji swiftly ordered a severe punishment, decreeing that the perpetrator's hands and feet be amputated. This decisive action underscored Shivaji's unwavering dedication to upholding the safety and dignity of women throughout his reign, setting a precedent for his administration's policies and values.

Shivaji's respect for women extended beyond matters of justice. In a legendary incident involving the daughter-in-law of the Subhedar of Kalyan, Shivaji exemplified grace and compassion even in the midst of victory. Though tradition dictated that she be treated as spoils of war, Shivaji chose to honour her with respect and generosity. His remark upon her beauty as motherly, coupled with his decision to gift her before sending her back to her family, demonstrated his commitment to treating all individuals with dignity and humanity, regardless of circumstance.

Jijabai's influence, coupled with Shivaji's innate sense of justice and valour, shaped a leader who prioritised the safety, dignity, and rights of all individuals, particularly women. His progressive governance and strategic prowess cemented his legacy as one of India's most revered historical figures, inspiring admiration, and reverence for generations to come.

Similarly on the other hand,

The story of the great Gautama Prince, who later became known as Buddha, underscores the significance of one's perceptions. Initially sheltered from life's harsh realities and only exposed to glory and goodness, the Prince later questioned the essence of his existence.

He pondered over the nature of suffering and embarked on a journey of introspection and meditation. Despite his privileged upbringing, his quest for truth led him to discover inner peace and enlightenment, ultimately earning him the title of Buddha. It shows that regardless of one's environment, asking the right questions and exploring life's mysteries can lead to profound insights and transformation.

Never underestimate the power of your inner essence, which complements your outward appearance. The connection between yourself and others is not just physical but also rooted in the energy that unites us all. The sense of fulfilment comes from within, just as it does from external sources. Ultimately, it's your emotions and perceptions that shape your reality.

While you see with your eyes, hear from your ears, taste from your mouth/tongue, feel through the touch of skin, and smell through your nose.

The way we take information is through visual, auditory, kinaesthetic, olfactory, or gustatory mediums. We all have our ways of absorbing information. While we take in all this information from different sources and different means, we delete some of the unwanted information, some information is distorted, and the other is generalised.

And then we compartmentalise this information under internal presentations based on smell, sound, pictures, feelings, taste, or even self-talk. This segregated memory now becomes a part of our data based on which state of mind, and behaviours are built.

- Surround yourself with prose and poetry that uplift and nourish your soul. Engage in books that guide you on a journey of self-discovery and understanding. Choose movies that resonate with your spirit and leave you feeling inspired.

- Keep company with people who respect, celebrate, and love you, offering you a sense of peace and belonging. Engage in activities that align with your true purpose, approaching them with grace and love, which will ultimately lead to inner peace and tranquillity.

- Avoid consuming repetitive negative news and media. Refrain from dwelling on topics that do not contribute positively to your well-being or have any meaningful impact. Instead, focus your thoughts and energy on pursuits that bring joy, fulfilment, and positivity into your life.

- Even the music you hear has the power to turn your reality. As we hear music it does influence our emotions causing us to feel in a certain way.

It's upon you how to code the outer manifestation into the inner world, which is taken care of by the mind. The mind is guided by the will. If the inner energy is strong, it will ultimately guide the inner experience as well.

One's values and attitudes are instrumental in shaping their actions. It's crucial to educate and nurture the youth to uphold principles of dignity and compassion. Rather than reacting impulsively, it's essential to address pain with resolution. True worth is revealed through patience and tolerance.

The pledges made by renowned leaders like Mahatma Gandhi, Abraham Lincoln, Atal Bihari Vajpayee, Swami Vivekananda, A. P. J. Abdul Kalam Nelson Mandela & many more highlight the significance of virtues in processing information. When guided by divine will, these virtues become the cornerstone of one's inner world, shaping their life's journey.

Life encompasses a spectrum of emotions—from happiness to sadness—each tinting the canvas of the mind. The energy we radiate reflects our inner alignment.

You see, to shape up the world within, sometimes you need a strong will and determination as your perception will be driven by your very core energy. Ensure to shape your world by people who influence you positively and take that shining Sankalpa to ensure to illuminate your life and radiate to others too.

Chapter Twenty Four

Inner Voice

Be attentive to the voice of your heart and soul, as it manifests in various forms such as feelings, words, visuals, smells, or tastes. By staying present and aware, you take an inward journey, connecting with your life force.

Being alone isn't negative, but the sensation of loneliness isn't desirable. Whether surrounded by noise and people in a club or by oneself, the crucial aspect is hearing one's own voice. The emptiness of being in a crowd yet feeling lonely holds no value.

The hustle and bustle of Mumbai, often dubbed the "city that never sleeps," is epitomised by its local train commute. For many, including myself, navigating through the crowded train stations and enduring long hours of travel had become a routine part of daily life.

One particular day, as I approached a central line station, I was greeted with a usual sight - the stairs leading to the platform were flooded with people. The thought of squeezing myself into that mass of bodies crossed my mind, but I hesitated. Instead, I chose to step back and observe.

As I watched the chaotic scene unfold before me, a wave of empathy washed over me. I couldn't help but feel sorry for both me and the countless others who were forced to endure such conditions day in and day out. The suffocating crowds, the constant jostling, the lack of personal space - it was a dark reminder of the challenges faced by millions of Mumbaikars on a daily basis.

In that moment of reflection, I realised the importance of staying aware amidst the chaos. By choosing to step back and observe, I not only avoided potential trouble for myself, but also gained a deeper understanding of the human experience in a city as dynamic and demanding as Mumbai. It was a lesson in mindfulness, reminding me to prioritise my well-being and create space for myself even in the most crowded of environments.

As I finally made my way to the platform, weaving through the throngs of people with renewed purpose, I had a newfound sense of awareness about where I stood, and what I wanted to achieve.

Certainly, the human mind often experiences a duality of voices, one urging us towards positive actions while the other tempting us towards less constructive choices. Take, for instance, the decision to study. One voice may encourage diligent focus and commitment to learning, while the other may suggest indulging in the immediate gratification of watching a Netflix series.

This inner conflict is a classic dichotomy of the angel and devil on one's shoulders, each representing opposing impulses and desires. It's a struggle between our higher moral instincts and our base desires.

However, true strength lies in discerning and following our authentic selves beyond the tug-of-war between these two voices. It's about cultivating a strong resolve, or Sankalpa, to align our actions with what is genuinely beneficial for our personal growth and well-being.

A balanced individual recognizes and acknowledges both voices within, but ultimately chooses to heed the call of their inner truth. By doing so, they navigate through life's choices with clarity and integrity, making a path that is guided by their highest aspirations and values.

Physical Wellness

To achieve physical wellness, it's essential to cultivate empathy and develop habits that respect and understand the space we share with others.

This includes practising good hygiene habits, such as regular handwashing and maintaining cleanliness in our surroundings.

Additionally, showing consideration for others, like offering a seat to elders or individuals with disabilities, or allowing others to enter the lift before ourselves, demonstrates empathy and kindness.

In social interactions, it's important to approach people with genuine care and respect. Instead of making potentially uncomfortable or judgmental comments about someone's appearance, such as weight changes, it's better to simply greet them with kindness and ask how they are doing. This gesture acknowledges the inherent value of each individual and fosters a sense of connection and respect. Just as we greet others with "Namaste," which signifies recognizing the divine within them, showing empathy and genuine concern for others contributes to a healthier and more compassionate community.

Mental Wellness

Words possess the power to cast spells, hence the term "spellings." It's crucial to be mindful of the words we speak, as they have the potential to uplift or tear down individuals. Rather than using words to harm, it's far more beneficial to focus our efforts on building others up.

Positive affirmations such as "Thank you," "You are doing great," "You are awesome," "You are smart," and "You are strong" can work wonders in boosting someone's confidence and morale. By choosing to use language that encourages and empowers, we contribute to the growth and well-being of those around us.

These words serve as reminders to be mindful of others. As we cultivate mindfulness, we naturally encourage others to treat us with the same consideration. This brings us closer to our authentic selves, which inherently holds greatness. Moreover, it's essential to monitor our internal dialogue, the constant chatter within and around us. By practising gratitude, kindness, and letting go of negative thoughts, we nurture a more positive and balanced mindset.

Prayers & blessings as well as selfless service are some means to work on our mental wellness.

Herd Mentality

Nature often provides subtle hints for us to connect with and understand. Animals, for instance, exhibit remarkable intuition; they instinctively react to potential dangers. The challenge in humans lies not in our inability to comprehend these cues, but rather in our lack of openness to respond.

In today's society, there's a prevalent herd mentality, where individuals tend to follow the crowd without questioning. Our minds become clouded by the multitude of voices we encounter. Amidst this cacophony, we often neglect our inner voice, which is crucial for self-understanding.

In the digital age, the influx of information from various media sources further complicates matters. Our cell phones constantly bombard us with notifications, each vying for our attention. It's imperative to discern which voices truly matter amidst this noise.

Social media adds to this phenomenon, presenting curated versions of people's lives. It's easy to fall into the trap of comparing oneself to others, especially when confronted with idealised images and filtered realities. However, indulging in self-pity serves no purpose; instead, we should seek inspiration and positive influence from others.

If someone's glamorous social media posts evoke feelings of inadequacy, it's essential to recognize the effort behind those images and channel any negative emotions into motivation for self-improvement. Ultimately, we must prioritise listening to our own authentic voice amidst the clamour of external influences, steering clear of the pitfalls of false comparisons and self-doubt.

What happened is for good,

Everything that is happening is for good,

All that will happen will also be for the good.

The inner voice coming from much within is more of an understanding. Words possess a unique power like casting a spell; when spoken with genuine intention, they hold the potential to manifest into reality.

Every human is a living God.

It's crucial to recognize that the energy we pray for in our faith also resides within us all. When we show disrespect, we're not just disrespecting others but also the divine. The inner voice, arising from within, embodies our authentic self and signifies a deep understanding of our core and mission.

Your Inner voice

Speaking about the inner voice, and how it can be channelised for your own benefit.

Instead of trying to silence it, seek to understand the inner workings of your mind by externalising its voice. Imagine giving it a physical form and letting it express itself outwardly like any other person. Consider how you'd feel if someone started speaking to you the way your inner voice does. How would you interact with someone who vocalises your internal thoughts? Soon enough, you'd likely ask them to depart and never return.

And the same is true for the voice inside your head. Why is it talking? It's you who's talking, and it's you who's listening. And when the voice argues with itself, who is it arguing with? Who could possibly win? Notice that the voice takes both sides of the conversation. It doesn't care which side it takes, just as long as it gets to keep on talking. In such scenarios, use this voice for empowerment. Consider, while your body may feel the cold and you might not be able to change the temperature, when your mind acknowledges, "It's cold!" you can respond with, "We're nearly home, just a few more minutes." This simple acknowledgment can improve your mood. Similarly, in the world of thought, there's always a way to exert control and refine your experiences.

Energy -

Meditation channels the energy of tranquillity and serenity, guiding us towards a deeper comprehension of realities beyond the ordinary. Within ourselves, we encounter two distinct voices - one positive and one negative. The strength of our resolve, or Sankalpa, determines which voice dominates our consciousness, leading us closer to manifesting our intentions.

When your determination towards your goals is as unyielding as a solid vow, there's a likelihood that you'll encounter the encouraging "VOICE" that aligns with your genuine intentions. Even if fleeting doubts or moments of weakness arise, they may momentarily deter you, but ultimately, you'll persist on the journey towards success.

Over time, we often find ourselves losing focus on our priorities. In such instances, the prevailing voice within us may be overshadowed by the negativity stemming from various commitments and responsibilities we're managing. This can lead to a clouded perspective, attracting unwanted influences and distractions. However, by remaining attuned to our Sankalpa and staying mindful of the voices we hear, we can strengthen our inner guidance, allowing it to prevail with clarity and resilience.

PART V

Chapter Twenty Five

Holistic Way To Realise Your Resolutions

We have uncovered a new and effective way to make a resolution, which in effect can bring a change in all quadrants of your life. Sometimes addressing one quadrant of your life plays a domino effect and affects other quadrants, creating a fulfilling experience, as I mentioned about my Sankalpa for Health. But most often, you have to focus on individual quadrants and evaluate where you are, and what you are missing.

I have created a ready reckoner which are parameters that need to be addressed in every quadrant of your life. My purpose through this book is to make you aware of where you are, and what you are capable of being. I do not offer solutions but show you the way.

Holistic Way To Realise Your Resolutions

Spiritual Well being	Mental Health	Physical Health	Financial
☐ Prayer and Blessing	☐ Priority & Focus	☐ Clear GUT	☐ Mental Wealth
☐ Service, Help others	☐ Practice Meditation	☐ Food habits – Last meal -3 to hrs before sleep	☐ Credit Card – 20% of monthly income
☐ Peace & Bliss	☐ Watch Breath	☐ Exercise	☐ Money Values
☐ Be kind	☐ Positive Intent	☐ Schedule	☐ Budgeting & Savings
☐ Practice Detachment	☐ Emotional Wellbeing	☐ Breathing Practise	☐ Feel Good about Money
☐ Meditation 24/7	☐ Acceptance	☐ Follow Balanced Nutrition	☐ Donate & help
☐ Donate	☐ Practice Happiness	☐ Learn Macros & Nutrition	☐ Money mindset
☐ Values	☐ Life Essential skills	☐ Sleep	☐ Financial Goals
☐ Practise HVEFC	☐ Practise HVEFC	☐ Hydration – Water drink well	☐ Accept Money / Wealth
		☐ Mindful of Posture	☐ How much of Money "Number" specific
		☐ Practise HVEFC	☐ Practise HVEFC

The Resolution 2.0 "Sankalpa"

The four aspects of life that really matter are listed in the chart. −

Check the boxes and see what you do, and what is missing. In case, if you feel you need to fix any blank boxes, plant a Sankalpa − take a Resolution to fix it.

Our life journeys are fraught with wills, desires, aspirations, goals, and expectations- fancy words for how to live a life. But, at the core what we all look at is a happy, and content life. We all seek attention, admiration, and acknowledgment, but more often do find it externally leading to disappointments. It's all about expectations and validations. But all that we seek is within us, and with this right frame of mind, and a purposeful Sankalpa, you will be able to live a blessed life.

The energy is beyond sight, sound, and touch. It's a sense that can be felt and lies deep within you.

The Resolution 2.0 "Sankalpa" − is the way to realise the dreams, goals, and vision that you have always aspired for, in the light to make it possible by taking a holistic sankalpa that would fix all the aspects of Life.

Life is a piece of Energy, it's up to you to Channelise it to make it work for You & Community, towards the Greater Good.

Vishal M. Shevle

YOUR RESOLUTION "THE 2.0 WAY"

Express and let it begin

Body - Physical Fitness	Mind - Mental Well-being
Spiritual - Energy/Soul	Wealth - Financial Well-being

Advice, kindly take 1 Resolution for each quadrant or
it's also ok to take 1 Resolution that takes care of all Quadrants

To get clarity you can put your thoughts below
"Script your Resolution"

Script your Resolution

www.ingramcontent.com/pod-product-compliance
Lightning Source LLC
LaVergne TN
LVHW091712070526
838199LV00050B/2365